I0003355

PostgreSQL 9.6 Vol4: Server Programming

A catalogue record for this book is available from the Hong Kong Public Libraries.

Published in Hong Kong by Samurai Media Limited.

Email: info@samuraimedia.org

ISBN 978-988-8406-71-5

Copyright 1996 to 2016 The PostgreSQL Global Development Group

PostgreSQL is Copyright 1996 to 2016 by the PostgreSQL Global Development Group.
Postgres95 is Copyright 1994 to 1995 by the Regents of the University of California.
Permission to use, copy, modify, and distribute this software and its documentation for any purpose, without fee, and without a written agreement is hereby granted, provided that the above copyright notice and this paragraph and the following two paragraphs appear in all copies.

IN NO EVENT SHALL THE UNIVERSITY OF CALIFORNIA BE LIABLE TO ANY PARTY FOR DIRECT, INDIRECT, SPECIAL, INCIDENTAL, OR CONSEQUENTIAL DAMAGES, INCLUDING LOST PROFITS, ARISING OUT OF THE USE OF THIS SOFTWARE AND ITS DOCUMENTATION, EVEN IF THE UNIVERSITY OF CALIFORNIA HAS BEEN ADVISED OF THE POSSIBILITY OF SUCH DAMAGE.

THE UNIVERSITY OF CALIFORNIA SPECIFICALLY DISCLAIMS ANYWARRANTIES, INCLUDING, BUT NOT LIMITED TO, THE IMPLIED WARRANTIES OF MERCHANTABILITY AND FITNESS FOR A PARTICULAR PURPOSE. THE SOFTWARE PROVIDED HEREUNDER IS ON AN AS-IS BASIS, AND THE UNIVERSITY OF CALIFORNIA HAS NO OBLIGATIONS TO PROVIDE MAINTENANCE, SUPPORT, UPDATES, ENHANCEMENTS, OR MODIFICATIONS.

Minor modifications for publication Copyright 2016 Samurai Media Limited.

Background Cover Image by https://www.flickr.com/people/webtreatsetc/
The blue and white elephant logo is Copyright by Jeff MacDonald

Table of Contents

V. Server Programming

This part is about extending the server functionality with user-defined functions, data types, triggers, etc. These are advanced topics which should probably be approached only after all the other user documentation about PostgreSQL has been understood. Later chapters in this part describe the server-side programming languages available in the PostgreSQL distribution as well as general issues concerning server-side programming languages. It is essential to read at least the earlier sections of Chapter 36 (covering functions) before diving into the material about server-side programming languages.

Chapter 36. Extending SQL

In the sections that follow, we will discuss how you can extend the PostgreSQL SQL query language by adding:

- functions (starting in Section 36.3)
- aggregates (starting in Section 36.10)
- data types (starting in Section 36.11)
- operators (starting in Section 36.12)
- operator classes for indexes (starting in Section 36.14)
- packages of related objects (starting in Section 36.15)

36.1. How Extensibility Works

PostgreSQL is extensible because its operation is catalog-driven. If you are familiar with standard relational database systems, you know that they store information about databases, tables, columns, etc., in what are commonly known as system catalogs. (Some systems call this the data dictionary.) The catalogs appear to the user as tables like any other, but the DBMS stores its internal bookkeeping in them. One key difference between PostgreSQL and standard relational database systems is that PostgreSQL stores much more information in its catalogs: not only information about tables and columns, but also information about data types, functions, access methods, and so on. These tables can be modified by the user, and since PostgreSQL bases its operation on these tables, this means that PostgreSQL can be extended by users. By comparison, conventional database systems can only be extended by changing hardcoded procedures in the source code or by loading modules specially written by the DBMS vendor.

The PostgreSQL server can moreover incorporate user-written code into itself through dynamic loading. That is, the user can specify an object code file (e.g., a shared library) that implements a new type or function, and PostgreSQL will load it as required. Code written in SQL is even more trivial to add to the server. This ability to modify its operation "on the fly" makes PostgreSQL uniquely suited for rapid prototyping of new applications and storage structures.

36.2. The PostgreSQL Type System

PostgreSQL data types are divided into base types, composite types, domains, and pseudo-types.

36.2.1. Base Types

Base types are those, like `int4`, that are implemented below the level of the SQL language (typically in a low-level language such as C). They generally correspond to what are often known as abstract data types. PostgreSQL can only operate on such types through functions provided by the user and only understands the behavior of such types to the extent that the user describes them. Base types are further subdivided into scalar and array types. For each scalar type, a corresponding array type is automatically created that can hold variable-size arrays of that scalar type.

36.2.2. Composite Types

Composite types, or row types, are created whenever the user creates a table. It is also possible to use CREATE TYPE to define a "stand-alone" composite type with no associated table. A composite type is simply a list of types with associated field names. A value of a composite type is a row or record of field values. The user can access the component fields from SQL queries. Refer to Section 8.16 for more information on composite types.

36.2.3. Domains

A domain is based on a particular base type and for many purposes is interchangeable with its base type. However, a domain can have constraints that restrict its valid values to a subset of what the underlying base type would allow.

Domains can be created using the SQL command CREATE DOMAIN. Their creation and use is not discussed in this chapter.

36.2.4. Pseudo-Types

There are a few "pseudo-types" for special purposes. Pseudo-types cannot appear as columns of tables or attributes of composite types, but they can be used to declare the argument and result types of functions. This provides a mechanism within the type system to identify special classes of functions. Table 8-25 lists the existing pseudo-types.

36.2.5. Polymorphic Types

Five pseudo-types of special interest are `anyelement`, `anyarray`, `anynonarray`, `anyenum`, and `anyrange`, which are collectively called *polymorphic types*. Any function declared using these types is said to be a *polymorphic function*. A polymorphic function can operate on many different data types, with the specific data type(s) being determined by the data types actually passed to it in a particular call.

Polymorphic arguments and results are tied to each other and are resolved to a specific data type when a query calling a polymorphic function is parsed. Each position (either argument or return value) declared as `anyelement` is allowed to have any specific actual data type, but in any given call they must all be the *same* actual type. Each position declared as `anyarray` can have any array data type, but similarly they must all be the same type. And similarly, positions declared as `anyrange` must all be the same range type. Furthermore, if there are positions declared `anyarray` and others declared `anyelement`, the actual array type in the `anyarray` positions must be an array whose elements are the same type appearing in the `anyelement` positions. Similarly, if there are positions declared `anyrange` and others declared `anyelement`, the actual range type in the `anyrange` positions must be a range whose subtype is the same type appearing in the `anyelement` positions. `anynonarray` is treated exactly the same as `anyelement`, but adds the additional constraint that the actual type must not be an array type. `anyenum` is treated exactly the same as `anyelement`, but adds the additional constraint that the actual type must be an enum type.

Thus, when more than one argument position is declared with a polymorphic type, the net effect is that only certain combinations of actual argument types are allowed. For example, a function declared as `equal(anyelement, anyelement)` will take any two input values, so long as they are of the same data type.

When the return value of a function is declared as a polymorphic type, there must be at least one argument position that is also polymorphic, and the actual data type supplied as the argument determines the actual result type for that call. For example, if there were not already an array subscripting mechanism, one could define a function that implements subscripting as `subscript(anyarray, integer) returns anyelement`. This declaration constrains the actual first argument to be an array type, and allows the parser to infer the correct result type from the actual first argument's type. Another example is that a function declared as `f(anyarray) returns anyenum` will only accept arrays of enum types.

Note that `anynonarray` and `anyenum` do not represent separate type variables; they are the same type as `anyelement`, just with an additional constraint. For example, declaring a function as `f(anyelement, anyenum)` is equivalent to declaring it as `f(anyenum, anyenum)`: both actual arguments have to be the same enum type.

A variadic function (one taking a variable number of arguments, as in Section 36.4.5) can be polymorphic: this is accomplished by declaring its last parameter as `VARIADIC anyarray`. For purposes of argument matching and determining the actual result type, such a function behaves the same as if you had written the appropriate number of `anynonarray` parameters.

36.3. User-defined Functions

PostgreSQL provides four kinds of functions:

- query language functions (functions written in SQL) (Section 36.4)
- procedural language functions (functions written in, for example, PL/pgSQL or PL/Tcl) (Section 36.7)
- internal functions (Section 36.8)
- C-language functions (Section 36.9)

Every kind of function can take base types, composite types, or combinations of these as arguments (parameters). In addition, every kind of function can return a base type or a composite type. Functions can also be defined to return sets of base or composite values.

Many kinds of functions can take or return certain pseudo-types (such as polymorphic types), but the available facilities vary. Consult the description of each kind of function for more details.

It's easiest to define SQL functions, so we'll start by discussing those. Most of the concepts presented for SQL functions will carry over to the other types of functions.

Throughout this chapter, it can be useful to look at the reference page of the CREATE FUNCTION command to understand the examples better. Some examples from this chapter can be found in `funcs.sql` and `funcs.c` in the `src/tutorial` directory in the PostgreSQL source distribution.

36.4. Query Language (SQL) Functions

SQL functions execute an arbitrary list of SQL statements, returning the result of the last query in the list. In the simple (non-set) case, the first row of the last query's result will be returned. (Bear in mind that "the first row" of a multirow result is not well-defined unless you use ORDER BY.) If the last query happens to return no rows at all, the null value will be returned.

Alternatively, an SQL function can be declared to return a set (that is, multiple rows) by specifying the function's return type as SETOF *sometype*, or equivalently by declaring it as RETURNS TABLE (*columns*). In this case all rows of the last query's result are returned. Further details appear below.

The body of an SQL function must be a list of SQL statements separated by semicolons. A semicolon after the last statement is optional. Unless the function is declared to return void, the last statement must be a SELECT, or an INSERT, UPDATE, or DELETE that has a RETURNING clause.

Any collection of commands in the SQL language can be packaged together and defined as a function. Besides SELECT queries, the commands can include data modification queries (INSERT, UPDATE, and DELETE), as well as other SQL commands. (You cannot use transaction control commands, e.g. COMMIT, SAVEPOINT, and some utility commands, e.g. VACUUM, in SQL functions.) However, the final command must be a SELECT or have a RETURNING clause that returns whatever is specified as the function's return type. Alternatively, if you want to define a SQL function that performs actions but has no useful value to return, you can define it as returning void. For example, this function removes rows with negative salaries from the emp table:

```
CREATE FUNCTION clean_emp() RETURNS void AS '
    DELETE FROM emp
        WHERE salary < 0;
' LANGUAGE SQL;

SELECT clean_emp();

 clean_emp
-----------

(1 row)
```

> **Note:** The entire body of a SQL function is parsed before any of it is executed. While a SQL function can contain commands that alter the system catalogs (e.g., CREATE TABLE), the effects of such commands will not be visible during parse analysis of later commands in the function. Thus, for example, CREATE TABLE foo (...); INSERT INTO foo VALUES(...); will not work as desired if packaged up into a single SQL function, since foo won't exist yet when the INSERT command is parsed. It's recommended to use PL/PgSQL instead of a SQL function in this type of situation.

The syntax of the CREATE FUNCTION command requires the function body to be written as a string constant. It is usually most convenient to use dollar quoting (see Section 4.1.2.4) for the string constant. If you choose to use regular single-quoted string constant syntax, you must double single quote marks (') and backslashes (\) (assuming escape string syntax) in the body of the function (see Section 4.1.2.1).

36.4.1. Arguments for SQL Functions

Arguments of a SQL function can be referenced in the function body using either names or numbers. Examples of both methods appear below.

To use a name, declare the function argument as having a name, and then just write that name in the function body. If the argument name is the same as any column name in the current SQL command within the function, the column name will take precedence. To override this, qualify the argument name with the name of the function itself, that is *function_name.argument_name*. (If this would conflict with a qualified column name, again the column name wins. You can avoid the ambiguity by choosing a different alias for the table within the SQL command.)

In the older numeric approach, arguments are referenced using the syntax $n: $1 refers to the first input argument, $2 to the second, and so on. This will work whether or not the particular argument was declared with a name.

If an argument is of a composite type, then the dot notation, e.g., *argname.fieldname* or $1.*fieldname*, can be used to access attributes of the argument. Again, you might need to qualify the argument's name with the function name to make the form with an argument name unambiguous.

SQL function arguments can only be used as data values, not as identifiers. Thus for example this is reasonable:

```
INSERT INTO mytable VALUES ($1);
```

but this will not work:

```
INSERT INTO $1 VALUES (42);
```

> **Note:** The ability to use names to reference SQL function arguments was added in PostgreSQL 9.2. Functions to be used in older servers must use the $n notation.

36.4.2. SQL Functions on Base Types

The simplest possible SQL function has no arguments and simply returns a base type, such as integer:

```
CREATE FUNCTION one() RETURNS integer AS $$
    SELECT 1 AS result;
$$ LANGUAGE SQL;

-- Alternative syntax for string literal:
CREATE FUNCTION one() RETURNS integer AS '
```

```
        SELECT 1 AS result;
' LANGUAGE SQL;

SELECT one();

 one
-----
   1
```

Notice that we defined a column alias within the function body for the result of the function (with the name `result`), but this column alias is not visible outside the function. Hence, the result is labeled `one` instead of `result`.

It is almost as easy to define SQL functions that take base types as arguments:

```
CREATE FUNCTION add_em(x integer, y integer) RETURNS integer AS $$
    SELECT x + y;
$$ LANGUAGE SQL;

SELECT add_em(1, 2) AS answer;

 answer
--------
      3
```

Alternatively, we could dispense with names for the arguments and use numbers:

```
CREATE FUNCTION add_em(integer, integer) RETURNS integer AS $$
    SELECT $1 + $2;
$$ LANGUAGE SQL;

SELECT add_em(1, 2) AS answer;

 answer
--------
      3
```

Here is a more useful function, which might be used to debit a bank account:

```
CREATE FUNCTION tf1 (accountno integer, debit numeric) RETURNS integer AS $$
    UPDATE bank
        SET balance = balance - debit
        WHERE accountno = tf1.accountno;
    SELECT 1;
$$ LANGUAGE SQL;
```

A user could execute this function to debit account 17 by $100.00 as follows:

```
SELECT tf1(17, 100.0);
```

In this example, we chose the name `accountno` for the first argument, but this is the same as the name of a column in the `bank` table. Within the `UPDATE` command, `accountno` refers to the column `bank.accountno`, so `tf1.accountno` must be used to refer to the argument. We could of course avoid this by using a different name for the argument.

In practice one would probably like a more useful result from the function than a constant 1, so a more likely definition is:

```
CREATE FUNCTION tf1 (accountno integer, debit numeric) RETURNS integer AS $$
    UPDATE bank
        SET balance = balance - debit
        WHERE accountno = tf1.accountno;
    SELECT balance FROM bank WHERE accountno = tf1.accountno;
$$ LANGUAGE SQL;
```

which adjusts the balance and returns the new balance. The same thing could be done in one command using `RETURNING`:

```
CREATE FUNCTION tf1 (accountno integer, debit numeric) RETURNS integer AS $$
    UPDATE bank
        SET balance = balance - debit
        WHERE accountno = tf1.accountno
    RETURNING balance;
$$ LANGUAGE SQL;
```

36.4.3. SQL Functions on Composite Types

When writing functions with arguments of composite types, we must not only specify which argument we want but also the desired attribute (field) of that argument. For example, suppose that `emp` is a table containing employee data, and therefore also the name of the composite type of each row of the table. Here is a function `double_salary` that computes what someone's salary would be if it were doubled:

```
CREATE TABLE emp (
    name        text,
    salary      numeric,
    age         integer,
    cubicle     point
);

INSERT INTO emp VALUES ('Bill', 4200, 45, '(2,1)');

CREATE FUNCTION double_salary(emp) RETURNS numeric AS $$
    SELECT $1.salary * 2 AS salary;
$$ LANGUAGE SQL;

SELECT name, double_salary(emp.*) AS dream
    FROM emp
    WHERE emp.cubicle ~= point '(2,1)';
```

```
name | dream
------+-------
Bill |  8400
```

Notice the use of the syntax `$1.salary` to select one field of the argument row value. Also notice how the calling `SELECT` command uses `*` to select the entire current row of a table as a composite value. The table row can alternatively be referenced using just the table name, like this:

```
SELECT name, double_salary(emp) AS dream
    FROM emp
    WHERE emp.cubicle ~= point '(2,1)';
```

but this usage is deprecated since it's easy to get confused.

Sometimes it is handy to construct a composite argument value on-the-fly. This can be done with the `ROW` construct. For example, we could adjust the data being passed to the function:

```
SELECT name, double_salary(ROW(name, salary*1.1, age, cubicle)) AS dream
    FROM emp;
```

It is also possible to build a function that returns a composite type. This is an example of a function that returns a single `emp` row:

```
CREATE FUNCTION new_emp() RETURNS emp AS $$
    SELECT text 'None' AS name,
        1000.0 AS salary,
        25 AS age,
        point '(2,2)' AS cubicle;
$$ LANGUAGE SQL;
```

In this example we have specified each of the attributes with a constant value, but any computation could have been substituted for these constants.

Note two important things about defining the function:

- The select list order in the query must be exactly the same as that in which the columns appear in the table associated with the composite type. (Naming the columns, as we did above, is irrelevant to the system.)

- You must typecast the expressions to match the definition of the composite type, or you will get errors like this:

  ```
  ERROR:  function declared to return emp returns varchar instead of text at column 1
  ```

A different way to define the same function is:

```
CREATE FUNCTION new_emp() RETURNS emp AS $$
    SELECT ROW('None', 1000.0, 25, '(2,2)')::emp;
$$ LANGUAGE SQL;
```

Here we wrote a SELECT that returns just a single column of the correct composite type. This isn't really better in this situation, but it is a handy alternative in some cases — for example, if we need to compute the result by calling another function that returns the desired composite value.

We could call this function directly in either of two ways:

```
SELECT new_emp();

          new_emp
--------------------------
 (None,1000.0,25,"(2,2)")

SELECT * FROM new_emp();

 name | salary | age | cubicle
------+--------+-----+---------
 None | 1000.0 |  25 | (2,2)
```

The second way is described more fully in Section 36.4.7.

When you use a function that returns a composite type, you might want only one field (attribute) from its result. You can do that with syntax like this:

```
SELECT (new_emp()).name;

 name
------
 None
```

The extra parentheses are needed to keep the parser from getting confused. If you try to do it without them, you get something like this:

```
SELECT new_emp().name;
ERROR:  syntax error at or near "."
LINE 1: SELECT new_emp().name;
                        ^
```

Another option is to use functional notation for extracting an attribute. The simple way to explain this is that we can use the notations *attribute(table)* and *table.attribute* interchangeably.

```
SELECT name(new_emp());

 name
------
 None

-- This is the same as:
-- SELECT emp.name AS youngster FROM emp WHERE emp.age < 30;

SELECT name(emp) AS youngster FROM emp WHERE age(emp) < 30;

 youngster
-----------
```

```
Sam
Andy
```

> **Tip:** The equivalence between functional notation and attribute notation makes it possible to use functions on composite types to emulate "computed fields". For example, using the previous definition for `double_salary(emp)`, we can write
>
> ```
> SELECT emp.name, emp.double_salary FROM emp;
> ```
>
> An application using this wouldn't need to be directly aware that `double_salary` isn't a real column of the table. (You can also emulate computed fields with views.)
>
> Because of this behavior, it's unwise to give a function that takes a single composite-type argument the same name as any of the fields of that composite type.

Another way to use a function returning a composite type is to pass the result to another function that accepts the correct row type as input:

```
CREATE FUNCTION getname(emp) RETURNS text AS $$
    SELECT $1.name;
$$ LANGUAGE SQL;

SELECT getname(new_emp());
 getname
---------
 None
(1 row)
```

Still another way to use a function that returns a composite type is to call it as a table function, as described in Section 36.4.7.

36.4.4. SQL Functions with Output Parameters

An alternative way of describing a function's results is to define it with *output parameters*, as in this example:

```
CREATE FUNCTION add_em (IN x int, IN y int, OUT sum int)
AS 'SELECT x + y'
LANGUAGE SQL;

SELECT add_em(3,7);
 add_em
--------
     10
(1 row)
```

This is not essentially different from the version of `add_em` shown in Section 36.4.2. The real value of output parameters is that they provide a convenient way of defining functions that return several columns. For example,

```
CREATE FUNCTION sum_n_product (x int, y int, OUT sum int, OUT product int)
AS 'SELECT x + y, x * y'
LANGUAGE SQL;
```

```
 SELECT * FROM sum_n_product(11,42);
 sum | product
-----+---------
  53 |     462
(1 row)
```

What has essentially happened here is that we have created an anonymous composite type for the result of the function. The above example has the same end result as

```
CREATE TYPE sum_prod AS (sum int, product int);
```

```
CREATE FUNCTION sum_n_product (int, int) RETURNS sum_prod
AS 'SELECT $1 + $2, $1 * $2'
LANGUAGE SQL;
```

but not having to bother with the separate composite type definition is often handy. Notice that the names attached to the output parameters are not just decoration, but determine the column names of the anonymous composite type. (If you omit a name for an output parameter, the system will choose a name on its own.)

Notice that output parameters are not included in the calling argument list when invoking such a function from SQL. This is because PostgreSQL considers only the input parameters to define the function's calling signature. That means also that only the input parameters matter when referencing the function for purposes such as dropping it. We could drop the above function with either of

```
DROP FUNCTION sum_n_product (x int, y int, OUT sum int, OUT product int);
DROP FUNCTION sum_n_product (int, int);
```

Parameters can be marked as IN (the default), OUT, INOUT, or VARIADIC. An INOUT parameter serves as both an input parameter (part of the calling argument list) and an output parameter (part of the result record type). VARIADIC parameters are input parameters, but are treated specially as described next.

36.4.5. SQL Functions with Variable Numbers of Arguments

SQL functions can be declared to accept variable numbers of arguments, so long as all the "optional" arguments are of the same data type. The optional arguments will be passed to the function as an array. The function is declared by marking the last parameter as VARIADIC; this parameter must be declared as being of an array type. For example:

```
CREATE FUNCTION mleast(VARIADIC arr numeric[]) RETURNS numeric AS $$
    SELECT min($1[i]) FROM generate_subscripts($1, 1) g(i);
```

```
$$ LANGUAGE SQL;

SELECT mleast(10, -1, 5, 4.4);
 mleast
--------
     -1
(1 row)
```

Effectively, all the actual arguments at or beyond the VARIADIC position are gathered up into a one-dimensional array, as if you had written

```
SELECT mleast(ARRAY[10, -1, 5, 4.4]);    -- doesn't work
```

You can't actually write that, though — or at least, it will not match this function definition. A parameter marked VARIADIC matches one or more occurrences of its element type, not of its own type.

Sometimes it is useful to be able to pass an already-constructed array to a variadic function; this is particularly handy when one variadic function wants to pass on its array parameter to another one. You can do that by specifying VARIADIC in the call:

```
SELECT mleast(VARIADIC ARRAY[10, -1, 5, 4.4]);
```

This prevents expansion of the function's variadic parameter into its element type, thereby allowing the array argument value to match normally. VARIADIC can only be attached to the last actual argument of a function call.

Specifying VARIADIC in the call is also the only way to pass an empty array to a variadic function, for example:

```
SELECT mleast(VARIADIC ARRAY[]::numeric[]);
```

Simply writing SELECT mleast() does not work because a variadic parameter must match at least one actual argument. (You could define a second function also named mleast, with no parameters, if you wanted to allow such calls.)

The array element parameters generated from a variadic parameter are treated as not having any names of their own. This means it is not possible to call a variadic function using named arguments (Section 4.3), except when you specify VARIADIC. For example, this will work:

```
SELECT mleast(VARIADIC arr => ARRAY[10, -1, 5, 4.4]);
```

but not these:

```
SELECT mleast(arr => 10);
SELECT mleast(arr => ARRAY[10, -1, 5, 4.4]);
```

36.4.6. SQL Functions with Default Values for Arguments

Functions can be declared with default values for some or all input arguments. The default values are inserted whenever the function is called with insufficiently many actual arguments. Since arguments can only be omitted from the end of the actual argument list, all parameters after a parameter with a default value have to have default values as well. (Although the use of named argument notation could allow this restriction to be relaxed, it's still enforced so that positional argument notation works sensibly.)

For example:

```
CREATE FUNCTION foo(a int, b int DEFAULT 2, c int DEFAULT 3)
RETURNS int
LANGUAGE SQL
AS $$
    SELECT $1 + $2 + $3;
$$;

SELECT foo(10, 20, 30);
 foo
-----
  60
(1 row)

SELECT foo(10, 20);
 foo
-----
  33
(1 row)

SELECT foo(10);
 foo
-----
  15
(1 row)

SELECT foo();  -- fails since there is no default for the first argument
ERROR:  function foo() does not exist
```

The = sign can also be used in place of the key word DEFAULT.

36.4.7. SQL Functions as Table Sources

All SQL functions can be used in the FROM clause of a query, but it is particularly useful for functions returning composite types. If the function is defined to return a base type, the table function produces a one-column table. If the function is defined to return a composite type, the table function produces a column for each attribute of the composite type.

Here is an example:

```
CREATE TABLE foo (fooid int, foosubid int, fooname text);
INSERT INTO foo VALUES (1, 1, 'Joe');
INSERT INTO foo VALUES (1, 2, 'Ed');
INSERT INTO foo VALUES (2, 1, 'Mary');

CREATE FUNCTION getfoo(int) RETURNS foo AS $$
    SELECT * FROM foo WHERE fooid = $1;
```

```
$$ LANGUAGE SQL;

SELECT *, upper(fooname) FROM getfoo(1) AS t1;

 fooid | foosubid | fooname | upper
-------+----------+---------+-------
     1 |        1 | Joe     | JOE
(1 row)
```

As the example shows, we can work with the columns of the function's result just the same as if they were columns of a regular table.

Note that we only got one row out of the function. This is because we did not use SETOF. That is described in the next section.

36.4.8. SQL Functions Returning Sets

When an SQL function is declared as returning SETOF *sometype*, the function's final query is executed to completion, and each row it outputs is returned as an element of the result set.

This feature is normally used when calling the function in the FROM clause. In this case each row returned by the function becomes a row of the table seen by the query. For example, assume that table foo has the same contents as above, and we say:

```
CREATE FUNCTION getfoo(int) RETURNS SETOF foo AS $$
    SELECT * FROM foo WHERE fooid = $1;
$$ LANGUAGE SQL;

SELECT * FROM getfoo(1) AS t1;
```

Then we would get:

```
 fooid | foosubid | fooname
-------+----------+---------
     1 |        1 | Joe
     1 |        2 | Ed
(2 rows)
```

It is also possible to return multiple rows with the columns defined by output parameters, like this:

```
CREATE TABLE tab (y int, z int);
INSERT INTO tab VALUES (1, 2), (3, 4), (5, 6), (7, 8);

CREATE FUNCTION sum_n_product_with_tab (x int, OUT sum int, OUT product int)
RETURNS SETOF record
AS $$
    SELECT $1 + tab.y, $1 * tab.y FROM tab;
$$ LANGUAGE SQL;

SELECT * FROM sum_n_product_with_tab(10);
 sum | product
```

```
-----+---------
  11 |      10
  13 |      30
  15 |      50
  17 |      70
(4 rows)
```

The key point here is that you must write RETURNS SETOF record to indicate that the function returns multiple rows instead of just one. If there is only one output parameter, write that parameter's type instead of record.

It is frequently useful to construct a query's result by invoking a set-returning function multiple times, with the parameters for each invocation coming from successive rows of a table or subquery. The preferred way to do this is to use the LATERAL key word, which is described in Section 7.2.1.5. Here is an example using a set-returning function to enumerate elements of a tree structure:

```
SELECT * FROM nodes;
   name     | parent
-----------+--------
 Top       |
 Child1    | Top
 Child2    | Top
 Child3    | Top
 SubChild1 | Child1
 SubChild2 | Child1
(6 rows)

CREATE FUNCTION listchildren(text) RETURNS SETOF text AS $$
    SELECT name FROM nodes WHERE parent = $1
$$ LANGUAGE SQL STABLE;

SELECT * FROM listchildren('Top');
 listchildren
--------------
 Child1
 Child2
 Child3
(3 rows)

SELECT name, child FROM nodes, LATERAL listchildren(name) AS child;
  name   |   child
--------+-----------
 Top    | Child1
 Top    | Child2
 Top    | Child3
 Child1 | SubChild1
 Child1 | SubChild2
(5 rows)
```

This example does not do anything that we couldn't have done with a simple join, but in more complex calculations the option to put some of the work into a function can be quite convenient.

Currently, functions returning sets can also be called in the select list of a query. For each row that the query generates by itself, the function returning set is invoked, and an output row is generated for each element of the function's result set. Note, however, that this capability is deprecated and might be removed in future releases. The previous example could also be done with queries like these:

```
SELECT listchildren('Top');
 listchildren
--------------
 Child1
 Child2
 Child3
(3 rows)

SELECT name, listchildren(name) FROM nodes;
  name  | listchildren
--------+--------------
 Top    | Child1
 Top    | Child2
 Top    | Child3
 Child1 | SubChild1
 Child1 | SubChild2
(5 rows)
```

In the last SELECT, notice that no output row appears for Child2, Child3, etc. This happens because listchildren returns an empty set for those arguments, so no result rows are generated. This is the same behavior as we got from an inner join to the function result when using the LATERAL syntax.

> **Note:** If a function's last command is INSERT, UPDATE, or DELETE with RETURNING, that command will always be executed to completion, even if the function is not declared with SETOF or the calling query does not fetch all the result rows. Any extra rows produced by the RETURNING clause are silently dropped, but the commanded table modifications still happen (and are all completed before returning from the function).

> **Note:** The key problem with using set-returning functions in the select list, rather than the FROM clause, is that putting more than one set-returning function in the same select list does not behave very sensibly. (What you actually get if you do so is a number of output rows equal to the least common multiple of the numbers of rows produced by each set-returning function.) The LATERAL syntax produces less surprising results when calling multiple set-returning functions, and should usually be used instead.

36.4.9. SQL Functions Returning TABLE

There is another way to declare a function as returning a set, which is to use the syntax RETURNS TABLE(*columns*). This is equivalent to using one or more OUT parameters plus marking the function as returning SETOF record (or SETOF a single output parameter's type, as appropriate). This notation is specified in recent versions of the SQL standard, and thus may be more portable than using SETOF.

For example, the preceding sum-and-product example could also be done this way:

```
CREATE FUNCTION sum_n_product_with_tab (x int)
RETURNS TABLE(sum int, product int) AS $$
    SELECT $1 + tab.y, $1 * tab.y FROM tab;
$$ LANGUAGE SQL;
```

It is not allowed to use explicit OUT or INOUT parameters with the RETURNS TABLE notation — you must put all the output columns in the TABLE list.

36.4.10. Polymorphic SQL Functions

SQL functions can be declared to accept and return the polymorphic types anyelement, anyarray, anynonarray, anyenum, and anyrange. See Section 36.2.5 for a more detailed explanation of polymorphic functions. Here is a polymorphic function make_array that builds up an array from two arbitrary data type elements:

```
CREATE FUNCTION make_array(anyelement, anyelement) RETURNS anyarray AS $$
    SELECT ARRAY[$1, $2];
$$ LANGUAGE SQL;

SELECT make_array(1, 2) AS intarray, make_array('a'::text, 'b') AS textarray;
 intarray | textarray
----------+-----------
 {1,2}    | {a,b}
(1 row)
```

Notice the use of the typecast 'a'::text to specify that the argument is of type text. This is required if the argument is just a string literal, since otherwise it would be treated as type unknown, and array of unknown is not a valid type. Without the typecast, you will get errors like this:

```
ERROR:  could not determine polymorphic type because input has type "unknown"
```

It is permitted to have polymorphic arguments with a fixed return type, but the converse is not. For example:

```
CREATE FUNCTION is_greater(anyelement, anyelement) RETURNS boolean AS $$
    SELECT $1 > $2;
$$ LANGUAGE SQL;

SELECT is_greater(1, 2);
 is_greater
------------
 f
(1 row)

CREATE FUNCTION invalid_func() RETURNS anyelement AS $$
    SELECT 1;
$$ LANGUAGE SQL;
ERROR:  cannot determine result data type
```

```
DETAIL:  A function returning a polymorphic type must have at least one polymorphic
```

Polymorphism can be used with functions that have output arguments. For example:

```
CREATE FUNCTION dup (f1 anyelement, OUT f2 anyelement, OUT f3 anyarray)
AS 'select $1, array[$1,$1]' LANGUAGE SQL;

SELECT * FROM dup(22);
 f2 |   f3
----+---------
 22 | {22,22}
(1 row)
```

Polymorphism can also be used with variadic functions. For example:

```
CREATE FUNCTION anyleast (VARIADIC anyarray) RETURNS anyelement AS $$
    SELECT min($1[i]) FROM generate_subscripts($1, 1) g(i);
$$ LANGUAGE SQL;

SELECT anyleast(10, -1, 5, 4);
 anyleast
----------
       -1
(1 row)

SELECT anyleast('abc'::text, 'def');
 anyleast
----------
 abc
(1 row)

CREATE FUNCTION concat_values(text, VARIADIC anyarray) RETURNS text AS $$
    SELECT array_to_string($2, $1);
$$ LANGUAGE SQL;

SELECT concat_values('|', 1, 4, 2);
 concat_values
---------------
 1|4|2
(1 row)
```

36.4.11. SQL Functions with Collations

When a SQL function has one or more parameters of collatable data types, a collation is identified for each function call depending on the collations assigned to the actual arguments, as described in Section 23.2. If a collation is successfully identified (i.e., there are no conflicts of implicit collations among the arguments) then all the collatable parameters are treated as having that collation implicitly. This will affect the behavior of collation-sensitive operations within the function. For example, using the `anyleast` function described above, the result of

```
SELECT anyleast('abc'::text, 'ABC');
```

will depend on the database's default collation. In C locale the result will be ABC, but in many other locales it will be abc. The collation to use can be forced by adding a COLLATE clause to any of the arguments, for example

```
SELECT anyleast('abc'::text, 'ABC' COLLATE "C");
```

Alternatively, if you wish a function to operate with a particular collation regardless of what it is called with, insert COLLATE clauses as needed in the function definition. This version of `anyleast` would always use en_US locale to compare strings:

```
CREATE FUNCTION anyleast (VARIADIC anyarray) RETURNS anyelement AS $$
    SELECT min($1[i] COLLATE "en_US") FROM generate_subscripts($1, 1) g(i);
$$ LANGUAGE SQL;
```

But note that this will throw an error if applied to a non-collatable data type.

If no common collation can be identified among the actual arguments, then a SQL function treats its parameters as having their data types' default collation (which is usually the database's default collation, but could be different for parameters of domain types).

The behavior of collatable parameters can be thought of as a limited form of polymorphism, applicable only to textual data types.

36.5. Function Overloading

More than one function can be defined with the same SQL name, so long as the arguments they take are different. In other words, function names can be *overloaded*. When a query is executed, the server will determine which function to call from the data types and the number of the provided arguments. Overloading can also be used to simulate functions with a variable number of arguments, up to a finite maximum number.

When creating a family of overloaded functions, one should be careful not to create ambiguities. For instance, given the functions:

```
CREATE FUNCTION test(int, real) RETURNS ...
CREATE FUNCTION test(smallint, double precision) RETURNS ...
```

it is not immediately clear which function would be called with some trivial input like `test(1, 1.5)`. The currently implemented resolution rules are described in Chapter 10, but it is unwise to design a system that subtly relies on this behavior.

A function that takes a single argument of a composite type should generally not have the same name as any attribute (field) of that type. Recall that `attribute(table)` is considered equivalent to `table.attribute`. In the case that there is an ambiguity between a function on a composite type and an attribute of the composite type, the attribute will always be used. It is possible to override that choice by schema-qualifying the function name (that is, `schema.func(table)`) but it's better to avoid the problem by not choosing conflicting names.

Another possible conflict is between variadic and non-variadic functions. For instance, it is possible to create both `foo(numeric)` and `foo(VARIADIC numeric[])`. In this case it is unclear which one should be matched to a call providing a single numeric argument, such as `foo(10.1)`. The rule is that the function appearing earlier in the search path is used, or if the two functions are in the same schema, the non-variadic one is preferred.

When overloading C-language functions, there is an additional constraint: The C name of each function in the family of overloaded functions must be different from the C names of all other functions, either internal or dynamically loaded. If this rule is violated, the behavior is not portable. You might get a run-time linker error, or one of the functions will get called (usually the internal one). The alternative form of the `AS` clause for the SQL `CREATE FUNCTION` command decouples the SQL function name from the function name in the C source code. For instance:

```
CREATE FUNCTION test(int) RETURNS int
    AS 'filename', 'test_1arg'
    LANGUAGE C;
CREATE FUNCTION test(int, int) RETURNS int
    AS 'filename', 'test_2arg'
    LANGUAGE C;
```

The names of the C functions here reflect one of many possible conventions.

36.6. Function Volatility Categories

Every function has a *volatility* classification, with the possibilities being VOLATILE, STABLE, or IMMUTABLE. VOLATILE is the default if the CREATE FUNCTION command does not specify a category. The volatility category is a promise to the optimizer about the behavior of the function:

- A VOLATILE function can do anything, including modifying the database. It can return different results on successive calls with the same arguments. The optimizer makes no assumptions about the behavior of such functions. A query using a volatile function will re-evaluate the function at every row where its value is needed.

- A STABLE function cannot modify the database and is guaranteed to return the same results given the same arguments for all rows within a single statement. This category allows the optimizer to optimize multiple calls of the function to a single call. In particular, it is safe to use an expression containing such a function in an index scan condition. (Since an index scan will evaluate the comparison value only once, not once at each row, it is not valid to use a VOLATILE function in an index scan condition.)

- An IMMUTABLE function cannot modify the database and is guaranteed to return the same results given the same arguments forever. This category allows the optimizer to pre-evaluate the function when a query calls it with constant arguments. For example, a query like SELECT ... WHERE x = 2 + 2 can be simplified on sight to SELECT ... WHERE x = 4, because the function underlying the integer addition operator is marked IMMUTABLE.

For best optimization results, you should label your functions with the strictest volatility category that is valid for them.

Any function with side-effects *must* be labeled VOLATILE, so that calls to it cannot be optimized away. Even a function with no side-effects needs to be labeled VOLATILE if its value can change within a single query; some examples are random(), currval(), timeofday().

Another important example is that the current_timestamp family of functions qualify as STABLE, since their values do not change within a transaction.

There is relatively little difference between STABLE and IMMUTABLE categories when considering simple interactive queries that are planned and immediately executed: it doesn't matter a lot whether a function is executed once during planning or once during query execution startup. But there is a big difference if the plan is saved and reused later. Labeling a function IMMUTABLE when it really isn't might allow it to be prematurely folded to a constant during planning, resulting in a stale value being re-used during subsequent uses of the plan. This is a hazard when using prepared statements or when using function languages that cache plans (such as PL/pgSQL).

For functions written in SQL or in any of the standard procedural languages, there is a second important property determined by the volatility category, namely the visibility of any data changes that have been made by the SQL command that is calling the function. A VOLATILE function will see such changes, a STABLE or IMMUTABLE function will not. This behavior is implemented using the snapshotting behavior of MVCC (see Chapter 13): STABLE and IMMUTABLE functions use a snapshot established as of the start of the calling query, whereas VOLATILE functions obtain a fresh snapshot at the start of each query they execute.

> **Note:** Functions written in C can manage snapshots however they want, but it's usually a good idea to make C functions work this way too.

Because of this snapshotting behavior, a function containing only SELECT commands can safely be marked STABLE, even if it selects from tables that might be undergoing modifications by concurrent queries. PostgreSQL will execute all commands of a STABLE function using the snapshot established for the calling query, and so it will see a fixed view of the database throughout that query.

The same snapshotting behavior is used for SELECT commands within IMMUTABLE functions. It is generally unwise to select from database tables within an IMMUTABLE function at all, since the immutability will be broken if the table contents ever change. However, PostgreSQL does not enforce that you do not do that.

A common error is to label a function IMMUTABLE when its results depend on a configuration parameter. For example, a function that manipulates timestamps might well have results that depend on the TimeZone setting. For safety, such functions should be labeled STABLE instead.

> **Note:** PostgreSQL requires that STABLE and IMMUTABLE functions contain no SQL commands other than SELECT to prevent data modification. (This is not a completely bulletproof test, since such functions could still call VOLATILE functions that modify the database. If you do that, you will find that the STABLE or IMMUTABLE function does not notice the database changes applied by the called function, since they are hidden from its snapshot.)

36.7. Procedural Language Functions

PostgreSQL allows user-defined functions to be written in other languages besides SQL and C. These other languages are generically called *procedural languages* (PLs). Procedural languages aren't built into the PostgreSQL server; they are offered by loadable modules. See Chapter 40 and following chapters for more information.

36.8. Internal Functions

Internal functions are functions written in C that have been statically linked into the PostgreSQL server. The "body" of the function definition specifies the C-language name of the function, which need not be the same as the name being declared for SQL use. (For reasons of backward compatibility, an empty body is accepted as meaning that the C-language function name is the same as the SQL name.)

Normally, all internal functions present in the server are declared during the initialization of the database cluster (see Section 18.2), but a user could use CREATE FUNCTION to create additional alias names for an internal function. Internal functions are declared in CREATE FUNCTION with language name internal. For instance, to create an alias for the sqrt function:

```
CREATE FUNCTION square_root(double precision) RETURNS double precision
    AS 'dsqrt'
    LANGUAGE internal
    STRICT;
```

(Most internal functions expect to be declared "strict".)

> **Note:** Not all "predefined" functions are "internal" in the above sense. Some predefined functions are written in SQL.

36.9. C-Language Functions

User-defined functions can be written in C (or a language that can be made compatible with C, such as C++). Such functions are compiled into dynamically loadable objects (also called shared libraries) and are loaded by the server on demand. The dynamic loading feature is what distinguishes "C language" functions from "internal" functions — the actual coding conventions are essentially the same for both. (Hence, the standard internal function library is a rich source of coding examples for user-defined C functions.)

Two different calling conventions are currently used for C functions. The newer "version 1" calling convention is indicated by writing a PG_FUNCTION_INFO_V1() macro call for the function, as illustrated below. Lack of such a macro indicates an old-style ("version 0") function. The language name specified in CREATE FUNCTION is C in either case. Old-style functions are now deprecated because of portability problems and lack of functionality, but they are still supported for compatibility reasons.

36.9.1. Dynamic Loading

The first time a user-defined function in a particular loadable object file is called in a session, the dynamic loader loads that object file into memory so that the function can be called. The CREATE FUNCTION for a user-defined C function must therefore specify two pieces of information for the function: the name of the loadable object file, and the C name (link symbol) of the specific function to call within that object file. If the C name is not explicitly specified then it is assumed to be the same as the SQL function name.

The following algorithm is used to locate the shared object file based on the name given in the CREATE FUNCTION command:

1. If the name is an absolute path, the given file is loaded.

2. If the name starts with the string $libdir, that part is replaced by the PostgreSQL package library directory name, which is determined at build time.

3. If the name does not contain a directory part, the file is searched for in the path specified by the configuration variable dynamic_library_path.

4. Otherwise (the file was not found in the path, or it contains a non-absolute directory part), the dynamic loader will try to take the name as given, which will most likely fail. (It is unreliable to depend on the current working directory.)

If this sequence does not work, the platform-specific shared library file name extension (often .so) is appended to the given name and this sequence is tried again. If that fails as well, the load will fail.

It is recommended to locate shared libraries either relative to $libdir or through the dynamic library path. This simplifies version upgrades if the new installation is at a different location. The actual directory that $libdir stands for can be found out with the command pg_config --pkglibdir.

The user ID the PostgreSQL server runs as must be able to traverse the path to the file you intend to load. Making the file or a higher-level directory not readable and/or not executable by the postgres user is a common mistake.

In any case, the file name that is given in the CREATE FUNCTION command is recorded literally in the system catalogs, so if the file needs to be loaded again the same procedure is applied.

> **Note:** PostgreSQL will not compile a C function automatically. The object file must be compiled before it is referenced in a CREATE FUNCTION command. See Section 36.9.6 for additional information.

To ensure that a dynamically loaded object file is not loaded into an incompatible server, PostgreSQL checks that the file contains a "magic block" with the appropriate contents. This allows the server to detect obvious incompatibilities, such as code compiled for a different major version of PostgreSQL. A magic block is required as of PostgreSQL 8.2. To include a magic block, write this in one (and only one) of the module source files, after having included the header fmgr.h:

```
#ifdef PG_MODULE_MAGIC
PG_MODULE_MAGIC;
#endif
```

The #ifdef test can be omitted if the code doesn't need to compile against pre-8.2 PostgreSQL releases.

After it is used for the first time, a dynamically loaded object file is retained in memory. Future calls in the same session to the function(s) in that file will only incur the small overhead of a symbol table lookup. If you need to force a reload of an object file, for example after recompiling it, begin a fresh session.

Optionally, a dynamically loaded file can contain initialization and finalization functions. If the file includes a function named _PG_init, that function will be called immediately after loading the file. The function receives no parameters and should return void. If the file includes a function named _PG_fini, that function will be called immediately before unloading the file. Likewise, the function receives no parameters and should return void. Note that _PG_fini will only be called during an unload of the file, not during process termination. (Presently, unloads are disabled and will never occur, but this may change in the future.)

36.9.2. Base Types in C-Language Functions

To know how to write C-language functions, you need to know how PostgreSQL internally represents base data types and how they can be passed to and from functions. Internally, PostgreSQL regards a base type as a "blob of memory". The user-defined functions that you define over a type in turn define the way that PostgreSQL can operate on it. That is, PostgreSQL will only store and retrieve the data from disk and use your user-defined functions to input, process, and output the data.

Base types can have one of three internal formats:

- pass by value, fixed-length
- pass by reference, fixed-length
- pass by reference, variable-length

By-value types can only be 1, 2, or 4 bytes in length (also 8 bytes, if sizeof(Datum) is 8 on your machine). You should be careful to define your types such that they will be the same size (in bytes) on all architectures. For example, the long type is dangerous because it is 4 bytes on some machines and 8 bytes on others, whereas int type is 4 bytes on most Unix machines. A reasonable implementation of the int4 type on Unix machines might be:

```
/* 4-byte integer, passed by value */
typedef int int4;
```

(The actual PostgreSQL C code calls this type int32, because it is a convention in C that int*xx* means *xx bits*. Note therefore also that the C type int8 is 1 byte in size. The SQL type int8 is called int64 in C. See also Table 36-1.)

On the other hand, fixed-length types of any size can be passed by-reference. For example, here is a sample implementation of a PostgreSQL type:

```
/* 16-byte structure, passed by reference */
typedef struct
{
    double  x, y;
} Point;
```

Only pointers to such types can be used when passing them in and out of PostgreSQL functions. To return a value of such a type, allocate the right amount of memory with `palloc`, fill in the allocated memory, and return a pointer to it. (Also, if you just want to return the same value as one of your input arguments that's of the same data type, you can skip the extra `palloc` and just return the pointer to the input value.)

Finally, all variable-length types must also be passed by reference. All variable-length types must begin with an opaque length field of exactly 4 bytes, which will be set by `SET_VARSIZE`; never set this field directly! All data to be stored within that type must be located in the memory immediately following that length field. The length field contains the total length of the structure, that is, it includes the size of the length field itself.

Another important point is to avoid leaving any uninitialized bits within data type values; for example, take care to zero out any alignment padding bytes that might be present in structs. Without this, logically-equivalent constants of your data type might be seen as unequal by the planner, leading to inefficient (though not incorrect) plans.

Warning

Never modify the contents of a pass-by-reference input value. If you do so you are likely to corrupt on-disk data, since the pointer you are given might point directly into a disk buffer. The sole exception to this rule is explained in Section 36.10.

As an example, we can define the type `text` as follows:

```
typedef struct {
    int32 length;
    char data[FLEXIBLE_ARRAY_MEMBER];
} text;
```

The `[FLEXIBLE_ARRAY_MEMBER]` notation means that the actual length of the data part is not specified by this declaration.

When manipulating variable-length types, we must be careful to allocate the correct amount of memory and set the length field correctly. For example, if we wanted to store 40 bytes in a `text` structure, we might use a code fragment like this:

```
#include "postgres.h"
...
char buffer[40]; /* our source data */
...
text *destination = (text *) palloc(VARHDRSZ + 40);
SET_VARSIZE(destination, VARHDRSZ + 40);
memcpy(destination->data, buffer, 40);
...
```

`VARHDRSZ` is the same as `sizeof(int32)`, but it's considered good style to use the macro `VARHDRSZ` to refer to the size of the overhead for a variable-length type. Also, the length field *must* be set using the `SET_VARSIZE` macro, not by simple assignment.

Table 36-1 specifies which C type corresponds to which SQL type when writing a C-language function that uses a built-in type of PostgreSQL. The "Defined In" column gives the header file that needs to be included to get the type definition. (The actual definition might be in a different file that is included by the listed file. It is recommended that users stick to the defined interface.) Note that you should always include `postgres.h` first in any source file, because it declares a number of things that you will need anyway.

Table 36-1. Equivalent C Types for Built-in SQL Types

SQL Type	C Type	Defined In
`abstime`	`AbsoluteTime`	`utils/nabstime.h`
`bigint` (`int8`)	`int64`	`postgres.h`
`boolean`	`bool`	`postgres.h` (maybe compiler built-in)
`box`	`BOX*`	`utils/geo_decls.h`
`bytea`	`bytea*`	`postgres.h`
`"char"`	`char`	(compiler built-in)
`character`	`BpChar*`	`postgres.h`
`cid`	`CommandId`	`postgres.h`
`date`	`DateADT`	`utils/date.h`
`smallint` (`int2`)	`int16`	`postgres.h`
`int2vector`	`int2vector*`	`postgres.h`
`integer` (`int4`)	`int32`	`postgres.h`
`real` (`float4`)	`float4*`	`postgres.h`
`double precision` (`float8`)	`float8*`	`postgres.h`
`interval`	`Interval*`	`datatype/timestamp.h`
`lseg`	`LSEG*`	`utils/geo_decls.h`
`name`	`Name`	`postgres.h`
`oid`	`Oid`	`postgres.h`
`oidvector`	`oidvector*`	`postgres.h`
`path`	`PATH*`	`utils/geo_decls.h`
`point`	`POINT*`	`utils/geo_decls.h`
`regproc`	`regproc`	`postgres.h`
`reltime`	`RelativeTime`	`utils/nabstime.h`
`text`	`text*`	`postgres.h`
`tid`	`ItemPointer`	`storage/itemptr.h`
`time`	`TimeADT`	`utils/date.h`
`time with time zone`	`TimeTzADT`	`utils/date.h`
`timestamp`	`Timestamp*`	`datatype/timestamp.h`
`tinterval`	`TimeInterval`	`utils/nabstime.h`
`varchar`	`VarChar*`	`postgres.h`
`xid`	`TransactionId`	`postgres.h`

Now that we've gone over all of the possible structures for base types, we can show some examples of real functions.

36.9.3. Version 0 Calling Conventions

We present the "old style" calling convention first — although this approach is now deprecated, it's easier to get a handle on initially. In the version-0 method, the arguments and result of the C function are just declared in normal C style, but being careful to use the C representation of each SQL data type as shown above.

Here are some examples:

```
#include "postgres.h"
#include <string.h>
#include "utils/geo_decls.h"

#ifdef PG_MODULE_MAGIC
PG_MODULE_MAGIC;
#endif

/* by value */

int
add_one(int arg)
{
    return arg + 1;
}

/* by reference, fixed length */

float8 *
add_one_float8(float8 *arg)
{
    float8    *result = (float8 *) palloc(sizeof(float8));

    *result = *arg + 1.0;

    return result;
}

Point *
makepoint(Point *pointx, Point *pointy)
{
    Point     *new_point = (Point *) palloc(sizeof(Point));

    new_point->x = pointx->x;
    new_point->y = pointy->y;

    return new_point;
}

/* by reference, variable length */

text *
copytext(text *t)
{
```

```
    /*
     * VARSIZE is the total size of the struct in bytes.
     */
    text *new_t = (text *) palloc(VARSIZE(t));
    SET_VARSIZE(new_t, VARSIZE(t));
    /*
     * VARDATA is a pointer to the data region of the struct.
     */
    memcpy((void *) VARDATA(new_t), /* destination */
           (void *) VARDATA(t),     /* source */
           VARSIZE(t) - VARHDRSZ);  /* how many bytes */
    return new_t;
}

text *
concat_text(text *arg1, text *arg2)
{
    int32 new_text_size = VARSIZE(arg1) + VARSIZE(arg2) - VARHDRSZ;
    text *new_text = (text *) palloc(new_text_size);

    SET_VARSIZE(new_text, new_text_size);
    memcpy(VARDATA(new_text), VARDATA(arg1), VARSIZE(arg1) - VARHDRSZ);
    memcpy(VARDATA(new_text) + (VARSIZE(arg1) - VARHDRSZ),
           VARDATA(arg2), VARSIZE(arg2) - VARHDRSZ);
    return new_text;
}
```

Supposing that the above code has been prepared in file `funcs.c` and compiled into a shared object, we could define the functions to PostgreSQL with commands like this:

```
CREATE FUNCTION add_one(integer) RETURNS integer
     AS 'DIRECTORY/funcs', 'add_one'
     LANGUAGE C STRICT;

-- note overloading of SQL function name "add_one"
CREATE FUNCTION add_one(double precision) RETURNS double precision
     AS 'DIRECTORY/funcs', 'add_one_float8'
     LANGUAGE C STRICT;

CREATE FUNCTION makepoint(point, point) RETURNS point
     AS 'DIRECTORY/funcs', 'makepoint'
     LANGUAGE C STRICT;

CREATE FUNCTION copytext(text) RETURNS text
     AS 'DIRECTORY/funcs', 'copytext'
     LANGUAGE C STRICT;

CREATE FUNCTION concat_text(text, text) RETURNS text
     AS 'DIRECTORY/funcs', 'concat_text'
     LANGUAGE C STRICT;
```

Here, *DIRECTORY* stands for the directory of the shared library file (for instance the PostgreSQL tutorial directory, which contains the code for the examples used in this section). (Better style would be to use just 'funcs' in the AS clause, after having added *DIRECTORY* to the search path. In any case, we can omit the system-specific extension for a shared library, commonly .so or .sl.)

Notice that we have specified the functions as "strict", meaning that the system should automatically assume a null result if any input value is null. By doing this, we avoid having to check for null inputs in the function code. Without this, we'd have to check for null values explicitly, by checking for a null pointer for each pass-by-reference argument. (For pass-by-value arguments, we don't even have a way to check!)

Although this calling convention is simple to use, it is not very portable; on some architectures there are problems with passing data types that are smaller than int this way. Also, there is no simple way to return a null result, nor to cope with null arguments in any way other than making the function strict. The version-1 convention, presented next, overcomes these objections.

36.9.4. Version 1 Calling Conventions

The version-1 calling convention relies on macros to suppress most of the complexity of passing arguments and results. The C declaration of a version-1 function is always:

```
Datum funcname(PG_FUNCTION_ARGS)
```

In addition, the macro call:

```
PG_FUNCTION_INFO_V1(funcname);
```

must appear in the same source file. (Conventionally, it's written just before the function itself.) This macro call is not needed for internal-language functions, since PostgreSQL assumes that all internal functions use the version-1 convention. It is, however, required for dynamically-loaded functions.

In a version-1 function, each actual argument is fetched using a PG_GETARG_*xxx*() macro that corresponds to the argument's data type, and the result is returned using a PG_RETURN_*xxx*() macro for the return type. PG_GETARG_*xxx*() takes as its argument the number of the function argument to fetch, where the count starts at 0. PG_RETURN_*xxx*() takes as its argument the actual value to return.

Here we show the same functions as above, coded in version-1 style:

```
#include "postgres.h"
#include <string.h>
#include "fmgr.h"
#include "utils/geo_decls.h"

#ifdef PG_MODULE_MAGIC
PG_MODULE_MAGIC;
#endif

/* by value */

PG_FUNCTION_INFO_V1(add_one);

Datum
```

```
add_one(PG_FUNCTION_ARGS)
{
    int32    arg = PG_GETARG_INT32(0);

    PG_RETURN_INT32(arg + 1);
}

/* by reference, fixed length */

PG_FUNCTION_INFO_V1(add_one_float8);

Datum
add_one_float8(PG_FUNCTION_ARGS)
{
    /* The macros for FLOAT8 hide its pass-by-reference nature. */
    float8   arg = PG_GETARG_FLOAT8(0);

    PG_RETURN_FLOAT8(arg + 1.0);
}

PG_FUNCTION_INFO_V1(makepoint);

Datum
makepoint(PG_FUNCTION_ARGS)
{
    /* Here, the pass-by-reference nature of Point is not hidden. */
    Point      *pointx = PG_GETARG_POINT_P(0);
    Point      *pointy = PG_GETARG_POINT_P(1);
    Point      *new_point = (Point *) palloc(sizeof(Point));

    new_point->x = pointx->x;
    new_point->y = pointy->y;

    PG_RETURN_POINT_P(new_point);
}

/* by reference, variable length */

PG_FUNCTION_INFO_V1(copytext);

Datum
copytext(PG_FUNCTION_ARGS)
{
    text       *t = PG_GETARG_TEXT_P(0);
    /*
     * VARSIZE is the total size of the struct in bytes.
     */
    text       *new_t = (text *) palloc(VARSIZE(t));
    SET_VARSIZE(new_t, VARSIZE(t));
    /*
     * VARDATA is a pointer to the data region of the struct.
     */
    memcpy((void *) VARDATA(new_t), /* destination */
```

```
                (void *) VARDATA(t),      /* source */
                VARSIZE(t) - VARHDRSZ);   /* how many bytes */
        PG_RETURN_TEXT_P(new_t);
}


PG_FUNCTION_INFO_V1(concat_text);

Datum
concat_text(PG_FUNCTION_ARGS)
{
        text   *arg1 = PG_GETARG_TEXT_P(0);
        text   *arg2 = PG_GETARG_TEXT_P(1);
        int32 new_text_size = VARSIZE(arg1) + VARSIZE(arg2) - VARHDRSZ;
        text *new_text = (text *) palloc(new_text_size);

        SET_VARSIZE(new_text, new_text_size);
        memcpy(VARDATA(new_text), VARDATA(arg1), VARSIZE(arg1) - VARHDRSZ);
        memcpy(VARDATA(new_text) + (VARSIZE(arg1) - VARHDRSZ),
                VARDATA(arg2), VARSIZE(arg2) - VARHDRSZ);
        PG_RETURN_TEXT_P(new_text);
}
```

The CREATE FUNCTION commands are the same as for the version-0 equivalents.

At first glance, the version-1 coding conventions might appear to be just pointless obscurantism. They do, however, offer a number of improvements, because the macros can hide unnecessary detail. An example is that in coding add_one_float8, we no longer need to be aware that float8 is a pass-by-reference type. Another example is that the GETARG macros for variable-length types allow for more efficient fetching of "toasted" (compressed or out-of-line) values.

One big improvement in version-1 functions is better handling of null inputs and results. The macro PG_ARGISNULL(*n*) allows a function to test whether each input is null. (Of course, doing this is only necessary in functions not declared "strict".) As with the PG_GETARG_*xxx*() macros, the input arguments are counted beginning at zero. Note that one should refrain from executing PG_GETARG_*xxx*() until one has verified that the argument isn't null. To return a null result, execute PG_RETURN_NULL(); this works in both strict and nonstrict functions.

Other options provided in the new-style interface are two variants of the PG_GETARG_*xxx*() macros. The first of these, PG_GETARG_*xxx*_COPY(), guarantees to return a copy of the specified argument that is safe for writing into. (The normal macros will sometimes return a pointer to a value that is physically stored in a table, which must not be written to. Using the PG_GETARG_*xxx*_COPY() macros guarantees a writable result.) The second variant consists of the PG_GETARG_*xxx*_SLICE() macros which take three arguments. The first is the number of the function argument (as above). The second and third are the offset and length of the segment to be returned. Offsets are counted from zero, and a negative length requests that the remainder of the value be returned. These macros provide more efficient access to parts of large values in the case where they have storage type "external". (The storage type of a column can be specified using ALTER TABLE *tablename* ALTER COLUMN *colname* SET STORAGE *storagetype*. *storagetype* is one of plain, external, extended, or main.)

Finally, the version-1 function call conventions make it possible to return set results (Section 36.9.9) and implement trigger functions (Chapter 37) and procedural-language call handlers (Chapter 54). Version-1 code is also more portable than version-0, because it does not break restrictions on function call protocol in the C standard. For more details see `src/backend/utils/fmgr/README` in the source distribution.

36.9.5. Writing Code

Before we turn to the more advanced topics, we should discuss some coding rules for PostgreSQL C-language functions. While it might be possible to load functions written in languages other than C into PostgreSQL, this is usually difficult (when it is possible at all) because other languages, such as C++, FORTRAN, or Pascal often do not follow the same calling convention as C. That is, other languages do not pass argument and return values between functions in the same way. For this reason, we will assume that your C-language functions are actually written in C.

The basic rules for writing and building C functions are as follows:

- Use `pg_config --includedir-server` to find out where the PostgreSQL server header files are installed on your system (or the system that your users will be running on).

- Compiling and linking your code so that it can be dynamically loaded into PostgreSQL always requires special flags. See Section 36.9.6 for a detailed explanation of how to do it for your particular operating system.

- Remember to define a "magic block" for your shared library, as described in Section 36.9.1.

- When allocating memory, use the PostgreSQL functions `palloc` and `pfree` instead of the corresponding C library functions `malloc` and `free`. The memory allocated by `palloc` will be freed automatically at the end of each transaction, preventing memory leaks.

- Always zero the bytes of your structures using `memset` (or allocate them with `palloc0` in the first place). Even if you assign to each field of your structure, there might be alignment padding (holes in the structure) that contain garbage values. Without this, it's difficult to support hash indexes or hash joins, as you must pick out only the significant bits of your data structure to compute a hash. The planner also sometimes relies on comparing constants via bitwise equality, so you can get undesirable planning results if logically-equivalent values aren't bitwise equal.

- Most of the internal PostgreSQL types are declared in `postgres.h`, while the function manager interfaces (`PG_FUNCTION_ARGS`, etc.) are in `fmgr.h`, so you will need to include at least these two files. For portability reasons it's best to include `postgres.h` *first*, before any other system or user header files. Including `postgres.h` will also include `elog.h` and `palloc.h` for you.

- Symbol names defined within object files must not conflict with each other or with symbols defined in the PostgreSQL server executable. You will have to rename your functions or variables if you get error messages to this effect.

36.9.6. Compiling and Linking Dynamically-loaded Functions

Before you are able to use your PostgreSQL extension functions written in C, they must be compiled and linked in a special way to produce a file that can be dynamically loaded by the server. To be precise, a *shared library* needs to be created.

For information beyond what is contained in this section you should read the documentation of your operating system, in particular the manual pages for the C compiler, `cc`, and the link editor, `ld`. In addition, the PostgreSQL source code contains several working examples in the `contrib` directory. If you rely on these examples you will make your modules dependent on the availability of the PostgreSQL source code, however.

Creating shared libraries is generally analogous to linking executables: first the source files are compiled into object files, then the object files are linked together. The object files need to be created as *position-independent code* (PIC), which conceptually means that they can be placed at an arbitrary location in memory when they are loaded by the executable. (Object files intended for executables are usually not compiled that way.) The command to link a shared library contains special flags to distinguish it from linking an executable (at least in theory — on some systems the practice is much uglier).

In the following examples we assume that your source code is in a file `foo.c` and we will create a shared library `foo.so`. The intermediate object file will be called `foo.o` unless otherwise noted. A shared library can contain more than one object file, but we only use one here.

FreeBSD

> The compiler flag to create PIC is `-fpic`. To create shared libraries the compiler flag is `-shared`.
>
> ```
> gcc -fpic -c foo.c
> gcc -shared -o foo.so foo.o
> ```
> This is applicable as of version 3.0 of FreeBSD.

HP-UX

> The compiler flag of the system compiler to create PIC is `+z`. When using GCC it's `-fpic`. The linker flag for shared libraries is `-b`. So:
>
> ```
> cc +z -c foo.c
> ```
> or:
>
> ```
> gcc -fpic -c foo.c
> ```
> and then:
>
> ```
> ld -b -o foo.sl foo.o
> ```
> HP-UX uses the extension `.sl` for shared libraries, unlike most other systems.

Linux

> The compiler flag to create PIC is `-fpic`. On some platforms in some situations `-fPIC` must be used if `-fpic` does not work. Refer to the GCC manual for more information. The compiler flag to create a shared library is `-shared`. A complete example looks like this:
>
> ```
> cc -fpic -c foo.c
> cc -shared -o foo.so foo.o
> ```

OS X

> Here is an example. It assumes the developer tools are installed.
>
> ```
> cc -c foo.c
> cc -bundle -flat_namespace -undefined suppress -o foo.so foo.o
> ```

NetBSD

The compiler flag to create PIC is `-fpic`. For ELF systems, the compiler with the flag `-shared` is used to link shared libraries. On the older non-ELF systems, `ld -Bshareable` is used.

```
gcc -fpic -c foo.c
gcc -shared -o foo.so foo.o
```

OpenBSD

The compiler flag to create PIC is `-fpic`. `ld -Bshareable` is used to link shared libraries.

```
gcc -fpic -c foo.c
ld -Bshareable -o foo.so foo.o
```

Solaris

The compiler flag to create PIC is `-KPIC` with the Sun compiler and `-fpic` with GCC. To link shared libraries, the compiler option is `-G` with either compiler or alternatively `-shared` with GCC.

```
cc -KPIC -c foo.c
cc -G -o foo.so foo.o
```

or

```
gcc -fpic -c foo.c
gcc -G -o foo.so foo.o
```

UnixWare

The compiler flag to create PIC is `-K PIC` with the SCO compiler and `-fpic` with GCC. To link shared libraries, the compiler option is `-G` with the SCO compiler and `-shared` with GCC.

```
cc -K PIC -c foo.c
cc -G -o foo.so foo.o
```

or

```
gcc -fpic -c foo.c
gcc -shared -o foo.so foo.o
```

Tip: If this is too complicated for you, you should consider using GNU Libtool[1], which hides the platform differences behind a uniform interface.

The resulting shared library file can then be loaded into PostgreSQL. When specifying the file name to the CREATE FUNCTION command, one must give it the name of the shared library file, not the intermediate object file. Note that the system's standard shared-library extension (usually `.so` or `.sl`) can be omitted from the CREATE FUNCTION command, and normally should be omitted for best portability.

Refer back to Section 36.9.1 about where the server expects to find the shared library files.

36.9.7. Composite-type Arguments

Composite types do not have a fixed layout like C structures. Instances of a composite type can contain null fields. In addition, composite types that are part of an inheritance hierarchy can have different fields than

---

1. http://www.gnu.org/software/libtool/

other members of the same inheritance hierarchy. Therefore, PostgreSQL provides a function interface for accessing fields of composite types from C.

Suppose we want to write a function to answer the query:

```
SELECT name, c_overpaid(emp, 1500) AS overpaid
    FROM emp
    WHERE name = 'Bill' OR name = 'Sam';
```

Using call conventions version 0, we can define c_overpaid as:

```
#include "postgres.h"
#include "executor/executor.h"  /* for GetAttributeByName() */

#ifdef PG_MODULE_MAGIC
PG_MODULE_MAGIC;
#endif

bool
c_overpaid(HeapTupleHeader t, /* the current row of emp */
           int32 limit)
{
    bool isnull;
    int32 salary;

    salary = DatumGetInt32(GetAttributeByName(t, "salary", &isnull));
    if (isnull)
        return false;
    return salary > limit;
}
```

In version-1 coding, the above would look like this:

```
#include "postgres.h"
#include "executor/executor.h"  /* for GetAttributeByName() */

#ifdef PG_MODULE_MAGIC
PG_MODULE_MAGIC;
#endif

PG_FUNCTION_INFO_V1(c_overpaid);

Datum
c_overpaid(PG_FUNCTION_ARGS)
{
    HeapTupleHeader   t = PG_GETARG_HEAPTUPLEHEADER(0);
    int32             limit = PG_GETARG_INT32(1);
    bool isnull;
    Datum salary;

    salary = GetAttributeByName(t, "salary", &isnull);
    if (isnull)
        PG_RETURN_BOOL(false);
    /* Alternatively, we might prefer to do PG_RETURN_NULL() for null salary. */
```

```
    PG_RETURN_BOOL(DatumGetInt32(salary) > limit);
}
```

GetAttributeByName is the PostgreSQL system function that returns attributes out of the specified row. It has three arguments: the argument of type HeapTupleHeader passed into the function, the name of the desired attribute, and a return parameter that tells whether the attribute is null. GetAttributeByName returns a Datum value that you can convert to the proper data type by using the appropriate DatumGet*XXX*() macro. Note that the return value is meaningless if the null flag is set; always check the null flag before trying to do anything with the result.

There is also GetAttributeByNum, which selects the target attribute by column number instead of name.

The following command declares the function c_overpaid in SQL:

```
CREATE FUNCTION c_overpaid(emp, integer) RETURNS boolean
    AS 'DIRECTORY/funcs', 'c_overpaid'
    LANGUAGE C STRICT;
```

Notice we have used STRICT so that we did not have to check whether the input arguments were NULL.

36.9.8. Returning Rows (Composite Types)

To return a row or composite-type value from a C-language function, you can use a special API that provides macros and functions to hide most of the complexity of building composite data types. To use this API, the source file must include:

```
#include "funcapi.h"
```

There are two ways you can build a composite data value (henceforth a "tuple"): you can build it from an array of Datum values, or from an array of C strings that can be passed to the input conversion functions of the tuple's column data types. In either case, you first need to obtain or construct a TupleDesc descriptor for the tuple structure. When working with Datums, you pass the TupleDesc to BlessTupleDesc, and then call heap_form_tuple for each row. When working with C strings, you pass the TupleDesc to TupleDescGetAttInMetadata, and then call BuildTupleFromCStrings for each row. In the case of a function returning a set of tuples, the setup steps can all be done once during the first call of the function.

Several helper functions are available for setting up the needed TupleDesc. The recommended way to do this in most functions returning composite values is to call:

```
TypeFuncClass get_call_result_type(FunctionCallInfo fcinfo,
                                   Oid *resultTypeId,
                                   TupleDesc *resultTupleDesc)
```

passing the same fcinfo struct passed to the calling function itself. (This of course requires that you use the version-1 calling conventions.) resultTypeId can be specified as NULL or as the address of a local variable to receive the function's result type OID. resultTupleDesc should be the address of a local TupleDesc variable. Check that the result is TYPEFUNC_COMPOSITE; if so, resultTupleDesc has been filled with the needed `TupleDesc`. (If it is not, you can report an error along the lines of "function returning record called in context that cannot accept type record".)

> **Tip:** `get_call_result_type` can resolve the actual type of a polymorphic function result; so it is useful in functions that return scalar polymorphic results, not only functions that return composites. The `resultTypeId` output is primarily useful for functions returning polymorphic scalars.

> **Note:** `get_call_result_type` has a sibling `get_expr_result_type`, which can be used to resolve the expected output type for a function call represented by an expression tree. This can be used when trying to determine the result type from outside the function itself. There is also `get_func_result_type`, which can be used when only the function's OID is available. However these functions are not able to deal with functions declared to return `record`, and `get_func_result_type` cannot resolve polymorphic types, so you should preferentially use `get_call_result_type`.

Older, now-deprecated functions for obtaining `TupleDesc`s are:

```
TupleDesc RelationNameGetTupleDesc(const char *relname)
```

to get a `TupleDesc` for the row type of a named relation, and:

```
TupleDesc TypeGetTupleDesc(Oid typeoid, List *colaliases)
```

to get a `TupleDesc` based on a type OID. This can be used to get a `TupleDesc` for a base or composite type. It will not work for a function that returns `record`, however, and it cannot resolve polymorphic types.

Once you have a `TupleDesc`, call:

```
TupleDesc BlessTupleDesc(TupleDesc tupdesc)
```

if you plan to work with Datums, or:

```
AttInMetadata *TupleDescGetAttInMetadata(TupleDesc tupdesc)
```

if you plan to work with C strings. If you are writing a function returning set, you can save the results of these functions in the `FuncCallContext` structure — use the `tuple_desc` or `attinmeta` field respectively.

When working with Datums, use:

```
HeapTuple heap_form_tuple(TupleDesc tupdesc, Datum *values, bool *isnull)
```

to build a `HeapTuple` given user data in Datum form.

When working with C strings, use:

```
HeapTuple BuildTupleFromCStrings(AttInMetadata *attinmeta, char **values)
```

to build a `HeapTuple` given user data in C string form. `values` is an array of C strings, one for each attribute of the return row. Each C string should be in the form expected by the input function of the attribute data type. In order to return a null value for one of the attributes, the corresponding pointer in the values array should be set to NULL. This function will need to be called again for each row you return.

Once you have built a tuple to return from your function, it must be converted into a Datum. Use:

```
HeapTupleGetDatum(HeapTuple tuple)
```

to convert a HeapTuple into a valid Datum. This Datum can be returned directly if you intend to return just a single row, or it can be used as the current return value in a set-returning function.

An example appears in the next section.

36.9.9. Returning Sets

There is also a special API that provides support for returning sets (multiple rows) from a C-language function. A set-returning function must follow the version-1 calling conventions. Also, source files must include funcapi.h, as above.

A set-returning function (SRF) is called once for each item it returns. The SRF must therefore save enough state to remember what it was doing and return the next item on each call. The structure FuncCallContext is provided to help control this process. Within a function, fcinfo->flinfo->fn_extra is used to hold a pointer to FuncCallContext across calls.

```
typedef struct
{
    /*
     * Number of times we've been called before
     *
     * call_cntr is initialized to 0 for you by SRF_FIRSTCALL_INIT(), and
     * incremented for you every time SRF_RETURN_NEXT() is called.
     */
    uint32 call_cntr;

    /*
     * OPTIONAL maximum number of calls
     *
     * max_calls is here for convenience only and setting it is optional.
     * If not set, you must provide alternative means to know when the
     * function is done.
     */
    uint32 max_calls;

    /*
     * OPTIONAL pointer to result slot
     *
     * This is obsolete and only present for backward compatibility, viz,
     * user-defined SRFs that use the deprecated TupleDescGetSlot().
     */
    TupleTableSlot *slot;

    /*
     * OPTIONAL pointer to miscellaneous user-provided context information
```

```
    *
    * user_fctx is for use as a pointer to your own data to retain
    * arbitrary context information between calls of your function.
    */
   void *user_fctx;

   /*
    * OPTIONAL pointer to struct containing attribute type input metadata
    *
    * attinmeta is for use when returning tuples (i.e., composite data types)
    * and is not used when returning base data types. It is only needed
    * if you intend to use BuildTupleFromCStrings() to create the return
    * tuple.
    */
   AttInMetadata *attinmeta;

   /*
    * memory context used for structures that must live for multiple calls
    *
    * multi_call_memory_ctx is set by SRF_FIRSTCALL_INIT() for you, and used
    * by SRF_RETURN_DONE() for cleanup. It is the most appropriate memory
    * context for any memory that is to be reused across multiple calls
    * of the SRF.
    */
   MemoryContext multi_call_memory_ctx;

   /*
    * OPTIONAL pointer to struct containing tuple description
    *
    * tuple_desc is for use when returning tuples (i.e., composite data types)
    * and is only needed if you are going to build the tuples with
    * heap_form_tuple() rather than with BuildTupleFromCStrings().  Note that
    * the TupleDesc pointer stored here should usually have been run through
    * BlessTupleDesc() first.
    */
   TupleDesc tuple_desc;

} FuncCallContext;
```

An SRF uses several functions and macros that automatically manipulate the `FuncCallContext` structure (and expect to find it via `fn_extra`). Use:

```
SRF_IS_FIRSTCALL()
```

to determine if your function is being called for the first or a subsequent time. On the first call (only) use:

```
SRF_FIRSTCALL_INIT()
```

to initialize the `FuncCallContext`. On every function call, including the first, use:

```
SRF_PERCALL_SETUP()
```

to properly set up for using the `FuncCallContext` and clearing any previously returned data left over from the previous pass.

If your function has data to return, use:

```
SRF_RETURN_NEXT(funcctx, result)
```

to return it to the caller. (`result` must be of type `Datum`, either a single value or a tuple prepared as described above.) Finally, when your function is finished returning data, use:

```
SRF_RETURN_DONE(funcctx)
```

to clean up and end the SRF.

The memory context that is current when the SRF is called is a transient context that will be cleared between calls. This means that you do not need to call `pfree` on everything you allocated using `palloc`; it will go away anyway. However, if you want to allocate any data structures to live across calls, you need to put them somewhere else. The memory context referenced by `multi_call_memory_ctx` is a suitable location for any data that needs to survive until the SRF is finished running. In most cases, this means that you should switch into `multi_call_memory_ctx` while doing the first-call setup.

Warning

While the actual arguments to the function remain unchanged between calls, if you detoast the argument values (which is normally done transparently by the `PG_GETARG_xxx` macro) in the transient context then the detoasted copies will be freed on each cycle. Accordingly, if you keep references to such values in your `user_fctx`, you must either copy them into the `multi_call_memory_ctx` after detoasting, or ensure that you detoast the values only in that context.

A complete pseudo-code example looks like the following:

```
Datum
my_set_returning_function(PG_FUNCTION_ARGS)
{
    FuncCallContext   *funcctx;
    Datum              result;
    further declarations as needed

    if (SRF_IS_FIRSTCALL())
    {
        MemoryContext oldcontext;

        funcctx = SRF_FIRSTCALL_INIT();
        oldcontext = MemoryContextSwitchTo(funcctx->multi_call_memory_ctx);
        /* One-time setup code appears here: */
        user code
        if returning composite
            build TupleDesc, and perhaps AttInMetadata
        endif returning composite
        user code
        MemoryContextSwitchTo(oldcontext);
    }
```

```
    /* Each-time setup code appears here: */
    user code
    funcctx = SRF_PERCALL_SETUP();
    user code

    /* this is just one way we might test whether we are done: */
    if (funcctx->call_cntr < funcctx->max_calls)
    {
        /* Here we want to return another item: */
        user code
        obtain result Datum
        SRF_RETURN_NEXT(funcctx, result);
    }
    else
    {
        /* Here we are done returning items and just need to clean up: */
        user code
        SRF_RETURN_DONE(funcctx);
    }
}
```

A complete example of a simple SRF returning a composite type looks like:

```
PG_FUNCTION_INFO_V1(retcomposite);

Datum
retcomposite(PG_FUNCTION_ARGS)
{
    FuncCallContext     *funcctx;
    int                  call_cntr;
    int                  max_calls;
    TupleDesc            tupdesc;
    AttInMetadata       *attinmeta;

    /* stuff done only on the first call of the function */
    if (SRF_IS_FIRSTCALL())
    {
        MemoryContext   oldcontext;

        /* create a function context for cross-call persistence */
        funcctx = SRF_FIRSTCALL_INIT();

        /* switch to memory context appropriate for multiple function calls */
        oldcontext = MemoryContextSwitchTo(funcctx->multi_call_memory_ctx);

        /* total number of tuples to be returned */
        funcctx->max_calls = PG_GETARG_UINT32(0);

        /* Build a tuple descriptor for our result type */
        if (get_call_result_type(fcinfo, NULL, &tupdesc) != TYPEFUNC_COMPOSITE)
            ereport(ERROR,
```

```
                    (errcode(ERRCODE_FEATURE_NOT_SUPPORTED),
                 errmsg("function returning record called in context "
                        "that cannot accept type record")));

        /*
         * generate attribute metadata needed later to produce tuples from raw
         * C strings
         */
        attinmeta = TupleDescGetAttInMetadata(tupdesc);
        funcctx->attinmeta = attinmeta;

        MemoryContextSwitchTo(oldcontext);
    }

    /* stuff done on every call of the function */
    funcctx = SRF_PERCALL_SETUP();

    call_cntr = funcctx->call_cntr;
    max_calls = funcctx->max_calls;
    attinmeta = funcctx->attinmeta;

    if (call_cntr < max_calls)    /* do when there is more left to send */
    {
        char       **values;
        HeapTuple    tuple;
        Datum        result;

        /*
         * Prepare a values array for building the returned tuple.
         * This should be an array of C strings which will
         * be processed later by the type input functions.
         */
        values = (char **) palloc(3 * sizeof(char *));
        values[0] = (char *) palloc(16 * sizeof(char));
        values[1] = (char *) palloc(16 * sizeof(char));
        values[2] = (char *) palloc(16 * sizeof(char));

        snprintf(values[0], 16, "%d", 1 * PG_GETARG_INT32(1));
        snprintf(values[1], 16, "%d", 2 * PG_GETARG_INT32(1));
        snprintf(values[2], 16, "%d", 3 * PG_GETARG_INT32(1));

        /* build a tuple */
        tuple = BuildTupleFromCStrings(attinmeta, values);

        /* make the tuple into a datum */
        result = HeapTupleGetDatum(tuple);

        /* clean up (this is not really necessary) */
        pfree(values[0]);
        pfree(values[1]);
        pfree(values[2]);
        pfree(values);
```

```
        SRF_RETURN_NEXT(funcctx, result);
    }
    else    /* do when there is no more left */
    {
        SRF_RETURN_DONE(funcctx);
    }
}
```

One way to declare this function in SQL is:

```
CREATE TYPE __retcomposite AS (f1 integer, f2 integer, f3 integer);

CREATE OR REPLACE FUNCTION retcomposite(integer, integer)
    RETURNS SETOF __retcomposite
    AS 'filename', 'retcomposite'
    LANGUAGE C IMMUTABLE STRICT;
```

A different way is to use OUT parameters:

```
CREATE OR REPLACE FUNCTION retcomposite(IN integer, IN integer,
    OUT f1 integer, OUT f2 integer, OUT f3 integer)
    RETURNS SETOF record
    AS 'filename', 'retcomposite'
    LANGUAGE C IMMUTABLE STRICT;
```

Notice that in this method the output type of the function is formally an anonymous `record` type.

The directory contrib/tablefunc module in the source distribution contains more examples of set-returning functions.

36.9.10. Polymorphic Arguments and Return Types

C-language functions can be declared to accept and return the polymorphic types `anyelement`, `anyarray`, `anynonarray`, `anyenum`, and `anyrange`. See Section 36.2.5 for a more detailed explanation of polymorphic functions. When function arguments or return types are defined as polymorphic types, the function author cannot know in advance what data type it will be called with, or need to return. There are two routines provided in `fmgr.h` to allow a version-1 C function to discover the actual data types of its arguments and the type it is expected to return. The routines are called `get_fn_expr_rettype(FmgrInfo *flinfo)` and `get_fn_expr_argtype(FmgrInfo *flinfo, int argnum)`. They return the result or argument type OID, or `InvalidOid` if the information is not available. The structure `flinfo` is normally accessed as `fcinfo->flinfo`. The parameter `argnum` is zero based. `get_call_result_type` can also be used as an alternative to `get_fn_expr_rettype`. There is also `get_fn_expr_variadic`, which can be used to find out whether variadic arguments have been merged into an array. This is primarily useful for `VARIADIC "any"` functions, since such merging will always have occurred for variadic functions taking ordinary array types.

For example, suppose we want to write a function to accept a single element of any type, and return a one-dimensional array of that type:

```
PG_FUNCTION_INFO_V1(make_array);
Datum
```

```
make_array(PG_FUNCTION_ARGS)
{
    ArrayType    *result;
    Oid          element_type = get_fn_expr_argtype(fcinfo->flinfo, 0);
    Datum        element;
    bool         isnull;
    int16        typlen;
    bool         typbyval;
    char         typalign;
    int          ndims;
    int          dims[MAXDIM];
    int          lbs[MAXDIM];

    if (!OidIsValid(element_type))
        elog(ERROR, "could not determine data type of input");

    /* get the provided element, being careful in case it's NULL */
    isnull = PG_ARGISNULL(0);
    if (isnull)
        element = (Datum) 0;
    else
        element = PG_GETARG_DATUM(0);

    /* we have one dimension */
    ndims = 1;
    /* and one element */
    dims[0] = 1;
    /* and lower bound is 1 */
    lbs[0] = 1;

    /* get required info about the element type */
    get_typlenbyvalalign(element_type, &typlen, &typbyval, &typalign);

    /* now build the array */
    result = construct_md_array(&element, &isnull, ndims, dims, lbs,
                                element_type, typlen, typbyval, typalign);

    PG_RETURN_ARRAYTYPE_P(result);
}
```

The following command declares the function make_array in SQL:

```
CREATE FUNCTION make_array(anyelement) RETURNS anyarray
    AS 'DIRECTORY/funcs', 'make_array'
    LANGUAGE C IMMUTABLE;
```

There is a variant of polymorphism that is only available to C-language functions: they can be declared to take parameters of type "any". (Note that this type name must be double-quoted, since it's also a SQL reserved word.) This works like anyelement except that it does not constrain different "any" arguments to be the same type, nor do they help determine the function's result type. A C-language function can also declare its final parameter to be VARIADIC "any". This will match one or more actual arguments of any type (not necessarily the same type). These arguments will *not* be gathered into an array as happens with normal variadic functions; they will just be passed to the function separately. The PG_NARGS() macro and the methods described above must be used to determine the number of actual arguments and their types when using this feature. Also, users of such a function might wish to use the VARIADIC keyword in their function call, with the expectation that the function would treat the array elements as separate arguments. The function itself must implement that behavior if wanted, after using get_fn_expr_variadic to detect that the actual argument was marked with VARIADIC.

36.9.11. Transform Functions

Some function calls can be simplified during planning based on properties specific to the function. For example, int4mul(n, 1) could be simplified to just n. To define such function-specific optimizations, write a *transform function* and place its OID in the protransform field of the primary function's pg_proc entry. The transform function must have the SQL signature protransform(internal) RETURNS internal. The argument, actually FuncExpr *, is a dummy node representing a call to the primary function. If the transform function's study of the expression tree proves that a simplified expression tree can substitute for all possible concrete calls represented thereby, build and return that simplified expression. Otherwise, return a NULL pointer (*not* a SQL null).

We make no guarantee that PostgreSQL will never call the primary function in cases that the transform function could simplify. Ensure rigorous equivalence between the simplified expression and an actual call to the primary function.

Currently, this facility is not exposed to users at the SQL level because of security concerns, so it is only practical to use for optimizing built-in functions.

36.9.12. Shared Memory and LWLocks

Add-ins can reserve LWLocks and an allocation of shared memory on server startup. The add-in's shared library must be preloaded by specifying it in shared_preload_libraries. Shared memory is reserved by calling:

```
void RequestAddinShmemSpace(int size)
```

from your _PG_init function.

LWLocks are reserved by calling:

```
void RequestNamedLWLockTranche(const char *tranche_name, int num_lwlocks)
```

from _PG_init. This will ensure that an array of num_lwlocks LWLocks is available under the name tranche_name. Use GetNamedLWLockTranche to get a pointer to this array.

To avoid possible race-conditions, each backend should use the LWLock AddinShmemInitLock when connecting to and initializing its allocation of shared memory, as shown here:

```
static mystruct *ptr = NULL;

if (!ptr)
```

```
{
        bool    found;

        LWLockAcquire(AddinShmemInitLock, LW_EXCLUSIVE);
        ptr = ShmemInitStruct("my struct name", size, &found);
        if (!found)
        {
                initialize contents of shmem area;
                acquire any requested LWLocks using:
                ptr->locks = GetNamedLWLockTranche("my tranche name");
        }
        LWLockRelease(AddinShmemInitLock);
}
```

36.9.13. Using C++ for Extensibility

Although the PostgreSQL backend is written in C, it is possible to write extensions in C++ if these guidelines are followed:

- All functions accessed by the backend must present a C interface to the backend; these C functions can then call C++ functions. For example, `extern C` linkage is required for backend-accessed functions. This is also necessary for any functions that are passed as pointers between the backend and C++ code.

- Free memory using the appropriate deallocation method. For example, most backend memory is allocated using `palloc()`, so use `pfree()` to free it. Using C++ `delete` in such cases will fail.

- Prevent exceptions from propagating into the C code (use a catch-all block at the top level of all `extern C` functions). This is necessary even if the C++ code does not explicitly throw any exceptions, because events like out-of-memory can still throw exceptions. Any exceptions must be caught and appropriate errors passed back to the C interface. If possible, compile C++ with `-fno-exceptions` to eliminate exceptions entirely; in such cases, you must check for failures in your C++ code, e.g. check for NULL returned by `new()`.

- If calling backend functions from C++ code, be sure that the C++ call stack contains only plain old data structures (POD). This is necessary because backend errors generate a distant `longjmp()` that does not properly unroll a C++ call stack with non-POD objects.

In summary, it is best to place C++ code behind a wall of `extern C` functions that interface to the backend, and avoid exception, memory, and call stack leakage.

36.10. User-defined Aggregates

Aggregate functions in PostgreSQL are defined in terms of *state values* and *state transition functions*. That is, an aggregate operates using a state value that is updated as each successive input row is processed. To define a new aggregate function, one selects a data type for the state value, an initial value for the state, and a state transition function. The state transition function takes the previous state value and the aggregate's input value(s) for the current row, and returns a new state value. A *final function* can also be specified, in case the desired result of the aggregate is different from the data that needs to be kept in the running state value. The final function takes the ending state value and returns whatever is wanted as the aggregate result. In principle, the transition and final functions are just ordinary functions that could also be used outside the context of the aggregate. (In practice, it's often helpful for performance reasons to create specialized transition functions that can only work when called as part of an aggregate.)

Thus, in addition to the argument and result data types seen by a user of the aggregate, there is an internal state-value data type that might be different from both the argument and result types.

If we define an aggregate that does not use a final function, we have an aggregate that computes a running function of the column values from each row. sum is an example of this kind of aggregate. sum starts at zero and always adds the current row's value to its running total. For example, if we want to make a sum aggregate to work on a data type for complex numbers, we only need the addition function for that data type. The aggregate definition would be:

```
CREATE AGGREGATE sum (complex)
(
    sfunc = complex_add,
    stype = complex,
    initcond = '(0,0)'
);
```

which we might use like this:

```
SELECT sum(a) FROM test_complex;

   sum
-----------
 (34,53.9)
```

(Notice that we are relying on function overloading: there is more than one aggregate named sum, but PostgreSQL can figure out which kind of sum applies to a column of type complex.)

The above definition of sum will return zero (the initial state value) if there are no nonnull input values. Perhaps we want to return null in that case instead — the SQL standard expects sum to behave that way. We can do this simply by omitting the initcond phrase, so that the initial state value is null. Ordinarily this would mean that the sfunc would need to check for a null state-value input. But for sum and some other simple aggregates like max and min, it is sufficient to insert the first nonnull input value into the state variable and then start applying the transition function at the second nonnull input value. PostgreSQL will do that automatically if the initial state value is null and the transition function is marked "strict" (i.e., not to be called for null inputs).

Another bit of default behavior for a "strict" transition function is that the previous state value is retained unchanged whenever a null input value is encountered. Thus, null values are ignored. If you need some other behavior for null inputs, do not declare your transition function as strict; instead code it to test for null inputs and do whatever is needed.

avg (average) is a more complex example of an aggregate. It requires two pieces of running state: the sum of the inputs and the count of the number of inputs. The final result is obtained by dividing these quantities. Average is typically implemented by using an array as the state value. For example, the built-in implementation of `avg(float8)` looks like:

```
CREATE AGGREGATE avg (float8)
(
    sfunc = float8_accum,
    stype = float8[],
    finalfunc = float8_avg,
    initcond = '{0,0,0}'
);
```

Note: `float8_accum` requires a three-element array, not just two elements, because it accumulates the sum of squares as well as the sum and count of the inputs. This is so that it can be used for some other aggregates as well as `avg`.

Aggregate function calls in SQL allow `DISTINCT` and `ORDER BY` options that control which rows are fed to the aggregate's transition function and in what order. These options are implemented behind the scenes and are not the concern of the aggregate's support functions.

For further details see the CREATE AGGREGATE command.

36.10.1. Moving-Aggregate Mode

Aggregate functions can optionally support *moving-aggregate mode*, which allows substantially faster execution of aggregate functions within windows with moving frame starting points. (See Section 3.5 and Section 4.2.8 for information about use of aggregate functions as window functions.) The basic idea is that in addition to a normal "forward" transition function, the aggregate provides an *inverse transition function*, which allows rows to be removed from the aggregate's running state value when they exit the window frame. For example a `sum` aggregate, which uses addition as the forward transition function, would use subtraction as the inverse transition function. Without an inverse transition function, the window function mechanism must recalculate the aggregate from scratch each time the frame starting point moves, resulting in run time proportional to the number of input rows times the average frame length. With an inverse transition function, the run time is only proportional to the number of input rows.

The inverse transition function is passed the current state value and the aggregate input value(s) for the earliest row included in the current state. It must reconstruct what the state value would have been if the given input row had never been aggregated, but only the rows following it. This sometimes requires that the forward transition function keep more state than is needed for plain aggregation mode. Therefore, the moving-aggregate mode uses a completely separate implementation from the plain mode: it has its own state data type, its own forward transition function, and its own final function if needed. These can be the same as the plain mode's data type and functions, if there is no need for extra state.

As an example, we could extend the `sum` aggregate given above to support moving-aggregate mode like this:

```
CREATE AGGREGATE sum (complex)
(
    sfunc = complex_add,
```

```
    stype = complex,
    initcond = '(0,0)',
    msfunc = complex_add,
    minvfunc = complex_sub,
    mstype = complex,
    minitcond = '(0,0)'
);
```

The parameters whose names begin with m define the moving-aggregate implementation. Except for the inverse transition function minvfunc, they correspond to the plain-aggregate parameters without m.

The forward transition function for moving-aggregate mode is not allowed to return null as the new state value. If the inverse transition function returns null, this is taken as an indication that the inverse function cannot reverse the state calculation for this particular input, and so the aggregate calculation will be redone from scratch for the current frame starting position. This convention allows moving-aggregate mode to be used in situations where there are some infrequent cases that are impractical to reverse out of the running state value. The inverse transition function can "punt" on these cases, and yet still come out ahead so long as it can work for most cases. As an example, an aggregate working with floating-point numbers might choose to punt when a NaN (not a number) input has to be removed from the running state value.

When writing moving-aggregate support functions, it is important to be sure that the inverse transition function can reconstruct the correct state value exactly. Otherwise there might be user-visible differences in results depending on whether the moving-aggregate mode is used. An example of an aggregate for which adding an inverse transition function seems easy at first, yet where this requirement cannot be met is sum over float4 or float8 inputs. A naive declaration of sum(float8) could be

```
CREATE AGGREGATE unsafe_sum (float8)
(
    stype = float8,
    sfunc = float8pl,
    mstype = float8,
    msfunc = float8pl,
    minvfunc = float8mi
);
```

This aggregate, however, can give wildly different results than it would have without the inverse transition function. For example, consider

```
SELECT
  unsafe_sum(x) OVER (ORDER BY n ROWS BETWEEN CURRENT ROW AND 1 FOLLOWING)
FROM (VALUES (1, 1.0e20::float8),
             (2, 1.0::float8)) AS v (n,x);
```

This query returns 0 as its second result, rather than the expected answer of 1. The cause is the limited precision of floating-point values: adding 1 to 1e20 results in 1e20 again, and so subtracting 1e20 from that yields 0, not 1. Note that this is a limitation of floating-point arithmetic in general, not a limitation of PostgreSQL.

36.10.2. Polymorphic and Variadic Aggregates

Aggregate functions can use polymorphic state transition functions or final functions, so that the same functions can be used to implement multiple aggregates. See Section 36.2.5 for an explanation of polymorphic functions. Going a step further, the aggregate function itself can be specified with polymorphic input type(s) and state type, allowing a single aggregate definition to serve for multiple input data types. Here is an example of a polymorphic aggregate:

```
CREATE AGGREGATE array_accum (anyelement)
(
    sfunc = array_append,
    stype = anyarray,
    initcond = '{}'
);
```

Here, the actual state type for any given aggregate call is the array type having the actual input type as elements. The behavior of the aggregate is to concatenate all the inputs into an array of that type. (Note: the built-in aggregate `array_agg` provides similar functionality, with better performance than this definition would have.)

Here's the output using two different actual data types as arguments:

```
SELECT attrelid::regclass, array_accum(attname)
    FROM pg_attribute
    WHERE attnum > 0 AND attrelid = 'pg_tablespace'::regclass
    GROUP BY attrelid;

   attrelid     |               array_accum
---------------+-------------------------------------------
 pg_tablespace | {spcname,spcowner,spcacl,spcoptions}
(1 row)

SELECT attrelid::regclass, array_accum(atttypid::regtype)
    FROM pg_attribute
    WHERE attnum > 0 AND attrelid = 'pg_tablespace'::regclass
    GROUP BY attrelid;

   attrelid     |         array_accum
---------------+--------------------------
 pg_tablespace | {name,oid,aclitem[],text[]}
(1 row)
```

Ordinarily, an aggregate function with a polymorphic result type has a polymorphic state type, as in the above example. This is necessary because otherwise the final function cannot be declared sensibly: it would need to have a polymorphic result type but no polymorphic argument type, which CREATE FUNCTION will reject on the grounds that the result type cannot be deduced from a call. But sometimes it is inconvenient to use a polymorphic state type. The most common case is where the aggregate support functions are to be written in C and the state type should be declared as `internal` because there is no SQL-level equivalent for it. To address this case, it is possible to declare the final function as taking extra "dummy" arguments that match the input arguments of the aggregate. Such dummy arguments are always passed as null values since no specific value is available when the final function is called. Their only use is to allow a polymorphic final function's result type to be connected to the aggregate's input type(s). For example, the definition of the built-in aggregate `array_agg` is equivalent to

```
CREATE FUNCTION array_agg_transfn(internal, anynonarray)
  RETURNS internal ...;
CREATE FUNCTION array_agg_finalfn(internal, anynonarray)
  RETURNS anyarray ...;

CREATE AGGREGATE array_agg (anynonarray)
(
    sfunc = array_agg_transfn,
    stype = internal,
    finalfunc = array_agg_finalfn,
    finalfunc_extra
);
```

Here, the `finalfunc_extra` option specifies that the final function receives, in addition to the state value, extra dummy argument(s) corresponding to the aggregate's input argument(s). The extra `anynonarray` argument allows the declaration of `array_agg_finalfn` to be valid.

An aggregate function can be made to accept a varying number of arguments by declaring its last argument as a `VARIADIC` array, in much the same fashion as for regular functions; see Section 36.4.5. The aggregate's transition function(s) must have the same array type as their last argument. The transition function(s) typically would also be marked `VARIADIC`, but this is not strictly required.

> **Note:** Variadic aggregates are easily misused in connection with the ORDER BY option (see Section 4.2.7), since the parser cannot tell whether the wrong number of actual arguments have been given in such a combination. Keep in mind that everything to the right of ORDER BY is a sort key, not an argument to the aggregate. For example, in
>
> ```
> SELECT myaggregate(a ORDER BY a, b, c) FROM ...
> ```
>
> the parser will see this as a single aggregate function argument and three sort keys. However, the user might have intended
>
> ```
> SELECT myaggregate(a, b, c ORDER BY a) FROM ...
> ```
>
> If myaggregate is variadic, both these calls could be perfectly valid.
>
> For the same reason, it's wise to think twice before creating aggregate functions with the same names and different numbers of regular arguments.

36.10.3. Ordered-Set Aggregates

The aggregates we have been describing so far are "normal" aggregates. PostgreSQL also supports *ordered-set aggregates*, which differ from normal aggregates in two key ways. First, in addition to ordinary aggregated arguments that are evaluated once per input row, an ordered-set aggregate can have "direct" arguments that are evaluated only once per aggregation operation. Second, the syntax for the ordinary aggregated arguments specifies a sort ordering for them explicitly. An ordered-set aggregate is usually used to implement a computation that depends on a specific row ordering, for instance rank or percentile, so that the sort ordering is a required aspect of any call. For example, the built-in definition of `percentile_disc` is equivalent to:

```
CREATE FUNCTION ordered_set_transition(internal, anyelement)
  RETURNS internal ...;
CREATE FUNCTION percentile_disc_final(internal, float8, anyelement)
  RETURNS anyelement ...;

CREATE AGGREGATE percentile_disc (float8 ORDER BY anyelement)
(
    sfunc = ordered_set_transition,
    stype = internal,
    finalfunc = percentile_disc_final,
    finalfunc_extra
);
```

This aggregate takes a `float8` direct argument (the percentile fraction) and an aggregated input that can be of any sortable data type. It could be used to obtain a median household income like this:

```
SELECT percentile_disc(0.5) WITHIN GROUP (ORDER BY income) FROM households;
 percentile_disc
-----------------
           50489
```

Here, `0.5` is a direct argument; it would make no sense for the percentile fraction to be a value varying across rows.

Unlike the case for normal aggregates, the sorting of input rows for an ordered-set aggregate is *not* done behind the scenes, but is the responsibility of the aggregate's support functions. The typical implementation approach is to keep a reference to a "tuplesort" object in the aggregate's state value, feed the incoming rows into that object, and then complete the sorting and read out the data in the final function. This design allows the final function to perform special operations such as injecting additional "hypothetical" rows into the data to be sorted. While normal aggregates can often be implemented with support functions written in PL/pgSQL or another PL language, ordered-set aggregates generally have to be written in C, since their state values aren't definable as any SQL data type. (In the above example, notice that the state value is declared as type `internal` — this is typical.)

The state transition function for an ordered-set aggregate receives the current state value plus the aggregated input values for each row, and returns the updated state value. This is the same definition as for normal aggregates, but note that the direct arguments (if any) are not provided. The final function receives the last state value, the values of the direct arguments if any, and (if `finalfunc_extra` is specified) null values corresponding to the aggregated input(s). As with normal aggregates, `finalfunc_extra` is only really useful if the aggregate is polymorphic; then the extra dummy argument(s) are needed to connect the final function's result type to the aggregate's input type(s).

Currently, ordered-set aggregates cannot be used as window functions, and therefore there is no need for them to support moving-aggregate mode.

36.10.4. Partial Aggregation

Optionally, an aggregate function can support *partial aggregation*. The idea of partial aggregation is to run the aggregate's state transition function over different subsets of the input data independently, and then to combine the state values resulting from those subsets to produce the same state value that would have resulted from scanning all the input in a single operation. This mode can be used for parallel aggregation by having different worker processes scan different portions of a table. Each worker produces a partial state value, and at the end those state values are combined to produce a final state value. (In the future this mode might also be used for purposes such as combining aggregations over local and remote tables; but that is not implemented yet.)

To support partial aggregation, the aggregate definition must provide a *combine function*, which takes two values of the aggregate's state type (representing the results of aggregating over two subsets of the input rows) and produces a new value of the state type, representing what the state would have been after aggregating over the combination of those sets of rows. It is unspecified what the relative order of the input rows from the two sets would have been. This means that it's usually impossible to define a useful combine function for aggregates that are sensitive to input row order.

As simple examples, MAX and MIN aggregates can be made to support partial aggregation by specifying the combine function as the same greater-of-two or lesser-of-two comparison function that is used as their transition function. SUM aggregates just need an addition function as combine function. (Again, this is the same as their transition function, unless the state value is wider than the input data type.)

The combine function is treated much like a transition function that happens to take a value of the state type, not of the underlying input type, as its second argument. In particular, the rules for dealing with null values and strict functions are similar. Also, if the aggregate definition specifies a non-null initcond, keep in mind that that will be used not only as the initial state for each partial aggregation run, but also as the initial state for the combine function, which will be called to combine each partial result into that state.

If the aggregate's state type is declared as internal, it is the combine function's responsibility that its result is allocated in the correct memory context for aggregate state values. This means in particular that when the first input is NULL it's invalid to simply return the second input, as that value will be in the wrong context and will not have sufficient lifespan.

When the aggregate's state type is declared as internal, it is usually also appropriate for the aggregate definition to provide a *serialization function* and a *deserialization function*, which allow such a state value to be copied from one process to another. Without these functions, parallel aggregation cannot be performed, and future applications such as local/remote aggregation will probably not work either.

A serialization function must take a single argument of type internal and return a result of type bytea, which represents the state value packaged up into a flat blob of bytes. Conversely, a deserialization function reverses that conversion. It must take two arguments of types bytea and internal, and return a result of type internal. (The second argument is unused and is always zero, but it is required for type-safety reasons.) The result of the deserialization function should simply be allocated in the current memory context, as unlike the combine function's result, it is not long-lived.

Worth noting also is that for an aggregate to be executed in parallel, the aggregate itself must be marked PARALLEL SAFE. The parallel-safety markings on its support functions are not consulted.

36.10.5. Support Functions for Aggregates

A function written in C can detect that it is being called as an aggregate support function by calling `AggCheckCallContext`, for example:

```
if (AggCheckCallContext(fcinfo, NULL))
```

One reason for checking this is that when it is true for a transition function, the first input must be a temporary state value and can therefore safely be modified in-place rather than allocating a new copy. See `int8inc()` for an example. (This is the *only* case where it is safe for a function to modify a pass-by-reference input. In particular, final functions for normal aggregates must not modify their inputs in any case, because in some cases they will be re-executed on the same final state value.)

Another support routine available to aggregate functions written in C is `AggGetAggref`, which returns the `Aggref` parse node that defines the aggregate call. This is mainly useful for ordered-set aggregates, which can inspect the substructure of the `Aggref` node to find out what sort ordering they are supposed to implement. Examples can be found in `orderedsetaggs.c` in the PostgreSQL source code.

36.11. User-defined Types

As described in Section 36.2, PostgreSQL can be extended to support new data types. This section describes how to define new base types, which are data types defined below the level of the SQL language. Creating a new base type requires implementing functions to operate on the type in a low-level language, usually C.

The examples in this section can be found in `complex.sql` and `complex.c` in the `src/tutorial` directory of the source distribution. See the `README` file in that directory for instructions about running the examples.

A user-defined type must always have input and output functions. These functions determine how the type appears in strings (for input by the user and output to the user) and how the type is organized in memory. The input function takes a null-terminated character string as its argument and returns the internal (in memory) representation of the type. The output function takes the internal representation of the type as argument and returns a null-terminated character string. If we want to do anything more with the type than merely store it, we must provide additional functions to implement whatever operations we'd like to have for the type.

Suppose we want to define a type `complex` that represents complex numbers. A natural way to represent a complex number in memory would be the following C structure:

```
typedef struct Complex {
    double      x;
    double      y;
} Complex;
```

We will need to make this a pass-by-reference type, since it's too large to fit into a single `Datum` value.

As the external string representation of the type, we choose a string of the form `(x,y)`.

The input and output functions are usually not hard to write, especially the output function. But when defining the external string representation of the type, remember that you must eventually write a complete and robust parser for that representation as your input function. For instance:

```
PG_FUNCTION_INFO_V1(complex_in);

Datum
complex_in(PG_FUNCTION_ARGS)
{
    char        *str = PG_GETARG_CSTRING(0);
    double      x,
                y;
    Complex     *result;

    if (sscanf(str, " ( %lf , %lf )", &x, &y) != 2)
        ereport(ERROR,
                (errcode(ERRCODE_INVALID_TEXT_REPRESENTATION),
                 errmsg("invalid input syntax for complex: \"%s\"",
                        str)));

    result = (Complex *) palloc(sizeof(Complex));
    result->x = x;
    result->y = y;
    PG_RETURN_POINTER(result);
}
```

The output function can simply be:

```
PG_FUNCTION_INFO_V1(complex_out);

Datum
complex_out(PG_FUNCTION_ARGS)
{
    Complex     *complex = (Complex *) PG_GETARG_POINTER(0);
    char        *result;

    result = psprintf("(%g,%g)", complex->x, complex->y);
    PG_RETURN_CSTRING(result);
}
```

You should be careful to make the input and output functions inverses of each other. If you do not, you will have severe problems when you need to dump your data into a file and then read it back in. This is a particularly common problem when floating-point numbers are involved.

Optionally, a user-defined type can provide binary input and output routines. Binary I/O is normally faster but less portable than textual I/O. As with textual I/O, it is up to you to define exactly what the external binary representation is. Most of the built-in data types try to provide a machine-independent binary representation. For complex, we will piggy-back on the binary I/O converters for type float8:

```
PG_FUNCTION_INFO_V1(complex_recv);

Datum
```

```
complex_recv(PG_FUNCTION_ARGS)
{
    StringInfo  buf = (StringInfo) PG_GETARG_POINTER(0);
    Complex     *result;

    result = (Complex *) palloc(sizeof(Complex));
    result->x = pq_getmsgfloat8(buf);
    result->y = pq_getmsgfloat8(buf);
    PG_RETURN_POINTER(result);
}


PG_FUNCTION_INFO_V1(complex_send);

Datum
complex_send(PG_FUNCTION_ARGS)
{
    Complex     *complex = (Complex *) PG_GETARG_POINTER(0);
    StringInfoData buf;

    pq_begintypsend(&buf);
    pq_sendfloat8(&buf, complex->x);
    pq_sendfloat8(&buf, complex->y);
    PG_RETURN_BYTEA_P(pq_endtypsend(&buf));
}
```

Once we have written the I/O functions and compiled them into a shared library, we can define the complex type in SQL. First we declare it as a shell type:

```
CREATE TYPE complex;
```

This serves as a placeholder that allows us to reference the type while defining its I/O functions. Now we can define the I/O functions:

```
CREATE FUNCTION complex_in(cstring)
    RETURNS complex
    AS 'filename'
    LANGUAGE C IMMUTABLE STRICT;

CREATE FUNCTION complex_out(complex)
    RETURNS cstring
    AS 'filename'
    LANGUAGE C IMMUTABLE STRICT;

CREATE FUNCTION complex_recv(internal)
   RETURNS complex
   AS 'filename'
   LANGUAGE C IMMUTABLE STRICT;

CREATE FUNCTION complex_send(complex)
   RETURNS bytea
   AS 'filename'
   LANGUAGE C IMMUTABLE STRICT;
```

Finally, we can provide the full definition of the data type:

```
CREATE TYPE complex (
    internallength = 16,
    input = complex_in,
    output = complex_out,
    receive = complex_recv,
    send = complex_send,
    alignment = double
);
```

When you define a new base type, PostgreSQL automatically provides support for arrays of that type. The array type typically has the same name as the base type with the underscore character (_) prepended.

Once the data type exists, we can declare additional functions to provide useful operations on the data type. Operators can then be defined atop the functions, and if needed, operator classes can be created to support indexing of the data type. These additional layers are discussed in following sections.

If the internal representation of the data type is variable-length, the internal representation must follow the standard layout for variable-length data: the first four bytes must be a `char[4]` field which is never accessed directly (customarily named `vl_len_`). You must use the `SET_VARSIZE()` macro to store the total size of the datum (including the length field itself) in this field and `VARSIZE()` to retrieve it. (These macros exist because the length field may be encoded depending on platform.)

For further details see the description of the CREATE TYPE command.

36.11.1. TOAST Considerations

If the values of your data type vary in size (in internal form), it's usually desirable to make the data type TOAST-able (see Section 65.2). You should do this even if the values are always too small to be compressed or stored externally, because TOAST can save space on small data too, by reducing header overhead.

To support TOAST storage, the C functions operating on the data type must always be careful to unpack any toasted values they are handed by using `PG_DETOAST_DATUM`. (This detail is customarily hidden by defining type-specific `GETARG_DATATYPE_P` macros.) Then, when running the CREATE TYPE command, specify the internal length as `variable` and select some appropriate storage option other than `plain`.

If data alignment is unimportant (either just for a specific function or because the data type specifies byte alignment anyway) then it's possible to avoid some of the overhead of `PG_DETOAST_DATUM`. You can use `PG_DETOAST_DATUM_PACKED` instead (customarily hidden by defining a `GETARG_DATATYPE_PP` macro) and using the macros `VARSIZE_ANY_EXHDR` and `VARDATA_ANY` to access a potentially-packed datum. Again, the data returned by these macros is not aligned even if the data type definition specifies an alignment. If the alignment is important you must go through the regular `PG_DETOAST_DATUM` interface.

> **Note:** Older code frequently declares `vl_len_` as an `int32` field instead of `char[4]`. This is OK as long as the struct definition has other fields that have at least `int32` alignment. But it is dangerous to use such a struct definition when working with a potentially unaligned datum; the compiler may take

it as license to assume the datum actually is aligned, leading to core dumps on architectures that are strict about alignment.

Another feature that's enabled by TOAST support is the possibility of having an *expanded* in-memory data representation that is more convenient to work with than the format that is stored on disk. The regular or "flat" varlena storage format is ultimately just a blob of bytes; it cannot for example contain pointers, since it may get copied to other locations in memory. For complex data types, the flat format may be quite expensive to work with, so PostgreSQL provides a way to "expand" the flat format into a representation that is more suited to computation, and then pass that format in-memory between functions of the data type.

To use expanded storage, a data type must define an expanded format that follows the rules given in `src/include/utils/expandeddatum.h`, and provide functions to "expand" a flat varlena value into expanded format and "flatten" the expanded format back to the regular varlena representation. Then ensure that all C functions for the data type can accept either representation, possibly by converting one into the other immediately upon receipt. This does not require fixing all existing functions for the data type at once, because the standard `PG_DETOAST_DATUM` macro is defined to convert expanded inputs into regular flat format. Therefore, existing functions that work with the flat varlena format will continue to work, though slightly inefficiently, with expanded inputs; they need not be converted until and unless better performance is important.

C functions that know how to work with an expanded representation typically fall into two categories: those that can only handle expanded format, and those that can handle either expanded or flat varlena inputs. The former are easier to write but may be less efficient overall, because converting a flat input to expanded form for use by a single function may cost more than is saved by operating on the expanded format. When only expanded format need be handled, conversion of flat inputs to expanded form can be hidden inside an argument-fetching macro, so that the function appears no more complex than one working with traditional varlena input. To handle both types of input, write an argument-fetching function that will detoast external, short-header, and compressed varlena inputs, but not expanded inputs. Such a function can be defined as returning a pointer to a union of the flat varlena format and the expanded format. Callers can use the `VARATT_IS_EXPANDED_HEADER()` macro to determine which format they received.

The TOAST infrastructure not only allows regular varlena values to be distinguished from expanded values, but also distinguishes "read-write" and "read-only" pointers to expanded values. C functions that only need to examine an expanded value, or will only change it in safe and non-semantically-visible ways, need not care which type of pointer they receive. C functions that produce a modified version of an input value are allowed to modify an expanded input value in-place if they receive a read-write pointer, but must not modify the input if they receive a read-only pointer; in that case they have to copy the value first, producing a new value to modify. A C function that has constructed a new expanded value should always return a read-write pointer to it. Also, a C function that is modifying a read-write expanded value in-place should take care to leave the value in a sane state if it fails partway through.

For examples of working with expanded values, see the standard array infrastructure, particularly `src/backend/utils/adt/array_expanded.c`.

36.12. User-defined Operators

Every operator is "syntactic sugar" for a call to an underlying function that does the real work; so you must first create the underlying function before you can create the operator. However, an operator is *not merely* syntactic sugar, because it carries additional information that helps the query planner optimize queries that use the operator. The next section will be devoted to explaining that additional information.

PostgreSQL supports left unary, right unary, and binary operators. Operators can be overloaded; that is, the same operator name can be used for different operators that have different numbers and types of operands. When a query is executed, the system determines the operator to call from the number and types of the provided operands.

Here is an example of creating an operator for adding two complex numbers. We assume we've already created the definition of type complex (see Section 36.11). First we need a function that does the work, then we can define the operator:

```
CREATE FUNCTION complex_add(complex, complex)
    RETURNS complex
    AS 'filename', 'complex_add'
    LANGUAGE C IMMUTABLE STRICT;

CREATE OPERATOR + (
    leftarg = complex,
    rightarg = complex,
    procedure = complex_add,
    commutator = +
);
```

Now we could execute a query like this:

```
SELECT (a + b) AS c FROM test_complex;

       c
-----------------
 (5.2,6.05)
 (133.42,144.95)
```

We've shown how to create a binary operator here. To create unary operators, just omit one of leftarg (for left unary) or rightarg (for right unary). The procedure clause and the argument clauses are the only required items in CREATE OPERATOR. The commutator clause shown in the example is an optional hint to the query optimizer. Further details about commutator and other optimizer hints appear in the next section.

36.13. Operator Optimization Information

A PostgreSQL operator definition can include several optional clauses that tell the system useful things about how the operator behaves. These clauses should be provided whenever appropriate, because they can make for considerable speedups in execution of queries that use the operator. But if you provide them, you must be sure that they are right! Incorrect use of an optimization clause can result in slow queries, subtly wrong output, or other Bad Things. You can always leave out an optimization clause if you are not sure about it; the only consequence is that queries might run slower than they need to.

Additional optimization clauses might be added in future versions of PostgreSQL. The ones described here are all the ones that release 9.6.0 understands.

36.13.1. COMMUTATOR

The COMMUTATOR clause, if provided, names an operator that is the commutator of the operator being defined. We say that operator A is the commutator of operator B if (x A y) equals (y B x) for all possible input values x, y. Notice that B is also the commutator of A. For example, operators < and > for a particular data type are usually each others' commutators, and operator + is usually commutative with itself. But operator − is usually not commutative with anything.

The left operand type of a commutable operator is the same as the right operand type of its commutator, and vice versa. So the name of the commutator operator is all that PostgreSQL needs to be given to look up the commutator, and that's all that needs to be provided in the COMMUTATOR clause.

It's critical to provide commutator information for operators that will be used in indexes and join clauses, because this allows the query optimizer to "flip around" such a clause to the forms needed for different plan types. For example, consider a query with a WHERE clause like tab1.x = tab2.y, where tab1.x and tab2.y are of a user-defined type, and suppose that tab2.y is indexed. The optimizer cannot generate an index scan unless it can determine how to flip the clause around to tab2.y = tab1.x, because the index-scan machinery expects to see the indexed column on the left of the operator it is given. PostgreSQL will *not* simply assume that this is a valid transformation — the creator of the = operator must specify that it is valid, by marking the operator with commutator information.

When you are defining a self-commutative operator, you just do it. When you are defining a pair of commutative operators, things are a little trickier: how can the first one to be defined refer to the other one, which you haven't defined yet? There are two solutions to this problem:

- One way is to omit the COMMUTATOR clause in the first operator that you define, and then provide one in the second operator's definition. Since PostgreSQL knows that commutative operators come in pairs, when it sees the second definition it will automatically go back and fill in the missing COMMUTATOR clause in the first definition.

- The other, more straightforward way is just to include COMMUTATOR clauses in both definitions. When PostgreSQL processes the first definition and realizes that COMMUTATOR refers to a nonexistent operator, the system will make a dummy entry for that operator in the system catalog. This dummy entry will have valid data only for the operator name, left and right operand types, and result type, since that's all that PostgreSQL can deduce at this point. The first operator's catalog entry will link to this dummy entry. Later, when you define the second operator, the system updates the dummy entry with the additional information from the second definition. If you try to use the dummy operator before it's been filled in, you'll just get an error message.

36.13.2. NEGATOR

The NEGATOR clause, if provided, names an operator that is the negator of the operator being defined. We say that operator A is the negator of operator B if both return Boolean results and (x A y) equals NOT (x B y) for all possible inputs x, y. Notice that B is also the negator of A. For example, < and >= are a negator pair for most data types. An operator can never validly be its own negator.

Unlike commutators, a pair of unary operators could validly be marked as each other's negators; that would mean (A x) equals NOT (B x) for all x, or the equivalent for right unary operators.

An operator's negator must have the same left and/or right operand types as the operator to be defined, so just as with COMMUTATOR, only the operator name need be given in the NEGATOR clause.

Providing a negator is very helpful to the query optimizer since it allows expressions like NOT (x = y) to be simplified into x <> y. This comes up more often than you might think, because NOT operations can be inserted as a consequence of other rearrangements.

Pairs of negator operators can be defined using the same methods explained above for commutator pairs.

36.13.3. RESTRICT

The RESTRICT clause, if provided, names a restriction selectivity estimation function for the operator. (Note that this is a function name, not an operator name.) RESTRICT clauses only make sense for binary operators that return boolean. The idea behind a restriction selectivity estimator is to guess what fraction of the rows in a table will satisfy a WHERE-clause condition of the form:

```
column OP constant
```

for the current operator and a particular constant value. This assists the optimizer by giving it some idea of how many rows will be eliminated by WHERE clauses that have this form. (What happens if the constant is on the left, you might be wondering? Well, that's one of the things that COMMUTATOR is for...)

Writing new restriction selectivity estimation functions is far beyond the scope of this chapter, but fortunately you can usually just use one of the system's standard estimators for many of your own operators. These are the standard restriction estimators:

eqsel for =
neqsel for <>
scalarltsel for < or <=
scalargtsel for > or >=

It might seem a little odd that these are the categories, but they make sense if you think about it. = will typically accept only a small fraction of the rows in a table; <> will typically reject only a small fraction. < will accept a fraction that depends on where the given constant falls in the range of values for that table column (which, it just so happens, is information collected by ANALYZE and made available to the selectivity estimator). <= will accept a slightly larger fraction than < for the same comparison constant, but they're close enough to not be worth distinguishing, especially since we're not likely to do better than a rough guess anyhow. Similar remarks apply to > and >=.

You can frequently get away with using either eqsel or neqsel for operators that have very high or very low selectivity, even if they aren't really equality or inequality. For example, the approximate-equality geometric operators use `eqsel` on the assumption that they'll usually only match a small fraction of the entries in a table.

You can use `scalarltsel` and `scalargtsel` for comparisons on data types that have some sensible means of being converted into numeric scalars for range comparisons. If possible, add the data type to those understood by the function `convert_to_scalar()` in `src/backend/utils/adt/selfuncs.c`. (Eventually, this function should be replaced by per-data-type functions identified through a column of the `pg_type` system catalog; but that hasn't happened yet.) If you do not do this, things will still work, but the optimizer's estimates won't be as good as they could be.

There are additional selectivity estimation functions designed for geometric operators in `src/backend/utils/adt/geo_selfuncs.c`: `areasel`, `positionsel`, and `contsel`. At this writing these are just stubs, but you might want to use them (or even better, improve them) anyway.

36.13.4. JOIN

The `JOIN` clause, if provided, names a join selectivity estimation function for the operator. (Note that this is a function name, not an operator name.) `JOIN` clauses only make sense for binary operators that return `boolean`. The idea behind a join selectivity estimator is to guess what fraction of the rows in a pair of tables will satisfy a `WHERE`-clause condition of the form:

```
table1.column1 OP table2.column2
```

for the current operator. As with the `RESTRICT` clause, this helps the optimizer very substantially by letting it figure out which of several possible join sequences is likely to take the least work.

As before, this chapter will make no attempt to explain how to write a join selectivity estimator function, but will just suggest that you use one of the standard estimators if one is applicable:

`eqjoinsel` for =
`neqjoinsel` for <>
`scalarltjoinsel` for < or <=
`scalargtjoinsel` for > or >=
`areajoinsel` for 2D area-based comparisons
`positionjoinsel` for 2D position-based comparisons
`contjoinsel` for 2D containment-based comparisons

36.13.5. HASHES

The `HASHES` clause, if present, tells the system that it is permissible to use the hash join method for a join based on this operator. `HASHES` only makes sense for a binary operator that returns `boolean`, and in practice the operator must represent equality for some data type or pair of data types.

The assumption underlying hash join is that the join operator can only return true for pairs of left and right values that hash to the same hash code. If two values get put in different hash buckets, the join will never compare them at all, implicitly assuming that the result of the join operator must be false. So it never makes sense to specify `HASHES` for operators that do not represent some form of equality. In most cases it is only practical to support hashing for operators that take the same data type on both sides. However, sometimes it is possible to design compatible hash functions for two or more data types; that is, functions that will generate the same hash codes for "equal" values, even though the values have different representations. For example, it's fairly simple to arrange this property when hashing integers of different widths.

To be marked HASHES, the join operator must appear in a hash index operator family. This is not enforced when you create the operator, since of course the referencing operator family couldn't exist yet. But attempts to use the operator in hash joins will fail at run time if no such operator family exists. The system needs the operator family to find the data-type-specific hash function(s) for the operator's input data type(s). Of course, you must also create suitable hash functions before you can create the operator family.

Care should be exercised when preparing a hash function, because there are machine-dependent ways in which it might fail to do the right thing. For example, if your data type is a structure in which there might be uninteresting pad bits, you cannot simply pass the whole structure to hash_any. (Unless you write your other operators and functions to ensure that the unused bits are always zero, which is the recommended strategy.) Another example is that on machines that meet the IEEE floating-point standard, negative zero and positive zero are different values (different bit patterns) but they are defined to compare equal. If a float value might contain negative zero then extra steps are needed to ensure it generates the same hash value as positive zero.

A hash-joinable operator must have a commutator (itself if the two operand data types are the same, or a related equality operator if they are different) that appears in the same operator family. If this is not the case, planner errors might occur when the operator is used. Also, it is a good idea (but not strictly required) for a hash operator family that supports multiple data types to provide equality operators for every combination of the data types; this allows better optimization.

> **Note:** The function underlying a hash-joinable operator must be marked immutable or stable. If it is volatile, the system will never attempt to use the operator for a hash join.

> **Note:** If a hash-joinable operator has an underlying function that is marked strict, the function must also be complete: that is, it should return true or false, never null, for any two nonnull inputs. If this rule is not followed, hash-optimization of IN operations might generate wrong results. (Specifically, IN might return false where the correct answer according to the standard would be null; or it might yield an error complaining that it wasn't prepared for a null result.)

36.13.6. MERGES

The MERGES clause, if present, tells the system that it is permissible to use the merge-join method for a join based on this operator. MERGES only makes sense for a binary operator that returns boolean, and in practice the operator must represent equality for some data type or pair of data types.

Merge join is based on the idea of sorting the left- and right-hand tables into order and then scanning them in parallel. So, both data types must be capable of being fully ordered, and the join operator must be one that can only succeed for pairs of values that fall at the "same place" in the sort order. In practice this means that the join operator must behave like equality. But it is possible to merge-join two distinct data types so long as they are logically compatible. For example, the smallint-versus-integer equality operator is merge-joinable. We only need sorting operators that will bring both data types into a logically compatible sequence.

To be marked MERGES, the join operator must appear as an equality member of a btree index operator family. This is not enforced when you create the operator, since of course the referencing operator family couldn't exist yet. But the operator will not actually be used for merge joins unless a matching operator family can be found. The MERGES flag thus acts as a hint to the planner that it's worth looking for a matching operator family.

A merge-joinable operator must have a commutator (itself if the two operand data types are the same, or a related equality operator if they are different) that appears in the same operator family. If this is not the case, planner errors might occur when the operator is used. Also, it is a good idea (but not strictly required) for a btree operator family that supports multiple data types to provide equality operators for every combination of the data types; this allows better optimization.

> **Note:** The function underlying a merge-joinable operator must be marked immutable or stable. If it is volatile, the system will never attempt to use the operator for a merge join.

36.14. Interfacing Extensions To Indexes

The procedures described thus far let you define new types, new functions, and new operators. However, we cannot yet define an index on a column of a new data type. To do this, we must define an *operator class* for the new data type. Later in this section, we will illustrate this concept in an example: a new operator class for the B-tree index method that stores and sorts complex numbers in ascending absolute value order.

Operator classes can be grouped into *operator families* to show the relationships between semantically compatible classes. When only a single data type is involved, an operator class is sufficient, so we'll focus on that case first and then return to operator families.

36.14.1. Index Methods and Operator Classes

The pg_am table contains one row for every index method (internally known as access method). Support for regular access to tables is built into PostgreSQL, but all index methods are described in pg_am. It is possible to add a new index access method by writing the necessary code and then creating a row in pg_am — but that is beyond the scope of this chapter (see Chapter 59).

The routines for an index method do not directly know anything about the data types that the index method will operate on. Instead, an *operator class* identifies the set of operations that the index method needs to use to work with a particular data type. Operator classes are so called because one thing they specify is the set of WHERE-clause operators that can be used with an index (i.e., can be converted into an index-scan qualification). An operator class can also specify some *support procedures* that are needed by the internal operations of the index method, but do not directly correspond to any WHERE-clause operator that can be used with the index.

It is possible to define multiple operator classes for the same data type and index method. By doing this, multiple sets of indexing semantics can be defined for a single data type. For example, a B-tree index requires a sort ordering to be defined for each data type it works on. It might be useful for a complex-number data type to have one B-tree operator class that sorts the data by complex absolute value, another that sorts by real part, and so on. Typically, one of the operator classes will be deemed most commonly useful and will be marked as the default operator class for that data type and index method.

The same operator class name can be used for several different index methods (for example, both B-tree and hash index methods have operator classes named `int4_ops`), but each such class is an independent entity and must be defined separately.

36.14.2. Index Method Strategies

The operators associated with an operator class are identified by "strategy numbers", which serve to identify the semantics of each operator within the context of its operator class. For example, B-trees impose a strict ordering on keys, lesser to greater, and so operators like "less than" and "greater than or equal to" are interesting with respect to a B-tree. Because PostgreSQL allows the user to define operators, PostgreSQL cannot look at the name of an operator (e.g., < or >=) and tell what kind of comparison it is. Instead, the index method defines a set of "strategies", which can be thought of as generalized operators. Each operator class specifies which actual operator corresponds to each strategy for a particular data type and interpretation of the index semantics.

The B-tree index method defines five strategies, shown in Table 36-2.

Table 36-2. B-tree Strategies

Operation	Strategy Number
less than	1
less than or equal	2
equal	3
greater than or equal	4
greater than	5

Hash indexes support only equality comparisons, and so they use only one strategy, shown in Table 36-3.

Table 36-3. Hash Strategies

Operation	Strategy Number
equal	1

GiST indexes are more flexible: they do not have a fixed set of strategies at all. Instead, the "consistency" support routine of each particular GiST operator class interprets the strategy numbers however it likes. As an example, several of the built-in GiST index operator classes index two-dimensional geometric objects, providing the "R-tree" strategies shown in Table 36-4. Four of these are true two-dimensional tests (overlaps, same, contains, contained by); four of them consider only the X direction; and the other four provide the same tests in the Y direction.

Table 36-4. GiST Two-Dimensional "R-tree" Strategies

Operation	Strategy Number
strictly left of	1
does not extend to right of	2
overlaps	3
does not extend to left of	4
strictly right of	5
same	6
contains	7
contained by	8
does not extend above	9
strictly below	10
strictly above	11
does not extend below	12

SP-GiST indexes are similar to GiST indexes in flexibility: they don't have a fixed set of strategies. Instead the support routines of each operator class interpret the strategy numbers according to the operator class's definition. As an example, the strategy numbers used by the built-in operator classes for points are shown in Table 36-5.

Table 36-5. SP-GiST Point Strategies

Operation	Strategy Number
strictly left of	1
strictly right of	5
same	6
contained by	8
strictly below	10
strictly above	11

GIN indexes are similar to GiST and SP-GiST indexes, in that they don't have a fixed set of strategies either. Instead the support routines of each operator class interpret the strategy numbers according to the operator class's definition. As an example, the strategy numbers used by the built-in operator classes for arrays are shown in Table 36-6.

Table 36-6. GIN Array Strategies

Operation	Strategy Number
overlap	1
contains	2
is contained by	3
equal	4

BRIN indexes are similar to GiST, SP-GiST and GIN indexes in that they don't have a fixed set of strategies either. Instead the support routines of each operator class interpret the strategy numbers according to the operator class's definition. As an example, the strategy numbers used by the built-in `Minmax` operator classes are shown in Table 36-7.

Table 36-7. BRIN Minmax Strategies

Operation	Strategy Number
less than	1
less than or equal	2
equal	3
greater than or equal	4
greater than	5

Notice that all the operators listed above return Boolean values. In practice, all operators defined as index method search operators must return type `boolean`, since they must appear at the top level of a `WHERE` clause to be used with an index. (Some index access methods also support *ordering operators*, which typically don't return Boolean values; that feature is discussed in Section 36.14.7.)

36.14.3. Index Method Support Routines

Strategies aren't usually enough information for the system to figure out how to use an index. In practice, the index methods require additional support routines in order to work. For example, the B-tree index method must be able to compare two keys and determine whether one is greater than, equal to, or less than the other. Similarly, the hash index method must be able to compute hash codes for key values. These operations do not correspond to operators used in qualifications in SQL commands; they are administrative routines used by the index methods, internally.

Just as with strategies, the operator class identifies which specific functions should play each of these roles for a given data type and semantic interpretation. The index method defines the set of functions it needs, and the operator class identifies the correct functions to use by assigning them to the "support function numbers" specified by the index method.

B-trees require a single support function, and allow a second one to be supplied at the operator class author's option, as shown in Table 36-8.

Table 36-8. B-tree Support Functions

Function	Support Number
Compare two keys and return an integer less than zero, zero, or greater than zero, indicating whether the first key is less than, equal to, or greater than the second	1
Return the addresses of C-callable sort support function(s), as documented in `utils/sortsupport.h` (optional)	2

Hash indexes require one support function, shown in Table 36-9.

Table 36-9. Hash Support Functions

Function	Support Number
Compute the hash value for a key	1

GiST indexes have nine support functions, two of which are optional, as shown in Table 36-10. (For more information see Chapter 61.)

Table 36-10. GiST Support Functions

Function	Description	Support Number
consistent	determine whether key satisfies the query qualifier	1
union	compute union of a set of keys	2
compress	compute a compressed representation of a key or value to be indexed	3
decompress	compute a decompressed representation of a compressed key	4
penalty	compute penalty for inserting new key into subtree with given subtree's key	5
picksplit	determine which entries of a page are to be moved to the new page and compute the union keys for resulting pages	6
equal	compare two keys and return true if they are equal	7
distance	determine distance from key to query value (optional)	8
fetch	compute original representation of a compressed key for index-only scans (optional)	9

SP-GiST indexes require five support functions, as shown in Table 36-11. (For more information see Chapter 62.)

Table 36-11. SP-GiST Support Functions

Function	Description	Support Number
config	provide basic information about the operator class	1

Function	Description	Support Number
choose	determine how to insert a new value into an inner tuple	2
picksplit	determine how to partition a set of values	3
inner_consistent	determine which sub-partitions need to be searched for a query	4
leaf_consistent	determine whether key satisfies the query qualifier	5

GIN indexes have six support functions, three of which are optional, as shown in Table 36-12. (For more information see Chapter 63.)

Table 36-12. GIN Support Functions

Function	Description	Support Number
compare	compare two keys and return an integer less than zero, zero, or greater than zero, indicating whether the first key is less than, equal to, or greater than the second	1
extractValue	extract keys from a value to be indexed	2
extractQuery	extract keys from a query condition	3
consistent	determine whether value matches query condition (Boolean variant) (optional if support function 6 is present)	4
comparePartial	compare partial key from query and key from index, and return an integer less than zero, zero, or greater than zero, indicating whether GIN should ignore this index entry, treat the entry as a match, or stop the index scan (optional)	5
triConsistent	determine whether value matches query condition (ternary variant) (optional if support function 4 is present)	6

BRIN indexes have four basic support functions, as shown in Table 36-13; those basic functions may require additional support functions to be provided. (For more information see Section 64.3.)

Table 36-13. BRIN Support Functions

Function	Description	Support Number
opcInfo	return internal information describing the indexed columns' summary data	1
add_value	add a new value to an existing summary index tuple	2
consistent	determine whether value matches query condition	3
union	compute union of two summary tuples	4

Unlike search operators, support functions return whichever data type the particular index method expects; for example in the case of the comparison function for B-trees, a signed integer. The number and types of the arguments to each support function are likewise dependent on the index method. For B-tree and hash the comparison and hashing support functions take the same input data types as do the operators included in the operator class, but this is not the case for most GiST, SP-GiST, GIN, and BRIN support functions.

36.14.4. An Example

Now that we have seen the ideas, here is the promised example of creating a new operator class. (You can find a working copy of this example in `src/tutorial/complex.c` and `src/tutorial/complex.sql` in the source distribution.) The operator class encapsulates operators that sort complex numbers in absolute value order, so we choose the name `complex_abs_ops`. First, we need a set of operators. The procedure for defining operators was discussed in Section 36.12. For an operator class on B-trees, the operators we require are:

- absolute-value less-than (strategy 1)
- absolute-value less-than-or-equal (strategy 2)
- absolute-value equal (strategy 3)
- absolute-value greater-than-or-equal (strategy 4)
- absolute-value greater-than (strategy 5)

The least error-prone way to define a related set of comparison operators is to write the B-tree comparison support function first, and then write the other functions as one-line wrappers around the support function. This reduces the odds of getting inconsistent results for corner cases. Following this approach, we first write:

```
#define Mag(c)   ((c)->x*(c)->x + (c)->y*(c)->y)

static int
complex_abs_cmp_internal(Complex *a, Complex *b)
{
    double      amag = Mag(a),
                bmag = Mag(b);
```

```
    if (amag < bmag)
        return -1;
    if (amag > bmag)
        return 1;
    return 0;
}
```

Now the less-than function looks like:

```
PG_FUNCTION_INFO_V1(complex_abs_lt);

Datum
complex_abs_lt(PG_FUNCTION_ARGS)
{
    Complex    *a = (Complex *) PG_GETARG_POINTER(0);
    Complex    *b = (Complex *) PG_GETARG_POINTER(1);

    PG_RETURN_BOOL(complex_abs_cmp_internal(a, b) < 0);
}
```

The other four functions differ only in how they compare the internal function's result to zero.

Next we declare the functions and the operators based on the functions to SQL:

```
CREATE FUNCTION complex_abs_lt(complex, complex) RETURNS bool
    AS 'filename', 'complex_abs_lt'
    LANGUAGE C IMMUTABLE STRICT;

CREATE OPERATOR < (
    leftarg = complex, rightarg = complex, procedure = complex_abs_lt,
    commutator = > , negator = >= ,
    restrict = scalarltsel, join = scalarltjoinsel
);
```

It is important to specify the correct commutator and negator operators, as well as suitable restriction and join selectivity functions, otherwise the optimizer will be unable to make effective use of the index. Note that the less-than, equal, and greater-than cases should use different selectivity functions.

Other things worth noting are happening here:

- There can only be one operator named, say, = and taking type `complex` for both operands. In this case we don't have any other operator = for `complex`, but if we were building a practical data type we'd probably want = to be the ordinary equality operation for complex numbers (and not the equality of the absolute values). In that case, we'd need to use some other operator name for `complex_abs_eq`.

- Although PostgreSQL can cope with functions having the same SQL name as long as they have different argument data types, C can only cope with one global function having a given name. So we shouldn't name the C function something simple like `abs_eq`. Usually it's a good practice to include the data type name in the C function name, so as not to conflict with functions for other data types.

- We could have made the SQL name of the function `abs_eq`, relying on PostgreSQL to distinguish it by argument data types from any other SQL function of the same name. To keep the example simple, we make the function have the same names at the C level and SQL level.

The next step is the registration of the support routine required by B-trees. The example C code that implements this is in the same file that contains the operator functions. This is how we declare the function:

```
CREATE FUNCTION complex_abs_cmp(complex, complex)
    RETURNS integer
    AS 'filename'
    LANGUAGE C IMMUTABLE STRICT;
```

Now that we have the required operators and support routine, we can finally create the operator class:

```
CREATE OPERATOR CLASS complex_abs_ops
    DEFAULT FOR TYPE complex USING btree AS
        OPERATOR        1        < ,
        OPERATOR        2        <= ,
        OPERATOR        3        = ,
        OPERATOR        4        >= ,
        OPERATOR        5        > ,
        FUNCTION        1        complex_abs_cmp(complex, complex);
```

And we're done! It should now be possible to create and use B-tree indexes on `complex` columns.

We could have written the operator entries more verbosely, as in:

```
        OPERATOR        1        < (complex, complex) ,
```

but there is no need to do so when the operators take the same data type we are defining the operator class for.

The above example assumes that you want to make this new operator class the default B-tree operator class for the `complex` data type. If you don't, just leave out the word `DEFAULT`.

36.14.5. Operator Classes and Operator Families

So far we have implicitly assumed that an operator class deals with only one data type. While there certainly can be only one data type in a particular index column, it is often useful to index operations that compare an indexed column to a value of a different data type. Also, if there is use for a cross-data-type operator in connection with an operator class, it is often the case that the other data type has a related operator class of its own. It is helpful to make the connections between related classes explicit, because this can aid the planner in optimizing SQL queries (particularly for B-tree operator classes, since the planner contains a great deal of knowledge about how to work with them).

To handle these needs, PostgreSQL uses the concept of an *operator family*. An operator family contains one or more operator classes, and can also contain indexable operators and corresponding support functions that belong to the family as a whole but not to any single class within the family. We say that such operators and functions are "loose" within the family, as opposed to being bound into a specific class. Typically each operator class contains single-data-type operators while cross-data-type operators are loose in the family.

All the operators and functions in an operator family must have compatible semantics, where the compatibility requirements are set by the index method. You might therefore wonder why bother to single out particular subsets of the family as operator classes; and indeed for many purposes the class divisions are irrelevant and the family is the only interesting grouping. The reason for defining operator classes is that they specify how much of the family is needed to support any particular index. If there is an index using an operator class, then that operator class cannot be dropped without dropping the index — but other parts of the operator family, namely other operator classes and loose operators, could be dropped. Thus, an operator class should be specified to contain the minimum set of operators and functions that are reasonably needed to work with an index on a specific data type, and then related but non-essential operators can be added as loose members of the operator family.

As an example, PostgreSQL has a built-in B-tree operator family `integer_ops`, which includes operator classes `int8_ops`, `int4_ops`, and `int2_ops` for indexes on `bigint` (`int8`), `integer` (`int4`), and `smallint` (`int2`) columns respectively. The family also contains cross-data-type comparison operators allowing any two of these types to be compared, so that an index on one of these types can be searched using a comparison value of another type. The family could be duplicated by these definitions:

```
CREATE OPERATOR FAMILY integer_ops USING btree;

CREATE OPERATOR CLASS int8_ops
DEFAULT FOR TYPE int8 USING btree FAMILY integer_ops AS
  -- standard int8 comparisons
  OPERATOR 1 < ,
  OPERATOR 2 <= ,
  OPERATOR 3 = ,
  OPERATOR 4 >= ,
  OPERATOR 5 > ,
  FUNCTION 1 btint8cmp(int8, int8) ,
  FUNCTION 2 btint8sortsupport(internal) ;

CREATE OPERATOR CLASS int4_ops
DEFAULT FOR TYPE int4 USING btree FAMILY integer_ops AS
  -- standard int4 comparisons
  OPERATOR 1 < ,
  OPERATOR 2 <= ,
  OPERATOR 3 = ,
  OPERATOR 4 >= ,
  OPERATOR 5 > ,
  FUNCTION 1 btint4cmp(int4, int4) ,
  FUNCTION 2 btint4sortsupport(internal) ;

CREATE OPERATOR CLASS int2_ops
DEFAULT FOR TYPE int2 USING btree FAMILY integer_ops AS
  -- standard int2 comparisons
  OPERATOR 1 < ,
  OPERATOR 2 <= ,
  OPERATOR 3 = ,
  OPERATOR 4 >= ,
  OPERATOR 5 > ,
  FUNCTION 1 btint2cmp(int2, int2) ,
  FUNCTION 2 btint2sortsupport(internal) ;
```

```
ALTER OPERATOR FAMILY integer_ops USING btree ADD
  -- cross-type comparisons int8 vs int2
  OPERATOR 1 < (int8, int2) ,
  OPERATOR 2 <= (int8, int2) ,
  OPERATOR 3 = (int8, int2) ,
  OPERATOR 4 >= (int8, int2) ,
  OPERATOR 5 > (int8, int2) ,
  FUNCTION 1 btint82cmp(int8, int2) ,

  -- cross-type comparisons int8 vs int4
  OPERATOR 1 < (int8, int4) ,
  OPERATOR 2 <= (int8, int4) ,
  OPERATOR 3 = (int8, int4) ,
  OPERATOR 4 >= (int8, int4) ,
  OPERATOR 5 > (int8, int4) ,
  FUNCTION 1 btint84cmp(int8, int4) ,

  -- cross-type comparisons int4 vs int2
  OPERATOR 1 < (int4, int2) ,
  OPERATOR 2 <= (int4, int2) ,
  OPERATOR 3 = (int4, int2) ,
  OPERATOR 4 >= (int4, int2) ,
  OPERATOR 5 > (int4, int2) ,
  FUNCTION 1 btint42cmp(int4, int2) ,

  -- cross-type comparisons int4 vs int8
  OPERATOR 1 < (int4, int8) ,
  OPERATOR 2 <= (int4, int8) ,
  OPERATOR 3 = (int4, int8) ,
  OPERATOR 4 >= (int4, int8) ,
  OPERATOR 5 > (int4, int8) ,
  FUNCTION 1 btint48cmp(int4, int8) ,

  -- cross-type comparisons int2 vs int8
  OPERATOR 1 < (int2, int8) ,
  OPERATOR 2 <= (int2, int8) ,
  OPERATOR 3 = (int2, int8) ,
  OPERATOR 4 >= (int2, int8) ,
  OPERATOR 5 > (int2, int8) ,
  FUNCTION 1 btint28cmp(int2, int8) ,

  -- cross-type comparisons int2 vs int4
  OPERATOR 1 < (int2, int4) ,
  OPERATOR 2 <= (int2, int4) ,
  OPERATOR 3 = (int2, int4) ,
  OPERATOR 4 >= (int2, int4) ,
  OPERATOR 5 > (int2, int4) ,
  FUNCTION 1 btint24cmp(int2, int4) ;
```

Notice that this definition "overloads" the operator strategy and support function numbers: each number occurs multiple times within the family. This is allowed so long as each instance of a particular number has distinct input data types. The instances that have both input types equal to an operator class's input type are the primary operators and support functions for that operator class, and in most cases should be declared as part of the operator class rather than as loose members of the family.

In a B-tree operator family, all the operators in the family must sort compatibly, meaning that the transitive laws hold across all the data types supported by the family: "if A = B and B = C, then A = C", and "if A < B and B < C, then A < C". Moreover, implicit or binary coercion casts between types represented in the operator family must not change the associated sort ordering. For each operator in the family there must be a support function having the same two input data types as the operator. It is recommended that a family be complete, i.e., for each combination of data types, all operators are included. Each operator class should include just the non-cross-type operators and support function for its data type.

To build a multiple-data-type hash operator family, compatible hash support functions must be created for each data type supported by the family. Here compatibility means that the functions are guaranteed to return the same hash code for any two values that are considered equal by the family's equality operators, even when the values are of different types. This is usually difficult to accomplish when the types have different physical representations, but it can be done in some cases. Furthermore, casting a value from one data type represented in the operator family to another data type also represented in the operator family via an implicit or binary coercion cast must not change the computed hash value. Notice that there is only one support function per data type, not one per equality operator. It is recommended that a family be complete, i.e., provide an equality operator for each combination of data types. Each operator class should include just the non-cross-type equality operator and the support function for its data type.

GiST, SP-GiST, and GIN indexes do not have any explicit notion of cross-data-type operations. The set of operators supported is just whatever the primary support functions for a given operator class can handle.

In BRIN, the requirements depends on the framework that provides the operator classes. For operator classes based on `minmax`, the behavior required is the same as for B-tree operator families: all the operators in the family must sort compatibly, and casts must not change the associated sort ordering.

> **Note:** Prior to PostgreSQL 8.3, there was no concept of operator families, and so any cross-data-type operators intended to be used with an index had to be bound directly into the index's operator class. While this approach still works, it is deprecated because it makes an index's dependencies too broad, and because the planner can handle cross-data-type comparisons more effectively when both data types have operators in the same operator family.

36.14.6. System Dependencies on Operator Classes

PostgreSQL uses operator classes to infer the properties of operators in more ways than just whether they can be used with indexes. Therefore, you might want to create operator classes even if you have no intention of indexing any columns of your data type.

In particular, there are SQL features such as ORDER BY and DISTINCT that require comparison and sorting of values. To implement these features on a user-defined data type, PostgreSQL looks for the default B-tree operator class for the data type. The "equals" member of this operator class defines the system's notion of equality of values for GROUP BY and DISTINCT, and the sort ordering imposed by the operator class defines the default ORDER BY ordering.

Comparison of arrays of user-defined types also relies on the semantics defined by the default B-tree operator class.

If there is no default B-tree operator class for a data type, the system will look for a default hash operator class. But since that kind of operator class only provides equality, in practice it is only enough to support array equality.

When there is no default operator class for a data type, you will get errors like "could not identify an ordering operator" if you try to use these SQL features with the data type.

> **Note:** In PostgreSQL versions before 7.4, sorting and grouping operations would implicitly use operators named =, <, and >. The new behavior of relying on default operator classes avoids having to make any assumption about the behavior of operators with particular names.

Another important point is that an operator that appears in a hash operator family is a candidate for hash joins, hash aggregation, and related optimizations. The hash operator family is essential here since it identifies the hash function(s) to use.

36.14.7. Ordering Operators

Some index access methods (currently, only GiST) support the concept of *ordering operators*. What we have been discussing so far are *search operators*. A search operator is one for which the index can be searched to find all rows satisfying WHERE *indexed_column operator constant*. Note that nothing is promised about the order in which the matching rows will be returned. In contrast, an ordering operator does not restrict the set of rows that can be returned, but instead determines their order. An ordering operator is one for which the index can be scanned to return rows in the order represented by ORDER BY *indexed_column operator constant*. The reason for defining ordering operators that way is that it supports nearest-neighbor searches, if the operator is one that measures distance. For example, a query like

```
SELECT * FROM places ORDER BY location <-> point '(101,456)' LIMIT 10;
```

finds the ten places closest to a given target point. A GiST index on the location column can do this efficiently because <-> is an ordering operator.

While search operators have to return Boolean results, ordering operators usually return some other type, such as float or numeric for distances. This type is normally not the same as the data type being indexed. To avoid hard-wiring assumptions about the behavior of different data types, the definition of an ordering operator is required to name a B-tree operator family that specifies the sort ordering of the result data type. As was stated in the previous section, B-tree operator families define PostgreSQL's notion of ordering, so this is a natural representation. Since the point <-> operator returns float8, it could be specified in an operator class creation command like this:

```
OPERATOR 15    <-> (point, point) FOR ORDER BY float_ops
```

where float_ops is the built-in operator family that includes operations on float8. This declaration states that the index is able to return rows in order of increasing values of the <-> operator.

36.14.8. Special Features of Operator Classes

There are two special features of operator classes that we have not discussed yet, mainly because they are not useful with the most commonly used index methods.

Normally, declaring an operator as a member of an operator class (or family) means that the index method can retrieve exactly the set of rows that satisfy a WHERE condition using the operator. For example:

```
SELECT * FROM table WHERE integer_column < 4;
```

can be satisfied exactly by a B-tree index on the integer column. But there are cases where an index is useful as an inexact guide to the matching rows. For example, if a GiST index stores only bounding boxes for geometric objects, then it cannot exactly satisfy a WHERE condition that tests overlap between nonrectangular objects such as polygons. Yet we could use the index to find objects whose bounding box overlaps the bounding box of the target object, and then do the exact overlap test only on the objects found by the index. If this scenario applies, the index is said to be "lossy" for the operator. Lossy index searches are implemented by having the index method return a *recheck* flag when a row might or might not really satisfy the query condition. The core system will then test the original query condition on the retrieved row to see whether it should be returned as a valid match. This approach works if the index is guaranteed to return all the required rows, plus perhaps some additional rows, which can be eliminated by performing the original operator invocation. The index methods that support lossy searches (currently, GiST, SP-GiST and GIN) allow the support functions of individual operator classes to set the recheck flag, and so this is essentially an operator-class feature.

Consider again the situation where we are storing in the index only the bounding box of a complex object such as a polygon. In this case there's not much value in storing the whole polygon in the index entry — we might as well store just a simpler object of type box. This situation is expressed by the STORAGE option in CREATE OPERATOR CLASS: we'd write something like:

```
CREATE OPERATOR CLASS polygon_ops
    DEFAULT FOR TYPE polygon USING gist AS
        ...
        STORAGE box;
```

At present, only the GiST, GIN and BRIN index methods support a STORAGE type that's different from the column data type. The GiST compress and decompress support routines must deal with data-type conversion when STORAGE is used. In GIN, the STORAGE type identifies the type of the "key" values, which normally is different from the type of the indexed column — for example, an operator class for integer-array columns might have keys that are just integers. The GIN extractValue and extractQuery support routines are responsible for extracting keys from indexed values. BRIN is similar to GIN: the STORAGE type identifies the type of the stored summary values, and operator classes' support procedures are responsible for interpreting the summary values correctly.

36.15. Packaging Related Objects into an Extension

A useful extension to PostgreSQL typically includes multiple SQL objects; for example, a new data type will require new functions, new operators, and probably new index operator classes. It is helpful to collect all these objects into a single package to simplify database management. PostgreSQL calls such a package an *extension*. To define an extension, you need at least a *script file* that contains the SQL commands to create the extension's objects, and a *control file* that specifies a few basic properties of the extension itself. If the extension includes C code, there will typically also be a shared library file into which the C code has been built. Once you have these files, a simple CREATE EXTENSION command loads the objects into your database.

The main advantage of using an extension, rather than just running the SQL script to load a bunch of "loose" objects into your database, is that PostgreSQL will then understand that the objects of the extension go together. You can drop all the objects with a single DROP EXTENSION command (no need to maintain a separate "uninstall" script). Even more useful, pg_dump knows that it should not dump the individual member objects of the extension — it will just include a CREATE EXTENSION command in dumps, instead. This vastly simplifies migration to a new version of the extension that might contain more or different objects than the old version. Note however that you must have the extension's control, script, and other files available when loading such a dump into a new database.

PostgreSQL will not let you drop an individual object contained in an extension, except by dropping the whole extension. Also, while you can change the definition of an extension member object (for example, via CREATE OR REPLACE FUNCTION for a function), bear in mind that the modified definition will not be dumped by pg_dump. Such a change is usually only sensible if you concurrently make the same change in the extension's script file. (But there are special provisions for tables containing configuration data; see Section 36.15.3.) In production situations, it's generally better to create an extension update script to perform changes to extension member objects.

The extension script may set privileges on objects that are part of the extension via GRANT and REVOKE statements. The final set of privileges for each object (if any are set) will be stored in the pg_init_privs system catalog. When pg_dump is used, the CREATE EXTENSION command will be included in the dump, followed by the set of GRANT and REVOKE statements necessary to set the privileges on the objects to what they were at the time the dump was taken.

PostgreSQL does not currently support extension scripts issuing CREATE POLICY or SECURITY LABEL statements. These are expected to be set after the extension has been created. All RLS policies and security labels on extension objects will be included in dumps created by pg_dump.

The extension mechanism also has provisions for packaging modification scripts that adjust the definitions of the SQL objects contained in an extension. For example, if version 1.1 of an extension adds one function and changes the body of another function compared to 1.0, the extension author can provide an *update script* that makes just those two changes. The ALTER EXTENSION UPDATE command can then be used to apply these changes and track which version of the extension is actually installed in a given database.

The kinds of SQL objects that can be members of an extension are shown in the description of ALTER EXTENSION. Notably, objects that are database-cluster-wide, such as databases, roles, and tablespaces, cannot be extension members since an extension is only known within one database. (Although an extension script is not prohibited from creating such objects, if it does so they will not be tracked as part of the extension.) Also notice that while a table can be a member of an extension, its subsidiary objects such as indexes are not directly considered members of the extension. Another important point is that schemas can belong to extensions, but not vice versa: an extension as such has an unqualified name and does not exist "within" any schema. The extension's member objects, however, will belong to schemas whenever appropriate for their object types. It may or may not be appropriate for an extension to own the schema(s) its member objects are within.

36.15.1. Extension Files

The CREATE EXTENSION command relies on a control file for each extension, which must be named the same as the extension with a suffix of .control, and must be placed in the installation's SHAREDIR/extension directory. There must also be at least one SQL script file, which follows the naming pattern *extension--version*.sql (for example, foo--1.0.sql for version 1.0 of extension foo). By default, the script file(s) are also placed in the SHAREDIR/extension directory; but the control file can specify a different directory for the script file(s).

The file format for an extension control file is the same as for the postgresql.conf file, namely a list of *parameter_name = value* assignments, one per line. Blank lines and comments introduced by # are allowed. Be sure to quote any value that is not a single word or number.

A control file can set the following parameters:

directory (string)

> The directory containing the extension's SQL script file(s). Unless an absolute path is given, the name is relative to the installation's SHAREDIR directory. The default behavior is equivalent to specifying directory = 'extension'.

default_version (string)

> The default version of the extension (the one that will be installed if no version is specified in CREATE EXTENSION). Although this can be omitted, that will result in CREATE EXTENSION failing if no VERSION option appears, so you generally don't want to do that.

comment (string)

> A comment (any string) about the extension. The comment is applied when initially creating an extension, but not during extension updates (since that might override user-added comments). Alternatively, the extension's comment can be set by writing a COMMENT command in the script file.

encoding (string)

> The character set encoding used by the script file(s). This should be specified if the script files contain any non-ASCII characters. Otherwise the files will be assumed to be in the database encoding.

module_pathname (string)

> The value of this parameter will be substituted for each occurrence of MODULE_PATHNAME in the script file(s). If it is not set, no substitution is made. Typically, this is set to $libdir/*shared_library_name* and then MODULE_PATHNAME is used in CREATE FUNCTION commands for C-language functions, so that the script files do not need to hard-wire the name of the shared library.

requires (string)

> A list of names of extensions that this extension depends on, for example requires = 'foo, bar'. Those extensions must be installed before this one can be installed.

superuser (boolean)

> If this parameter is true (which is the default), only superusers can create the extension or update it to a new version. If it is set to false, just the privileges required to execute the commands in the installation or update script are required.

`relocatable (boolean)`

> An extension is *relocatable* if it is possible to move its contained objects into a different schema after initial creation of the extension. The default is `false`, i.e. the extension is not relocatable. See Section 36.15.2 for more information.

`schema (string)`

> This parameter can only be set for non-relocatable extensions. It forces the extension to be loaded into exactly the named schema and not any other. The `schema` parameter is consulted only when initially creating an extension, not during extension updates. See Section 36.15.2 for more information.

In addition to the primary control file `extension.control`, an extension can have secondary control files named in the style `extension--version.control`. If supplied, these must be located in the script file directory. Secondary control files follow the same format as the primary control file. Any parameters set in a secondary control file override the primary control file when installing or updating to that version of the extension. However, the parameters `directory` and `default_version` cannot be set in a secondary control file.

An extension's SQL script files can contain any SQL commands, except for transaction control commands (`BEGIN`, `COMMIT`, etc) and commands that cannot be executed inside a transaction block (such as `VACUUM`). This is because the script files are implicitly executed within a transaction block.

An extension's SQL script files can also contain lines beginning with `\echo`, which will be ignored (treated as comments) by the extension mechanism. This provision is commonly used to throw an error if the script file is fed to psql rather than being loaded via `CREATE EXTENSION` (see example script in Section 36.15.5). Without that, users might accidentally load the extension's contents as "loose" objects rather than as an extension, a state of affairs that's a bit tedious to recover from.

While the script files can contain any characters allowed by the specified encoding, control files should contain only plain ASCII, because there is no way for PostgreSQL to know what encoding a control file is in. In practice this is only an issue if you want to use non-ASCII characters in the extension's comment. Recommended practice in that case is to not use the control file `comment` parameter, but instead use `COMMENT ON EXTENSION` within a script file to set the comment.

36.15.2. Extension Relocatability

Users often wish to load the objects contained in an extension into a different schema than the extension's author had in mind. There are three supported levels of relocatability:

- A fully relocatable extension can be moved into another schema at any time, even after it's been loaded into a database. This is done with the `ALTER EXTENSION SET SCHEMA` command, which automatically renames all the member objects into the new schema. Normally, this is only possible if the extension contains no internal assumptions about what schema any of its objects are in. Also, the extension's objects must all be in one schema to begin with (ignoring objects that do not belong to any schema, such as procedural languages). Mark a fully relocatable extension by setting `relocatable = true` in its control file.

- An extension might be relocatable during installation but not afterwards. This is typically the case if the extension's script file needs to reference the target schema explicitly, for example in setting `search_path` properties for SQL functions. For such an extension, set `relocatable = false` in its control file, and use `@extschema@` to refer to the target schema in the script file. All occurrences of this string will be replaced by the actual target schema's name before the script is executed. The user can set the target schema using the SCHEMA option of CREATE EXTENSION.

- If the extension does not support relocation at all, set relocatable = false in its control file, and also set schema to the name of the intended target schema. This will prevent use of the SCHEMA option of CREATE EXTENSION, unless it specifies the same schema named in the control file. This choice is typically necessary if the extension contains internal assumptions about schema names that can't be replaced by uses of @extschema@. The @extschema@ substitution mechanism is available in this case too, although it is of limited use since the schema name is determined by the control file.

In all cases, the script file will be executed with search_path initially set to point to the target schema; that is, CREATE EXTENSION does the equivalent of this:

```
SET LOCAL search_path TO @extschema@;
```

This allows the objects created by the script file to go into the target schema. The script file can change search_path if it wishes, but that is generally undesirable. search_path is restored to its previous setting upon completion of CREATE EXTENSION.

The target schema is determined by the schema parameter in the control file if that is given, otherwise by the SCHEMA option of CREATE EXTENSION if that is given, otherwise the current default object creation schema (the first one in the caller's search_path). When the control file schema parameter is used, the target schema will be created if it doesn't already exist, but in the other two cases it must already exist.

If any prerequisite extensions are listed in requires in the control file, their target schemas are appended to the initial setting of search_path. This allows their objects to be visible to the new extension's script file.

Although a non-relocatable extension can contain objects spread across multiple schemas, it is usually desirable to place all the objects meant for external use into a single schema, which is considered the extension's target schema. Such an arrangement works conveniently with the default setting of search_path during creation of dependent extensions.

36.15.3. Extension Configuration Tables

Some extensions include configuration tables, which contain data that might be added or changed by the user after installation of the extension. Ordinarily, if a table is part of an extension, neither the table's definition nor its content will be dumped by pg_dump. But that behavior is undesirable for a configuration table; any data changes made by the user need to be included in dumps, or the extension will behave differently after a dump and reload.

To solve this problem, an extension's script file can mark a table or a sequence it has created as a configuration relation, which will cause pg_dump to include the table's or the sequence's contents (not its definition) in dumps. To do that, call the function pg_extension_config_dump(regclass, text) after creating the table or the sequence, for example

```
CREATE TABLE my_config (key text, value text);
CREATE SEQUENCE my_config_seq;

SELECT pg_catalog.pg_extension_config_dump('my_config', '');
SELECT pg_catalog.pg_extension_config_dump('my_config_seq', '');
```

Any number of tables or sequences can be marked this way. Sequences associated with `serial` or `bigserial` columns can be marked as well.

When the second argument of `pg_extension_config_dump` is an empty string, the entire contents of the table are dumped by pg_dump. This is usually only correct if the table is initially empty as created by the extension script. If there is a mixture of initial data and user-provided data in the table, the second argument of `pg_extension_config_dump` provides a `WHERE` condition that selects the data to be dumped. For example, you might do

```
CREATE TABLE my_config (key text, value text, standard_entry boolean);

SELECT pg_catalog.pg_extension_config_dump('my_config', 'WHERE NOT standard_entry');
```

and then make sure that `standard_entry` is true only in the rows created by the extension's script.

For sequences, the second argument of `pg_extension_config_dump` has no effect.

More complicated situations, such as initially-provided rows that might be modified by users, can be handled by creating triggers on the configuration table to ensure that modified rows are marked correctly.

You can alter the filter condition associated with a configuration table by calling `pg_extension_config_dump` again. (This would typically be useful in an extension update script.) The only way to mark a table as no longer a configuration table is to dissociate it from the extension with `ALTER EXTENSION ... DROP TABLE`.

Note that foreign key relationships between these tables will dictate the order in which the tables are dumped out by pg_dump. Specifically, pg_dump will attempt to dump the referenced-by table before the referencing table. As the foreign key relationships are set up at CREATE EXTENSION time (prior to data being loaded into the tables) circular dependencies are not supported. When circular dependencies exist, the data will still be dumped out but the dump will not be able to be restored directly and user intervention will be required.

Sequences associated with `serial` or `bigserial` columns need to be directly marked to dump their state. Marking their parent relation is not enough for this purpose.

36.15.4. Extension Updates

One advantage of the extension mechanism is that it provides convenient ways to manage updates to the SQL commands that define an extension's objects. This is done by associating a version name or number with each released version of the extension's installation script. In addition, if you want users to be able to update their databases dynamically from one version to the next, you should provide *update scripts* that make the necessary changes to go from one version to the next. Update scripts have names following the pattern *extension--oldversion--newversion*.`sql` (for example, `foo--1.0--1.1.sql` contains the commands to modify version `1.0` of extension `foo` into version `1.1`).

Given that a suitable update script is available, the command `ALTER EXTENSION UPDATE` will update an installed extension to the specified new version. The update script is run in the same environment that `CREATE EXTENSION` provides for installation scripts: in particular, `search_path` is set up in the same way, and any new objects created by the script are automatically added to the extension.

If an extension has secondary control files, the control parameters that are used for an update script are those associated with the script's target (new) version.

The update mechanism can be used to solve an important special case: converting a "loose" collection of objects into an extension. Before the extension mechanism was added to PostgreSQL (in 9.1), many people wrote extension modules that simply created assorted unpackaged objects. Given an existing database containing such objects, how can we convert the objects into a properly packaged extension? Dropping them and then doing a plain CREATE EXTENSION is one way, but it's not desirable if the objects have dependencies (for example, if there are table columns of a data type created by the extension). The way to fix this situation is to create an empty extension, then use ALTER EXTENSION ADD to attach each pre-existing object to the extension, then finally create any new objects that are in the current extension version but were not in the unpackaged release. CREATE EXTENSION supports this case with its FROM *old_version* option, which causes it to not run the normal installation script for the target version, but instead the update script named *extension--old_version--target_version*.sql. The choice of the dummy version name to use as *old_version* is up to the extension author, though unpackaged is a common convention. If you have multiple prior versions you need to be able to update into extension style, use multiple dummy version names to identify them.

ALTER EXTENSION is able to execute sequences of update script files to achieve a requested update. For example, if only foo--1.0--1.1.sql and foo--1.1--2.0.sql are available, ALTER EXTENSION will apply them in sequence if an update to version 2.0 is requested when 1.0 is currently installed.

PostgreSQL doesn't assume anything about the properties of version names: for example, it does not know whether 1.1 follows 1.0. It just matches up the available version names and follows the path that requires applying the fewest update scripts. (A version name can actually be any string that doesn't contain -- or leading or trailing -.)

Sometimes it is useful to provide "downgrade" scripts, for example foo--1.1--1.0.sql to allow reverting the changes associated with version 1.1. If you do that, be careful of the possibility that a downgrade script might unexpectedly get applied because it yields a shorter path. The risky case is where there is a "fast path" update script that jumps ahead several versions as well as a downgrade script to the fast path's start point. It might take fewer steps to apply the downgrade and then the fast path than to move ahead one version at a time. If the downgrade script drops any irreplaceable objects, this will yield undesirable results.

To check for unexpected update paths, use this command:

```
SELECT * FROM pg_extension_update_paths('extension_name');
```

This shows each pair of distinct known version names for the specified extension, together with the update path sequence that would be taken to get from the source version to the target version, or NULL if there is no available update path. The path is shown in textual form with -- separators. You can use regexp_split_to_array(path,'--') if you prefer an array format.

36.15.5. Extension Example

Here is a complete example of an SQL-only extension, a two-element composite type that can store any type of value in its slots, which are named "k" and "v". Non-text values are automatically coerced to text for storage.

The script file pair--1.0.sql looks like this:

```
-- complain if script is sourced in psql, rather than via CREATE EXTENSION
\echo Use "CREATE EXTENSION pair" to load this file. \quit
```

```
CREATE TYPE pair AS ( k text, v text );

CREATE OR REPLACE FUNCTION pair(anyelement, text)
RETURNS pair LANGUAGE SQL AS 'SELECT ROW($1, $2)::pair';

CREATE OR REPLACE FUNCTION pair(text, anyelement)
RETURNS pair LANGUAGE SQL AS 'SELECT ROW($1, $2)::pair';

CREATE OR REPLACE FUNCTION pair(anyelement, anyelement)
RETURNS pair LANGUAGE SQL AS 'SELECT ROW($1, $2)::pair';

CREATE OR REPLACE FUNCTION pair(text, text)
RETURNS pair LANGUAGE SQL AS 'SELECT ROW($1, $2)::pair;';

CREATE OPERATOR ~> (LEFTARG = text, RIGHTARG = anyelement, PROCEDURE = pair);
CREATE OPERATOR ~> (LEFTARG = anyelement, RIGHTARG = text, PROCEDURE = pair);
CREATE OPERATOR ~> (LEFTARG = anyelement, RIGHTARG = anyelement, PROCEDURE = pair);
CREATE OPERATOR ~> (LEFTARG = text, RIGHTARG = text, PROCEDURE = pair);
```

The control file `pair.control` looks like this:

```
# pair extension
comment = 'A key/value pair data type'
default_version = '1.0'
relocatable = true
```

While you hardly need a makefile to install these two files into the correct directory, you could use a `Makefile` containing this:

```
EXTENSION = pair
DATA = pair--1.0.sql

PG_CONFIG = pg_config
PGXS := $(shell $(PG_CONFIG) --pgxs)
include $(PGXS)
```

This makefile relies on PGXS, which is described in Section 36.16. The command `make install` will install the control and script files into the correct directory as reported by pg_config.

Once the files are installed, use the CREATE EXTENSION command to load the objects into any particular database.

36.16. Extension Building Infrastructure

If you are thinking about distributing your PostgreSQL extension modules, setting up a portable build system for them can be fairly difficult. Therefore the PostgreSQL installation provides a build infrastructure for extensions, called PGXS, so that simple extension modules can be built simply against an already installed server. PGXS is mainly intended for extensions that include C code, although it can be used for pure-SQL extensions too. Note that PGXS is not intended to be a universal build system framework that can be used to build any software interfacing to PostgreSQL; it simply automates common build rules for simple server extension modules. For more complicated packages, you might need to write your own build system.

To use the PGXS infrastructure for your extension, you must write a simple makefile. In the makefile, you need to set some variables and include the global PGXS makefile. Here is an example that builds an extension module named `isbn_issn`, consisting of a shared library containing some C code, an extension control file, a SQL script, and a documentation text file:

```
MODULES = isbn_issn
EXTENSION = isbn_issn
DATA = isbn_issn--1.0.sql
DOCS = README.isbn_issn

PG_CONFIG = pg_config
PGXS := $(shell $(PG_CONFIG) --pgxs)
include $(PGXS)
```

The last three lines should always be the same. Earlier in the file, you assign variables or add custom make rules.

Set one of these three variables to specify what is built:

MODULES

list of shared-library objects to be built from source files with same stem (do not include library suffixes in this list)

MODULE_big

a shared library to build from multiple source files (list object files in `OBJS`)

PROGRAM

an executable program to build (list object files in `OBJS`)

The following variables can also be set:

EXTENSION

extension name(s); for each name you must provide an *extension*.control file, which will be installed into *prefix*/share/extension

MODULEDIR

subdirectory of *prefix*/share into which DATA and DOCS files should be installed (if not set, default is extension if EXTENSION is set, or contrib if not)

DATA

random files to install into *prefix*/share/$MODULEDIR

DATA_built

random files to install into *prefix*/share/$MODULEDIR, which need to be built first

DATA_TSEARCH

random files to install under *prefix*/share/tsearch_data

DOCS

random files to install under *prefix*/doc/$MODULEDIR

SCRIPTS

script files (not binaries) to install into *prefix*/bin

SCRIPTS_built

script files (not binaries) to install into *prefix*/bin, which need to be built first

REGRESS

list of regression test cases (without suffix), see below

REGRESS_OPTS

additional switches to pass to pg_regress

EXTRA_CLEAN

extra files to remove in make clean

PG_CPPFLAGS

will be added to CPPFLAGS

PG_LIBS

will be added to PROGRAM link line

SHLIB_LINK

will be added to MODULE_big link line

PG_CONFIG

path to pg_config program for the PostgreSQL installation to build against (typically just pg_config to use the first one in your PATH)

Put this makefile as Makefile in the directory which holds your extension. Then you can do make to compile, and then make install to install your module. By default, the extension is compiled and installed for the PostgreSQL installation that corresponds to the first pg_config program found in your PATH. You can use a different installation by setting PG_CONFIG to point to its pg_config program, either within the makefile or on the make command line.

You can also run make in a directory outside the source tree of your extension, if you want to keep the build directory separate. This procedure is also called a *VPATH* build. Here's how:

```
mkdir build_dir
cd build_dir
make -f /path/to/extension/source/tree/Makefile
make -f /path/to/extension/source/tree/Makefile install
```

Alternatively, you can set up a directory for a VPATH build in a similar way to how it is done for the core code. One way to do this is using the core script `config/prep_buildtree`. Once this has been done you can build by setting the `make` variable `VPATH` like this:

```
make VPATH=/path/to/extension/source/tree
make VPATH=/path/to/extension/source/tree install
```

This procedure can work with a greater variety of directory layouts.

The scripts listed in the `REGRESS` variable are used for regression testing of your module, which can be invoked by `make installcheck` after doing `make install`. For this to work you must have a running PostgreSQL server. The script files listed in `REGRESS` must appear in a subdirectory named `sql/` in your extension's directory. These files must have extension `.sql`, which must not be included in the `REGRESS` list in the makefile. For each test there should also be a file containing the expected output in a subdirectory named `expected/`, with the same stem and extension `.out`. `make installcheck` executes each test script with psql, and compares the resulting output to the matching expected file. Any differences will be written to the file `regression.diffs` in `diff -c` format. Note that trying to run a test that is missing its expected file will be reported as "trouble", so make sure you have all expected files.

> **Tip:** The easiest way to create the expected files is to create empty files, then do a test run (which will of course report differences). Inspect the actual result files found in the `results/` directory, then copy them to `expected/` if they match what you expect from the test.

Chapter 37. Triggers

This chapter provides general information about writing trigger functions. Trigger functions can be written in most of the available procedural languages, including PL/pgSQL (Chapter 41), PL/Tcl (Chapter 42), PL/Perl (Chapter 43), and PL/Python (Chapter 44). After reading this chapter, you should consult the chapter for your favorite procedural language to find out the language-specific details of writing a trigger in it.

It is also possible to write a trigger function in C, although most people find it easier to use one of the procedural languages. It is not currently possible to write a trigger function in the plain SQL function language.

37.1. Overview of Trigger Behavior

A trigger is a specification that the database should automatically execute a particular function whenever a certain type of operation is performed. Triggers can be attached to tables, views, and foreign tables.

On tables and foreign tables, triggers can be defined to execute either before or after any INSERT, UPDATE, or DELETE operation, either once per modified row, or once per SQL statement. If an INSERT contains an ON CONFLICT DO UPDATE clause, it is possible that the effects of a BEFORE insert trigger and a BEFORE update trigger can both be applied together, if a reference to an EXCLUDED column appears. UPDATE triggers can moreover be set to fire only if certain columns are mentioned in the SET clause of the UPDATE statement. Triggers can also fire for TRUNCATE statements. If a trigger event occurs, the trigger's function is called at the appropriate time to handle the event. Foreign tables do not support the TRUNCATE statement at all.

On views, triggers can be defined to execute instead of INSERT, UPDATE, or DELETE operations. INSTEAD OF triggers are fired once for each row that needs to be modified in the view. It is the responsibility of the trigger's function to perform the necessary modifications to the underlying base tables and, where appropriate, return the modified row as it will appear in the view. Triggers on views can also be defined to execute once per SQL statement, before or after INSERT, UPDATE, or DELETE operations.

The trigger function must be defined before the trigger itself can be created. The trigger function must be declared as a function taking no arguments and returning type trigger. (The trigger function receives its input through a specially-passed TriggerData structure, not in the form of ordinary function arguments.)

Once a suitable trigger function has been created, the trigger is established with CREATE TRIGGER. The same trigger function can be used for multiple triggers.

PostgreSQL offers both *per-row* triggers and *per-statement* triggers. With a per-row trigger, the trigger function is invoked once for each row that is affected by the statement that fired the trigger. In contrast, a per-statement trigger is invoked only once when an appropriate statement is executed, regardless of the number of rows affected by that statement. In particular, a statement that affects zero rows will still result in the execution of any applicable per-statement triggers. These two types of triggers are sometimes called *row-level* triggers and *statement-level* triggers, respectively. Triggers on TRUNCATE may only be defined at statement level. On views, triggers that fire before or after may only be defined at statement level, while triggers that fire instead of an INSERT, UPDATE, or DELETE may only be defined at row level.

Triggers are also classified according to whether they fire *before*, *after*, or *instead of* the operation. These are referred to as BEFORE triggers, AFTER triggers, and INSTEAD OF triggers respectively. Statement-level

BEFORE triggers naturally fire before the statement starts to do anything, while statement-level AFTER triggers fire at the very end of the statement. These types of triggers may be defined on tables or views. Row-level BEFORE triggers fire immediately before a particular row is operated on, while row-level AFTER triggers fire at the end of the statement (but before any statement-level AFTER triggers). These types of triggers may only be defined on tables and foreign tables. Row-level INSTEAD OF triggers may only be defined on views, and fire immediately as each row in the view is identified as needing to be operated on.

If an INSERT contains an ON CONFLICT DO UPDATE clause, it is possible that the effects of all row-level BEFORE INSERT triggers and all row-level BEFORE UPDATE triggers can both be applied in a way that is apparent from the final state of the updated row, if an EXCLUDED column is referenced. There need not be an EXCLUDED column reference for both sets of row-level BEFORE triggers to execute, though. The possibility of surprising outcomes should be considered when there are both BEFORE INSERT and BEFORE UPDATE row-level triggers that both affect a row being inserted/updated (this can still be problematic if the modifications are more or less equivalent if they're not also idempotent). Note that statement-level UPDATE triggers are executed when ON CONFLICT DO UPDATE is specified, regardless of whether or not any rows were affected by the UPDATE (and regardless of whether the alternative UPDATE path was ever taken). An INSERT with an ON CONFLICT DO UPDATE clause will execute statement-level BEFORE INSERT triggers first, then statement-level BEFORE UPDATE triggers, followed by statement-level AFTER UPDATE triggers and finally statement-level AFTER INSERT triggers.

Trigger functions invoked by per-statement triggers should always return NULL. Trigger functions invoked by per-row triggers can return a table row (a value of type HeapTuple) to the calling executor, if they choose. A row-level trigger fired before an operation has the following choices:

- It can return NULL to skip the operation for the current row. This instructs the executor to not perform the row-level operation that invoked the trigger (the insertion, modification, or deletion of a particular table row).

- For row-level INSERT and UPDATE triggers only, the returned row becomes the row that will be inserted or will replace the row being updated. This allows the trigger function to modify the row being inserted or updated.

A row-level BEFORE trigger that does not intend to cause either of these behaviors must be careful to return as its result the same row that was passed in (that is, the NEW row for INSERT and UPDATE triggers, the OLD row for DELETE triggers).

A row-level INSTEAD OF trigger should either return NULL to indicate that it did not modify any data from the view's underlying base tables, or it should return the view row that was passed in (the NEW row for INSERT and UPDATE operations, or the OLD row for DELETE operations). A nonnull return value is used to signal that the trigger performed the necessary data modifications in the view. This will cause the count of the number of rows affected by the command to be incremented. For INSERT and UPDATE operations, the trigger may modify the NEW row before returning it. This will change the data returned by INSERT RETURNING or UPDATE RETURNING, and is useful when the view will not show exactly the same data that was provided.

The return value is ignored for row-level triggers fired after an operation, and so they can return NULL.

If more than one trigger is defined for the same event on the same relation, the triggers will be fired in alphabetical order by trigger name. In the case of BEFORE and INSTEAD OF triggers, the possibly-modified row returned by each trigger becomes the input to the next trigger. If any BEFORE or INSTEAD OF trigger returns NULL, the operation is abandoned for that row and subsequent triggers are not fired (for that row).

A trigger definition can also specify a Boolean WHEN condition, which will be tested to see whether the trigger should be fired. In row-level triggers the WHEN condition can examine the old and/or new values of columns of the row. (Statement-level triggers can also have WHEN conditions, although the feature is not so useful for them.) In a BEFORE trigger, the WHEN condition is evaluated just before the function is or would be executed, so using WHEN is not materially different from testing the same condition at the beginning of the trigger function. However, in an AFTER trigger, the WHEN condition is evaluated just after the row update occurs, and it determines whether an event is queued to fire the trigger at the end of statement. So when an AFTER trigger's WHEN condition does not return true, it is not necessary to queue an event nor to re-fetch the row at end of statement. This can result in significant speedups in statements that modify many rows, if the trigger only needs to be fired for a few of the rows. INSTEAD OF triggers do not support WHEN conditions.

Typically, row-level BEFORE triggers are used for checking or modifying the data that will be inserted or updated. For example, a BEFORE trigger might be used to insert the current time into a timestamp column, or to check that two elements of the row are consistent. Row-level AFTER triggers are most sensibly used to propagate the updates to other tables, or make consistency checks against other tables. The reason for this division of labor is that an AFTER trigger can be certain it is seeing the final value of the row, while a BEFORE trigger cannot; there might be other BEFORE triggers firing after it. If you have no specific reason to make a trigger BEFORE or AFTER, the BEFORE case is more efficient, since the information about the operation doesn't have to be saved until end of statement.

If a trigger function executes SQL commands then these commands might fire triggers again. This is known as cascading triggers. There is no direct limitation on the number of cascade levels. It is possible for cascades to cause a recursive invocation of the same trigger; for example, an INSERT trigger might execute a command that inserts an additional row into the same table, causing the INSERT trigger to be fired again. It is the trigger programmer's responsibility to avoid infinite recursion in such scenarios.

When a trigger is being defined, arguments can be specified for it. The purpose of including arguments in the trigger definition is to allow different triggers with similar requirements to call the same function. As an example, there could be a generalized trigger function that takes as its arguments two column names and puts the current user in one and the current time stamp in the other. Properly written, this trigger function would be independent of the specific table it is triggering on. So the same function could be used for INSERT events on any table with suitable columns, to automatically track creation of records in a transaction table for example. It could also be used to track last-update events if defined as an UPDATE trigger.

Each programming language that supports triggers has its own method for making the trigger input data available to the trigger function. This input data includes the type of trigger event (e.g., INSERT or UPDATE) as well as any arguments that were listed in CREATE TRIGGER. For a row-level trigger, the input data also includes the NEW row for INSERT and UPDATE triggers, and/or the OLD row for UPDATE and DELETE triggers. Statement-level triggers do not currently have any way to examine the individual row(s) modified by the statement.

37.2. Visibility of Data Changes

If you execute SQL commands in your trigger function, and these commands access the table that the trigger is for, then you need to be aware of the data visibility rules, because they determine whether these

SQL commands will see the data change that the trigger is fired for. Briefly:

- Statement-level triggers follow simple visibility rules: none of the changes made by a statement are visible to statement-level BEFORE triggers, whereas all modifications are visible to statement-level AFTER triggers.

- The data change (insertion, update, or deletion) causing the trigger to fire is naturally *not* visible to SQL commands executed in a row-level BEFORE trigger, because it hasn't happened yet.

- However, SQL commands executed in a row-level BEFORE trigger *will* see the effects of data changes for rows previously processed in the same outer command. This requires caution, since the ordering of these change events is not in general predictable; a SQL command that affects multiple rows can visit the rows in any order.

- Similarly, a row-level INSTEAD OF trigger will see the effects of data changes made by previous firings of INSTEAD OF triggers in the same outer command.

- When a row-level AFTER trigger is fired, all data changes made by the outer command are already complete, and are visible to the invoked trigger function.

If your trigger function is written in any of the standard procedural languages, then the above statements apply only if the function is declared VOLATILE. Functions that are declared STABLE or IMMUTABLE will not see changes made by the calling command in any case.

Further information about data visibility rules can be found in Section 45.4. The example in Section 37.4 contains a demonstration of these rules.

37.3. Writing Trigger Functions in C

This section describes the low-level details of the interface to a trigger function. This information is only needed when writing trigger functions in C. If you are using a higher-level language then these details are handled for you. In most cases you should consider using a procedural language before writing your triggers in C. The documentation of each procedural language explains how to write a trigger in that language.

Trigger functions must use the "version 1" function manager interface.

When a function is called by the trigger manager, it is not passed any normal arguments, but it is passed a "context" pointer pointing to a `TriggerData` structure. C functions can check whether they were called from the trigger manager or not by executing the macro:

```
CALLED_AS_TRIGGER(fcinfo)
```

which expands to:

```
((fcinfo)->context != NULL && IsA((fcinfo)->context, TriggerData))
```

If this returns true, then it is safe to cast `fcinfo->context` to type `TriggerData *` and make use of the pointed-to `TriggerData` structure. The function must *not* alter the `TriggerData` structure or any of the data it points to.

struct `TriggerData` is defined in `commands/trigger.h`:

```
typedef struct TriggerData
{
    NodeTag        type;
    TriggerEvent   tg_event;
    Relation       tg_relation;
    HeapTuple      tg_trigtuple;
    HeapTuple      tg_newtuple;
    Trigger        *tg_trigger;
    Buffer         tg_trigtuplebuf;
    Buffer         tg_newtuplebuf;
} TriggerData;
```

where the members are defined as follows:

type

   Always `T_TriggerData`.

tg_event

   Describes the event for which the function is called. You can use the following macros to examine `tg_event`:

TRIGGER_FIRED_BEFORE(tg_event)

   Returns true if the trigger fired before the operation.

TRIGGER_FIRED_AFTER(tg_event)

   Returns true if the trigger fired after the operation.

TRIGGER_FIRED_INSTEAD(tg_event)

   Returns true if the trigger fired instead of the operation.

TRIGGER_FIRED_FOR_ROW(tg_event)

   Returns true if the trigger fired for a row-level event.

TRIGGER_FIRED_FOR_STATEMENT(tg_event)

   Returns true if the trigger fired for a statement-level event.

TRIGGER_FIRED_BY_INSERT(tg_event)

   Returns true if the trigger was fired by an INSERT command.

TRIGGER_FIRED_BY_UPDATE(tg_event)

   Returns true if the trigger was fired by an UPDATE command.

TRIGGER_FIRED_BY_DELETE(tg_event)

   Returns true if the trigger was fired by a DELETE command.

TRIGGER_FIRED_BY_TRUNCATE(tg_event)

   Returns true if the trigger was fired by a TRUNCATE command.

`tg_relation`

> A pointer to a structure describing the relation that the trigger fired for. Look at `utils/rel.h` for details about this structure. The most interesting things are `tg_relation->rd_att` (descriptor of the relation tuples) and `tg_relation->rd_rel->relname` (relation name; the type is not `char*` but `NameData`; use `SPI_getrelname(tg_relation)` to get a `char*` if you need a copy of the name).

`tg_trigtuple`

> A pointer to the row for which the trigger was fired. This is the row being inserted, updated, or deleted. If this trigger was fired for an `INSERT` or `DELETE` then this is what you should return from the function if you don't want to replace the row with a different one (in the case of `INSERT`) or skip the operation. For triggers on foreign tables, values of system columns herein are unspecified.

`tg_newtuple`

> A pointer to the new version of the row, if the trigger was fired for an `UPDATE`, and `NULL` if it is for an `INSERT` or a `DELETE`. This is what you have to return from the function if the event is an `UPDATE` and you don't want to replace this row by a different one or skip the operation. For triggers on foreign tables, values of system columns herein are unspecified.

`tg_trigger`

> A pointer to a structure of type `Trigger`, defined in `utils/reltrigger.h`:
>
> ```
> typedef struct Trigger
> {
>     Oid         tgoid;
>     char        *tgname;
>     Oid         tgfoid;
>     int16       tgtype;
>     char        tgenabled;
>     bool        tgisinternal;
>     Oid         tgconstrrelid;
>     Oid         tgconstrindid;
>     Oid         tgconstraint;
>     bool        tgdeferrable;
>     bool        tginitdeferred;
>     int16       tgnargs;
>     int16       tgnattr;
>     int16       *tgattr;
>     char        **tgargs;
>     char        *tgqual;
> } Trigger;
> ```
>
> where `tgname` is the trigger's name, `tgnargs` is the number of arguments in `tgargs`, and `tgargs` is an array of pointers to the arguments specified in the `CREATE TRIGGER` statement. The other members are for internal use only.

`tg_trigtuplebuf`

> The buffer containing `tg_trigtuple`, or `InvalidBuffer` if there is no such tuple or it is not stored in a disk buffer.

`tg_newtuplebuf`

The buffer containing `tg_newtuple`, or `InvalidBuffer` if there is no such tuple or it is not stored in a disk buffer.

A trigger function must return either a `HeapTuple` pointer or a `NULL` pointer (*not* an SQL null value, that is, do not set `isNull` true). Be careful to return either `tg_trigtuple` or `tg_newtuple`, as appropriate, if you don't want to modify the row being operated on.

37.4. A Complete Trigger Example

Here is a very simple example of a trigger function written in C. (Examples of triggers written in procedural languages can be found in the documentation of the procedural languages.)

The function `trigf` reports the number of rows in the table `ttest` and skips the actual operation if the command attempts to insert a null value into the column `x`. (So the trigger acts as a not-null constraint but doesn't abort the transaction.)

First, the table definition:

```
CREATE TABLE ttest (
    x integer
);
```

This is the source code of the trigger function:

```
#include "postgres.h"
#include "executor/spi.h"        /* this is what you need to work with SPI */
#include "commands/trigger.h"    /* ... triggers ... */
#include "utils/rel.h"           /* ... and relations */

PG_MODULE_MAGIC;

PG_FUNCTION_INFO_V1(trigf);

Datum
trigf(PG_FUNCTION_ARGS)
{
    TriggerData *trigdata = (TriggerData *) fcinfo->context;
    TupleDesc   tupdesc;
    HeapTuple   rettuple;
    char        *when;
    bool        checknull = false;
    bool        isnull;
    int         ret, i;

    /* make sure it's called as a trigger at all */
    if (!CALLED_AS_TRIGGER(fcinfo))
        elog(ERROR, "trigf: not called by trigger manager");
```

```
    /* tuple to return to executor */
    if (TRIGGER_FIRED_BY_UPDATE(trigdata->tg_event))
        rettuple = trigdata->tg_newtuple;
    else
        rettuple = trigdata->tg_trigtuple;

    /* check for null values */
    if (!TRIGGER_FIRED_BY_DELETE(trigdata->tg_event)
        && TRIGGER_FIRED_BEFORE(trigdata->tg_event))
        checknull = true;

    if (TRIGGER_FIRED_BEFORE(trigdata->tg_event))
        when = "before";
    else
        when = "after ";

    tupdesc = trigdata->tg_relation->rd_att;

    /* connect to SPI manager */
    if ((ret = SPI_connect()) < 0)
        elog(ERROR, "trigf (fired %s): SPI_connect returned %d", when, ret);

    /* get number of rows in table */
    ret = SPI_exec("SELECT count(*) FROM ttest", 0);

    if (ret < 0)
        elog(ERROR, "trigf (fired %s): SPI_exec returned %d", when, ret);

    /* count(*) returns int8, so be careful to convert */
    i = DatumGetInt64(SPI_getbinval(SPI_tuptable->vals[0],
                                    SPI_tuptable->tupdesc,
                                    1,
                                    &isnull));

    elog (INFO, "trigf (fired %s): there are %d rows in ttest", when, i);

    SPI_finish();

    if (checknull)
    {
        SPI_getbinval(rettuple, tupdesc, 1, &isnull);
        if (isnull)
            rettuple = NULL;
    }

    return PointerGetDatum(rettuple);
}
```

After you have compiled the source code (see Section 36.9.6), declare the function and the triggers:

```
CREATE FUNCTION trigf() RETURNS trigger
```

```
    AS 'filename'
    LANGUAGE C;

CREATE TRIGGER tbefore BEFORE INSERT OR UPDATE OR DELETE ON ttest
    FOR EACH ROW EXECUTE PROCEDURE trigf();

CREATE TRIGGER tafter AFTER INSERT OR UPDATE OR DELETE ON ttest
    FOR EACH ROW EXECUTE PROCEDURE trigf();
```

Now you can test the operation of the trigger:

```
=> INSERT INTO ttest VALUES (NULL);
INFO:  trigf (fired before): there are 0 rows in ttest
INSERT 0 0

-- Insertion skipped and AFTER trigger is not fired

=> SELECT * FROM ttest;
 x
---
(0 rows)

=> INSERT INTO ttest VALUES (1);
INFO:  trigf (fired before): there are 0 rows in ttest
INFO:  trigf (fired after ): there are 1 rows in ttest
                                          ^^^^^^^^
                             remember what we said about visibility.
INSERT 167793 1
vac=> SELECT * FROM ttest;
 x
---
 1
(1 row)

=> INSERT INTO ttest SELECT x * 2 FROM ttest;
INFO:  trigf (fired before): there are 1 rows in ttest
INFO:  trigf (fired after ): there are 2 rows in ttest
                                         ^^^^^^
                             remember what we said about visibility.
INSERT 167794 1
=> SELECT * FROM ttest;
 x
---
 1
 2
(2 rows)

=> UPDATE ttest SET x = NULL WHERE x = 2;
INFO:  trigf (fired before): there are 2 rows in ttest
UPDATE 0
=> UPDATE ttest SET x = 4 WHERE x = 2;
INFO:  trigf (fired before): there are 2 rows in ttest
```

```
INFO:  trigf (fired after ): there are 2 rows in ttest
UPDATE 1
vac=> SELECT * FROM ttest;
 x
---
 1
 4
(2 rows)

=> DELETE FROM ttest;
INFO:  trigf (fired before): there are 2 rows in ttest
INFO:  trigf (fired before): there are 1 rows in ttest
INFO:  trigf (fired after ): there are 0 rows in ttest
INFO:  trigf (fired after ): there are 0 rows in ttest
                                    ^^^^^^
                        remember what we said about visibility.
DELETE 2
=> SELECT * FROM ttest;
 x
---
(0 rows)
```

There are more complex examples in `src/test/regress/regress.c` and in spi.

Chapter 38. Event Triggers

To supplement the trigger mechanism discussed in Chapter 37, PostgreSQL also provides event triggers. Unlike regular triggers, which are attached to a single table and capture only DML events, event triggers are global to a particular database and are capable of capturing DDL events.

Like regular triggers, event triggers can be written in any procedural language that includes event trigger support, or in C, but not in plain SQL.

38.1. Overview of Event Trigger Behavior

An event trigger fires whenever the event with which it is associated occurs in the database in which it is defined. Currently, the only supported events are `ddl_command_start`, `ddl_command_end`, `table_rewrite` and `sql_drop`. Support for additional events may be added in future releases.

The `ddl_command_start` event occurs just before the execution of a CREATE, ALTER, DROP, SECURITY LABEL, COMMENT, GRANT or REVOKE command. No check whether the affected object exists or doesn't exist is performed before the event trigger fires. As an exception, however, this event does not occur for DDL commands targeting shared objects — databases, roles, and tablespaces — or for commands targeting event triggers themselves. The event trigger mechanism does not support these object types. `ddl_command_start` also occurs just before the execution of a SELECT INTO command, since this is equivalent to CREATE TABLE AS.

The `ddl_command_end` event occurs just after the execution of this same set of commands. To obtain more details on the DDL operations that took place, use the set-returning function `pg_event_trigger_ddl_commands()` from the `ddl_command_end` event trigger code (see Section 9.28). Note that the trigger fires after the actions have taken place (but before the transaction commits), and thus the system catalogs can be read as already changed.

The `sql_drop` event occurs just before the `ddl_command_end` event trigger for any operation that drops database objects. To list the objects that have been dropped, use the set-returning function `pg_event_trigger_dropped_objects()` from the `sql_drop` event trigger code (see Section 9.28). Note that the trigger is executed after the objects have been deleted from the system catalogs, so it's not possible to look them up anymore.

The `table_rewrite` event occurs just before a table is rewritten by some actions of the commands ALTER TABLE and ALTER TYPE. While other control statements are available to rewrite a table, like CLUSTER and VACUUM, the `table_rewrite` event is not triggered by them.

Event triggers (like other functions) cannot be executed in an aborted transaction. Thus, if a DDL command fails with an error, any associated `ddl_command_end` triggers will not be executed. Conversely, if a `ddl_command_start` trigger fails with an error, no further event triggers will fire, and no attempt will be made to execute the command itself. Similarly, if a `ddl_command_end` trigger fails with an error, the effects of the DDL statement will be rolled back, just as they would be in any other case where the containing transaction aborts.

For a complete list of commands supported by the event trigger mechanism, see Section 38.2.

Event triggers are created using the command CREATE EVENT TRIGGER. In order to create an event trigger, you must first create a function with the special return type `event_trigger`. This function need not (and may not) return a value; the return type serves merely as a signal that the function is to be invoked as an event trigger.

If more than one event trigger is defined for a particular event, they will fire in alphabetical order by trigger name.

A trigger definition can also specify a WHEN condition so that, for example, a `ddl_command_start` trigger can be fired only for particular commands which the user wishes to intercept. A common use of such triggers is to restrict the range of DDL operations which users may perform.

38.2. Event Trigger Firing Matrix

Table 38-1 lists all commands for which event triggers are supported.

Table 38-1. Event Trigger Support by Command Tag

Command Tag	`ddl_command_start`	`ddl_command_end`	`sql_drop`	`table_rewrite`	Notes
ALTER AGGREGATE	X	X	–	–	
ALTER COLLATION	X	X	–	–	
ALTER CONVERSION	X	X	–	–	
ALTER DOMAIN	X	X	–	–	
ALTER EXTENSION	X	X	–	–	
ALTER FOREIGN DATA WRAPPER	X	X	–	–	
ALTER FOREIGN TABLE	X	X	X	–	
ALTER FUNCTION	X	X	–	–	
ALTER LANGUAGE	X	X	–	–	
ALTER OPERATOR	X	X	–	–	
ALTER OPERATOR CLASS	X	X	–	–	

Command Tag	ddl_command_start	ddl_command_end	sql_drop	table_rewrite	Notes
ALTER OPERATOR FAMILY	X	X	–	–	
ALTER POLICY	X	X	–	–	
ALTER SCHEMA	X	X	–	–	
ALTER SEQUENCE	X	X	–	–	
ALTER SERVER	X	X	–	–	
ALTER TABLE	X	X	X	X	
ALTER TEXT SEARCH CONFIGURATION	X	X	–	–	
ALTER TEXT SEARCH DICTIONARY	X	X	–	–	
ALTER TEXT SEARCH PARSER	X	X	–	–	
ALTER TEXT SEARCH TEMPLATE	X	X	–	–	
ALTER TRIGGER	X	X	–	–	
ALTER TYPE	X	X	–	X	
ALTER USER MAPPING	X	X	–	–	
ALTER VIEW	X	X	–	–	
CREATE AGGREGATE	X	X	–	–	
COMMENT	X	X	–	–	Only for local objects
CREATE CAST	X	X	–	–	
CREATE COLLATION	X	X	–	–	
CREATE CONVERSION	X	X	–	–	

Command Tag	ddl_command_start	ddl_command_end	sql_drop	table_rewrite	Notes
CREATE DOMAIN	X	X	–	–	
CREATE EXTENSION	X	X	–	–	
CREATE FOREIGN DATA WRAPPER	X	X	–	–	
CREATE FOREIGN TABLE	X	X	–	–	
CREATE FUNCTION	X	X	–	–	
CREATE INDEX	X	X	–	–	
CREATE LANGUAGE	X	X	–	–	
CREATE OPERATOR	X	X	–	–	
CREATE OPERATOR CLASS	X	X	–	–	
CREATE OPERATOR FAMILY	X	X	–	–	
CREATE POLICY	X	X	–	–	
CREATE RULE	X	X	–	–	
CREATE SCHEMA	X	X	–	–	
CREATE SEQUENCE	X	X	–	–	
CREATE SERVER	X	X	–	–	
CREATE TABLE	X	X	–	–	
CREATE TABLE AS	X	X	–	–	
CREATE TEXT SEARCH CONFIGURATION	X	X	–	–	

Command Tag	ddl_command_start	ddl_command_end	sql_drop	table_rewrite	Notes
CREATE TEXT SEARCH DICTIONARY	X	X	–	–	
CREATE TEXT SEARCH PARSER	X	X	–	–	
CREATE TEXT SEARCH TEMPLATE	X	X	–	–	
CREATE TRIGGER	X	X	–	–	
CREATE TYPE	X	X	–	–	
CREATE USER MAPPING	X	X	–	–	
CREATE VIEW	X	X	–	–	
DROP AGGREGATE	X	X	X	–	
DROP CAST	X	X	X	–	
DROP COLLATION	X	X	X	–	
DROP CONVERSION	X	X	X	–	
DROP DOMAIN	X	X	X	–	
DROP EXTENSION	X	X	X	–	
DROP FOREIGN DATA WRAPPER	X	X	X	–	
DROP FOREIGN TABLE	X	X	X	–	
DROP FUNCTION	X	X	X	–	
DROP INDEX	X	X	X	–	
DROP LANGUAGE	X	X	X	–	
DROP OPERATOR	X	X	X	–	

Command Tag	ddl_command_start	ddl_command_end	sql_drop	table_rewrite	Notes
DROP OPERATOR CLASS	X	X	X	–	
DROP OPERATOR FAMILY	X	X	X	–	
DROP OWNED	X	X	X	–	
DROP POLICY	X	X	X	–	
DROP RULE	X	X	X	–	
DROP SCHEMA	X	X	X	–	
DROP SEQUENCE	X	X	X	–	
DROP SERVER	X	X	X	–	
DROP TABLE	X	X	X	–	
DROP TEXT SEARCH CONFIGURATION	X	X	X	–	
DROP TEXT SEARCH DICTIONARY	X	X	X	–	
DROP TEXT SEARCH PARSER	X	X	X	–	
DROP TEXT SEARCH TEMPLATE	X	X	X	–	
DROP TRIGGER	X	X	X	–	
DROP TYPE	X	X	X	–	
DROP USER MAPPING	X	X	X	–	
DROP VIEW	X	X	X	–	
GRANT	X	X	–	–	Only for local objects
IMPORT FOREIGN SCHEMA	X	X	–	–	
REVOKE	X	X	–	–	Only for local objects

Command Tag	ddl_command_start	ddl_command_end	sql_drop	table_rewrite	Notes
SECURITY LABEL	X	X	–	–	Only for local objects
SELECT INTO	X	X	–	–	

38.3. Writing Event Trigger Functions in C

This section describes the low-level details of the interface to an event trigger function. This information is only needed when writing event trigger functions in C. If you are using a higher-level language then these details are handled for you. In most cases you should consider using a procedural language before writing your event triggers in C. The documentation of each procedural language explains how to write an event trigger in that language.

Event trigger functions must use the "version 1" function manager interface.

When a function is called by the event trigger manager, it is not passed any normal arguments, but it is passed a "context" pointer pointing to a `EventTriggerData` structure. C functions can check whether they were called from the event trigger manager or not by executing the macro:

```
CALLED_AS_EVENT_TRIGGER(fcinfo)
```

which expands to:

```
((fcinfo)->context != NULL && IsA((fcinfo)->context, EventTriggerData))
```

If this returns true, then it is safe to cast `fcinfo->context` to type `EventTriggerData *` and make use of the pointed-to `EventTriggerData` structure. The function must *not* alter the `EventTriggerData` structure or any of the data it points to.

`struct EventTriggerData` is defined in `commands/event_trigger.h`:

```
typedef struct EventTriggerData
{
    NodeTag     type;
    const char *event;       /* event name */
    Node        *parsetree;  /* parse tree */
    const char *tag;         /* command tag */
} EventTriggerData;
```

where the members are defined as follows:

type

    Always `T_EventTriggerData`.

event

    Describes the event for which the function is called, one of `"ddl_command_start"`, `"ddl_command_end"`, `"sql_drop"`, `"table_rewrite"`. See Section 38.1 for the meaning of these events.

`parsetree`

> A pointer to the parse tree of the command. Check the PostgreSQL source code for details. The parse tree structure is subject to change without notice.

`tag`

> The command tag associated with the event for which the event trigger is run, for example `"CREATE FUNCTION"`.

An event trigger function must return a `NULL` pointer (*not* an SQL null value, that is, do not set `isNull` true).

38.4. A Complete Event Trigger Example

Here is a very simple example of an event trigger function written in C. (Examples of triggers written in procedural languages can be found in the documentation of the procedural languages.)

The function `noddl` raises an exception each time it is called. The event trigger definition associated the function with the `ddl_command_start` event. The effect is that all DDL commands (with the exceptions mentioned in Section 38.1) are prevented from running.

This is the source code of the trigger function:

```c
#include "postgres.h"
#include "commands/event_trigger.h"


PG_MODULE_MAGIC;

PG_FUNCTION_INFO_V1(noddl);

Datum
noddl(PG_FUNCTION_ARGS)
{
    EventTriggerData *trigdata;

    if (!CALLED_AS_EVENT_TRIGGER(fcinfo))  /* internal error */
        elog(ERROR, "not fired by event trigger manager");

    trigdata = (EventTriggerData *) fcinfo->context;

    ereport(ERROR,
        (errcode(ERRCODE_INSUFFICIENT_PRIVILEGE),
                errmsg("command \"%s\" denied", trigdata->tag)));

    PG_RETURN_NULL();
}
```

After you have compiled the source code (see Section 36.9.6), declare the function and the triggers:

```
CREATE FUNCTION noddl() RETURNS event_trigger
    AS 'noddl' LANGUAGE C;

CREATE EVENT TRIGGER noddl ON ddl_command_start
    EXECUTE PROCEDURE noddl();
```

Now you can test the operation of the trigger:

```
=# \dy
                    List of event triggers
 Name  |       Event        | Owner | Enabled | Procedure | Tags
-------+--------------------+-------+---------+-----------+------
 noddl | ddl_command_start  | dim   | enabled | noddl     |
(1 row)

=# CREATE TABLE foo(id serial);
ERROR:  command "CREATE TABLE" denied
```

In this situation, in order to be able to run some DDL commands when you need to do so, you have to either drop the event trigger or disable it. It can be convenient to disable the trigger for only the duration of a transaction:

```
BEGIN;
ALTER EVENT TRIGGER noddl DISABLE;
CREATE TABLE foo (id serial);
ALTER EVENT TRIGGER noddl ENABLE;
COMMIT;
```

(Recall that DDL commands on event triggers themselves are not affected by event triggers.)

38.5. A Table Rewrite Event Trigger Example

Thanks to the table_rewrite event, it is possible to implement a table rewriting policy only allowing the rewrite in maintenance windows.

Here's an example implementing such a policy.

```
CREATE OR REPLACE FUNCTION no_rewrite()
 RETURNS event_trigger
 LANGUAGE plpgsql AS
$$
---
--- Implement local Table Rewriting policy:
---    public.foo is not allowed rewriting, ever
---    other tables are only allowed rewriting between 1am and 6am
---    unless they have more than 100 blocks
---
DECLARE
```

```
    table_oid oid := pg_event_trigger_table_rewrite_oid();
    current_hour integer := extract('hour' from current_time);
    pages integer;
    max_pages integer := 100;
BEGIN
    IF pg_event_trigger_table_rewrite_oid() = 'public.foo'::regclass
    THEN
            RAISE EXCEPTION 'you"re not allowed to rewrite the table %',
                            table_oid::regclass;
    END IF;

    SELECT INTO pages relpages FROM pg_class WHERE oid = table_oid;
    IF pages > max_pages
    THEN
            RAISE EXCEPTION 'rewrites only allowed for table with less than % pages',
                            max_pages;
    END IF;

    IF current_hour NOT BETWEEN 1 AND 6
    THEN
            RAISE EXCEPTION 'rewrites only allowed between 1am and 6am';
    END IF;
END;
$$;

CREATE EVENT TRIGGER no_rewrite_allowed
                 ON table_rewrite
   EXECUTE PROCEDURE no_rewrite();
```

Chapter 39. The Rule System

This chapter discusses the rule system in PostgreSQL. Production rule systems are conceptually simple, but there are many subtle points involved in actually using them.

Some other database systems define active database rules, which are usually stored procedures and triggers. In PostgreSQL, these can be implemented using functions and triggers as well.

The rule system (more precisely speaking, the query rewrite rule system) is totally different from stored procedures and triggers. It modifies queries to take rules into consideration, and then passes the modified query to the query planner for planning and execution. It is very powerful, and can be used for many things such as query language procedures, views, and versions. The theoretical foundations and the power of this rule system are also discussed in *On Rules, Procedures, Caching and Views in Database Systems* and *A Unified Framework for Version Modeling Using Production Rules in a Database System.*

39.1. The Query Tree

To understand how the rule system works it is necessary to know when it is invoked and what its input and results are.

The rule system is located between the parser and the planner. It takes the output of the parser, one query tree, and the user-defined rewrite rules, which are also query trees with some extra information, and creates zero or more query trees as result. So its input and output are always things the parser itself could have produced and thus, anything it sees is basically representable as an SQL statement.

Now what is a query tree? It is an internal representation of an SQL statement where the single parts that it is built from are stored separately. These query trees can be shown in the server log if you set the configuration parameters `debug_print_parse`, `debug_print_rewritten`, or `debug_print_plan`. The rule actions are also stored as query trees, in the system catalog `pg_rewrite`. They are not formatted like the log output, but they contain exactly the same information.

Reading a raw query tree requires some experience. But since SQL representations of query trees are sufficient to understand the rule system, this chapter will not teach how to read them.

When reading the SQL representations of the query trees in this chapter it is necessary to be able to identify the parts the statement is broken into when it is in the query tree structure. The parts of a query tree are

the command type

This is a simple value telling which command (`SELECT`, `INSERT`, `UPDATE`, `DELETE`) produced the query tree.

the range table

The range table is a list of relations that are used in the query. In a `SELECT` statement these are the relations given after the `FROM` key word.

Every range table entry identifies a table or view and tells by which name it is called in the other parts of the query. In the query tree, the range table entries are referenced by number rather than by name, so here it doesn't matter if there are duplicate names as it would in an SQL statement. This can happen after the range tables of rules have been merged in. The examples in this chapter will not have this situation.

the result relation

> This is an index into the range table that identifies the relation where the results of the query go.
>
> SELECT queries don't have a result relation. (The special case of SELECT INTO is mostly identical to CREATE TABLE followed by INSERT ... SELECT, and is not discussed separately here.)
>
> For INSERT, UPDATE, and DELETE commands, the result relation is the table (or view!) where the changes are to take effect.

the target list

> The target list is a list of expressions that define the result of the query. In the case of a SELECT, these expressions are the ones that build the final output of the query. They correspond to the expressions between the key words SELECT and FROM. (* is just an abbreviation for all the column names of a relation. It is expanded by the parser into the individual columns, so the rule system never sees it.)
>
> DELETE commands don't need a normal target list because they don't produce any result. Instead, the rule system adds a special CTID entry to the empty target list, to allow the executor to find the row to be deleted. (CTID is added when the result relation is an ordinary table. If it is a view, a whole-row variable is added instead, as described in Section 39.2.4.)
>
> For INSERT commands, the target list describes the new rows that should go into the result relation. It consists of the expressions in the VALUES clause or the ones from the SELECT clause in INSERT ... SELECT. The first step of the rewrite process adds target list entries for any columns that were not assigned to by the original command but have defaults. Any remaining columns (with neither a given value nor a default) will be filled in by the planner with a constant null expression.
>
> For UPDATE commands, the target list describes the new rows that should replace the old ones. In the rule system, it contains just the expressions from the SET column = expression part of the command. The planner will handle missing columns by inserting expressions that copy the values from the old row into the new one. Just as for DELETE, the rule system adds a CTID or whole-row variable so that the executor can identify the old row to be updated.
>
> Every entry in the target list contains an expression that can be a constant value, a variable pointing to a column of one of the relations in the range table, a parameter, or an expression tree made of function calls, constants, variables, operators, etc.

the qualification

> The query's qualification is an expression much like one of those contained in the target list entries. The result value of this expression is a Boolean that tells whether the operation (INSERT, UPDATE, DELETE, or SELECT) for the final result row should be executed or not. It corresponds to the WHERE clause of an SQL statement.

the join tree

> The query's join tree shows the structure of the FROM clause. For a simple query like SELECT ... FROM a, b, c, the join tree is just a list of the FROM items, because we are allowed to join them in any order. But when JOIN expressions, particularly outer joins, are used, we have to join in the order shown by the joins. In that case, the join tree shows the structure of the JOIN expressions. The restrictions associated with particular JOIN clauses (from ON or USING expressions) are stored as qualification expressions attached to those join-tree nodes. It turns out to be convenient to store the

top-level WHERE expression as a qualification attached to the top-level join-tree item, too. So really the join tree represents both the FROM and WHERE clauses of a SELECT.

the others

The other parts of the query tree like the ORDER BY clause aren't of interest here. The rule system substitutes some entries there while applying rules, but that doesn't have much to do with the fundamentals of the rule system.

39.2. Views and the Rule System

Views in PostgreSQL are implemented using the rule system. In fact, there is essentially no difference between:

```
CREATE VIEW myview AS SELECT * FROM mytab;
```

compared against the two commands:

```
CREATE TABLE myview (same column list as mytab);
CREATE RULE "_RETURN" AS ON SELECT TO myview DO INSTEAD
    SELECT * FROM mytab;
```

because this is exactly what the CREATE VIEW command does internally. This has some side effects. One of them is that the information about a view in the PostgreSQL system catalogs is exactly the same as it is for a table. So for the parser, there is absolutely no difference between a table and a view. They are the same thing: relations.

39.2.1. How SELECT Rules Work

Rules ON SELECT are applied to all queries as the last step, even if the command given is an INSERT, UPDATE or DELETE. And they have different semantics from rules on the other command types in that they modify the query tree in place instead of creating a new one. So SELECT rules are described first.

Currently, there can be only one action in an ON SELECT rule, and it must be an unconditional SELECT action that is INSTEAD. This restriction was required to make rules safe enough to open them for ordinary users, and it restricts ON SELECT rules to act like views.

The examples for this chapter are two join views that do some calculations and some more views using them in turn. One of the two first views is customized later by adding rules for INSERT, UPDATE, and DELETE operations so that the final result will be a view that behaves like a real table with some magic functionality. This is not such a simple example to start from and this makes things harder to get into. But it's better to have one example that covers all the points discussed step by step rather than having many different ones that might mix up in mind.

For the example, we need a little min function that returns the lower of 2 integer values. We create that as:

```
CREATE FUNCTION min(integer, integer) RETURNS integer AS $$
    SELECT CASE WHEN $1 < $2 THEN $1 ELSE $2 END
$$ LANGUAGE SQL STRICT;
```

The real tables we need in the first two rule system descriptions are these:

```
CREATE TABLE shoe_data (
    shoename    text,           -- primary key
    sh_avail    integer,        -- available number of pairs
    slcolor     text,           -- preferred shoelace color
    slminlen    real,           -- minimum shoelace length
    slmaxlen    real,           -- maximum shoelace length
    slunit      text            -- length unit
);

CREATE TABLE shoelace_data (
    sl_name     text,           -- primary key
    sl_avail    integer,        -- available number of pairs
    sl_color    text,           -- shoelace color
    sl_len      real,           -- shoelace length
    sl_unit     text            -- length unit
);

CREATE TABLE unit (
    un_name     text,           -- primary key
    un_fact     real            -- factor to transform to cm
);
```

As you can see, they represent shoe-store data.

The views are created as:

```
CREATE VIEW shoe AS
    SELECT sh.shoename,
           sh.sh_avail,
           sh.slcolor,
           sh.slminlen,
           sh.slminlen * un.un_fact AS slminlen_cm,
           sh.slmaxlen,
           sh.slmaxlen * un.un_fact AS slmaxlen_cm,
           sh.slunit
      FROM shoe_data sh, unit un
     WHERE sh.slunit = un.un_name;

CREATE VIEW shoelace AS
    SELECT s.sl_name,
           s.sl_avail,
           s.sl_color,
           s.sl_len,
           s.sl_unit,
           s.sl_len * u.un_fact AS sl_len_cm
      FROM shoelace_data s, unit u
     WHERE s.sl_unit = u.un_name;

CREATE VIEW shoe_ready AS
    SELECT rsh.shoename,
```

```
        rsh.sh_avail,
        rsl.sl_name,
        rsl.sl_avail,
        min(rsh.sh_avail, rsl.sl_avail) AS total_avail
   FROM shoe rsh, shoelace rsl
  WHERE rsl.sl_color = rsh.slcolor
    AND rsl.sl_len_cm >= rsh.slminlen_cm
    AND rsl.sl_len_cm <= rsh.slmaxlen_cm;
```

The CREATE VIEW command for the shoelace view (which is the simplest one we have) will create a relation shoelace and an entry in pg_rewrite that tells that there is a rewrite rule that must be applied whenever the relation shoelace is referenced in a query's range table. The rule has no rule qualification (discussed later, with the non-SELECT rules, since SELECT rules currently cannot have them) and it is INSTEAD. Note that rule qualifications are not the same as query qualifications. The action of our rule has a query qualification. The action of the rule is one query tree that is a copy of the SELECT statement in the view creation command.

> **Note:** The two extra range table entries for NEW and OLD that you can see in the pg_rewrite entry aren't of interest for SELECT rules.

Now we populate unit, shoe_data and shoelace_data and run a simple query on a view:

```
INSERT INTO unit VALUES ('cm', 1.0);
INSERT INTO unit VALUES ('m', 100.0);
INSERT INTO unit VALUES ('inch', 2.54);

INSERT INTO shoe_data VALUES ('sh1', 2, 'black', 70.0, 90.0, 'cm');
INSERT INTO shoe_data VALUES ('sh2', 0, 'black', 30.0, 40.0, 'inch');
INSERT INTO shoe_data VALUES ('sh3', 4, 'brown', 50.0, 65.0, 'cm');
INSERT INTO shoe_data VALUES ('sh4', 3, 'brown', 40.0, 50.0, 'inch');

INSERT INTO shoelace_data VALUES ('sl1', 5, 'black', 80.0, 'cm');
INSERT INTO shoelace_data VALUES ('sl2', 6, 'black', 100.0, 'cm');
INSERT INTO shoelace_data VALUES ('sl3', 0, 'black', 35.0 , 'inch');
INSERT INTO shoelace_data VALUES ('sl4', 8, 'black', 40.0 , 'inch');
INSERT INTO shoelace_data VALUES ('sl5', 4, 'brown', 1.0 , 'm');
INSERT INTO shoelace_data VALUES ('sl6', 0, 'brown', 0.9 , 'm');
INSERT INTO shoelace_data VALUES ('sl7', 7, 'brown', 60 , 'cm');
INSERT INTO shoelace_data VALUES ('sl8', 1, 'brown', 40 , 'inch');

SELECT * FROM shoelace;
```

sl_name	sl_avail	sl_color	sl_len	sl_unit	sl_len_cm
sl1	5	black	80	cm	80
sl2	6	black	100	cm	100
sl7	7	brown	60	cm	60
sl3	0	black	35	inch	88.9
sl4	8	black	40	inch	101.6
sl8	1	brown	40	inch	101.6
sl5	4	brown	1	m	100

```
sl6          |          0 | brown   |   0.9 | m       |          90
(8 rows)
```

This is the simplest SELECT you can do on our views, so we take this opportunity to explain the basics of view rules. The SELECT * FROM shoelace was interpreted by the parser and produced the query tree:

```
SELECT shoelace.sl_name, shoelace.sl_avail,
       shoelace.sl_color, shoelace.sl_len,
       shoelace.sl_unit, shoelace.sl_len_cm
  FROM shoelace shoelace;
```

and this is given to the rule system. The rule system walks through the range table and checks if there are rules for any relation. When processing the range table entry for shoelace (the only one up to now) it finds the _RETURN rule with the query tree:

```
SELECT s.sl_name, s.sl_avail,
       s.sl_color, s.sl_len, s.sl_unit,
       s.sl_len * u.un_fact AS sl_len_cm
  FROM shoelace old, shoelace new,
       shoelace_data s, unit u
 WHERE s.sl_unit = u.un_name;
```

To expand the view, the rewriter simply creates a subquery range-table entry containing the rule's action query tree, and substitutes this range table entry for the original one that referenced the view. The resulting rewritten query tree is almost the same as if you had typed:

```
SELECT shoelace.sl_name, shoelace.sl_avail,
       shoelace.sl_color, shoelace.sl_len,
       shoelace.sl_unit, shoelace.sl_len_cm
  FROM (SELECT s.sl_name,
               s.sl_avail,
               s.sl_color,
               s.sl_len,
               s.sl_unit,
               s.sl_len * u.un_fact AS sl_len_cm
          FROM shoelace_data s, unit u
         WHERE s.sl_unit = u.un_name) shoelace;
```

There is one difference however: the subquery's range table has two extra entries shoelace old and shoelace new. These entries don't participate directly in the query, since they aren't referenced by the subquery's join tree or target list. The rewriter uses them to store the access privilege check information that was originally present in the range-table entry that referenced the view. In this way, the executor will still check that the user has proper privileges to access the view, even though there's no direct use of the view in the rewritten query.

That was the first rule applied. The rule system will continue checking the remaining range-table entries in the top query (in this example there are no more), and it will recursively check the range-table entries in the added subquery to see if any of them reference views. (But it won't expand old or new — otherwise we'd have infinite recursion!) In this example, there are no rewrite rules for `shoelace_data` or `unit`, so rewriting is complete and the above is the final result given to the planner.

Now we want to write a query that finds out for which shoes currently in the store we have the matching shoelaces (color and length) and where the total number of exactly matching pairs is greater or equal to two.

```
SELECT * FROM shoe_ready WHERE total_avail >= 2;

 shoename | sh_avail | sl_name | sl_avail | total_avail
----------+----------+---------+----------+-------------
 sh1      |        2 | sl1     |        5 |           2
 sh3      |        4 | sl7     |        7 |           4
(2 rows)
```

The output of the parser this time is the query tree:

```
SELECT shoe_ready.shoename, shoe_ready.sh_avail,
       shoe_ready.sl_name, shoe_ready.sl_avail,
       shoe_ready.total_avail
  FROM shoe_ready shoe_ready
 WHERE shoe_ready.total_avail >= 2;
```

The first rule applied will be the one for the `shoe_ready` view and it results in the query tree:

```
SELECT shoe_ready.shoename, shoe_ready.sh_avail,
       shoe_ready.sl_name, shoe_ready.sl_avail,
       shoe_ready.total_avail
  FROM (SELECT rsh.shoename,
               rsh.sh_avail,
               rsl.sl_name,
               rsl.sl_avail,
               min(rsh.sh_avail, rsl.sl_avail) AS total_avail
          FROM shoe rsh, shoelace rsl
         WHERE rsl.sl_color = rsh.slcolor
           AND rsl.sl_len_cm >= rsh.slminlen_cm
           AND rsl.sl_len_cm <= rsh.slmaxlen_cm) shoe_ready
 WHERE shoe_ready.total_avail >= 2;
```

Similarly, the rules for `shoe` and `shoelace` are substituted into the range table of the subquery, leading to a three-level final query tree:

```
SELECT shoe_ready.shoename, shoe_ready.sh_avail,
       shoe_ready.sl_name, shoe_ready.sl_avail,
       shoe_ready.total_avail
  FROM (SELECT rsh.shoename,
               rsh.sh_avail,
               rsl.sl_name,
               rsl.sl_avail,
               min(rsh.sh_avail, rsl.sl_avail) AS total_avail
          FROM (SELECT sh.shoename,
                       sh.sh_avail,
```

```
                sh.slcolor,
                sh.slminlen,
                sh.slminlen * un.un_fact AS slminlen_cm,
                sh.slmaxlen,
                sh.slmaxlen * un.un_fact AS slmaxlen_cm,
                sh.slunit
          FROM shoe_data sh, unit un
         WHERE sh.slunit = un.un_name) rsh,
        (SELECT s.sl_name,
                s.sl_avail,
                s.sl_color,
                s.sl_len,
                s.sl_unit,
                s.sl_len * u.un_fact AS sl_len_cm
          FROM shoelace_data s, unit u
         WHERE s.sl_unit = u.un_name) rsl
    WHERE rsl.sl_color = rsh.slcolor
      AND rsl.sl_len_cm >= rsh.slminlen_cm
      AND rsl.sl_len_cm <= rsh.slmaxlen_cm) shoe_ready
 WHERE shoe_ready.total_avail > 2;
```

It turns out that the planner will collapse this tree into a two-level query tree: the bottommost SELECT commands will be "pulled up" into the middle SELECT since there's no need to process them separately. But the middle SELECT will remain separate from the top, because it contains aggregate functions. If we pulled those up it would change the behavior of the topmost SELECT, which we don't want. However, collapsing the query tree is an optimization that the rewrite system doesn't have to concern itself with.

39.2.2. View Rules in Non-SELECT Statements

Two details of the query tree aren't touched in the description of view rules above. These are the command type and the result relation. In fact, the command type is not needed by view rules, but the result relation may affect the way in which the query rewriter works, because special care needs to be taken if the result relation is a view.

There are only a few differences between a query tree for a SELECT and one for any other command. Obviously, they have a different command type and for a command other than a SELECT, the result relation points to the range-table entry where the result should go. Everything else is absolutely the same. So having two tables t1 and t2 with columns a and b, the query trees for the two statements:

```
SELECT t2.b FROM t1, t2 WHERE t1.a = t2.a;
```

```
UPDATE t1 SET b = t2.b FROM t2 WHERE t1.a = t2.a;
```

are nearly identical. In particular:

- The range tables contain entries for the tables t1 and t2.

- The target lists contain one variable that points to column b of the range table entry for table t2.

- The qualification expressions compare the columns a of both range-table entries for equality.

- The join trees show a simple join between t1 and t2.

The consequence is, that both query trees result in similar execution plans: They are both joins over the two tables. For the UPDATE the missing columns from t1 are added to the target list by the planner and the final query tree will read as:

```
UPDATE t1 SET a = t1.a, b = t2.b FROM t2 WHERE t1.a = t2.a;
```

and thus the executor run over the join will produce exactly the same result set as:

```
SELECT t1.a, t2.b FROM t1, t2 WHERE t1.a = t2.a;
```

But there is a little problem in UPDATE: the part of the executor plan that does the join does not care what the results from the join are meant for. It just produces a result set of rows. The fact that one is a SELECT command and the other is an UPDATE is handled higher up in the executor, where it knows that this is an UPDATE, and it knows that this result should go into table t1. But which of the rows that are there has to be replaced by the new row?

To resolve this problem, another entry is added to the target list in UPDATE (and also in DELETE) statements: the current tuple ID (CTID). This is a system column containing the file block number and position in the block for the row. Knowing the table, the CTID can be used to retrieve the original row of t1 to be updated. After adding the CTID to the target list, the query actually looks like:

```
SELECT t1.a, t2.b, t1.ctid FROM t1, t2 WHERE t1.a = t2.a;
```

Now another detail of PostgreSQL enters the stage. Old table rows aren't overwritten, and this is why ROLLBACK is fast. In an UPDATE, the new result row is inserted into the table (after stripping the CTID) and in the row header of the old row, which the CTID pointed to, the cmax and xmax entries are set to the current command counter and current transaction ID. Thus the old row is hidden, and after the transaction commits the vacuum cleaner can eventually remove the dead row.

Knowing all that, we can simply apply view rules in absolutely the same way to any command. There is no difference.

39.2.3. The Power of Views in PostgreSQL

The above demonstrates how the rule system incorporates view definitions into the original query tree. In the second example, a simple SELECT from one view created a final query tree that is a join of 4 tables (unit was used twice with different names).

The benefit of implementing views with the rule system is, that the planner has all the information about which tables have to be scanned plus the relationships between these tables plus the restrictive qualifications from the views plus the qualifications from the original query in one single query tree. And this is still the situation when the original query is already a join over views. The planner has to decide which is the best path to execute the query, and the more information the planner has, the better this decision can be. And the rule system as implemented in PostgreSQL ensures, that this is all information available about the query up to that point.

39.2.4. Updating a View

What happens if a view is named as the target relation for an INSERT, UPDATE, or DELETE? Doing the substitutions described above would give a query tree in which the result relation points at a subquery range-table entry, which will not work. There are several ways in which PostgreSQL can support the appearance of updating a view, however.

If the subquery selects from a single base relation and is simple enough, the rewriter can automatically replace the subquery with the underlying base relation so that the INSERT, UPDATE, or DELETE is applied to the base relation in the appropriate way. Views that are "simple enough" for this are called *automatically updatable*. For detailed information on the kinds of view that can be automatically updated, see CREATE VIEW.

Alternatively, the operation may be handled by a user-provided INSTEAD OF trigger on the view. Rewriting works slightly differently in this case. For INSERT, the rewriter does nothing at all with the view, leaving it as the result relation for the query. For UPDATE and DELETE, it's still necessary to expand the view query to produce the "old" rows that the command will attempt to update or delete. So the view is expanded as normal, but another unexpanded range-table entry is added to the query to represent the view in its capacity as the result relation.

The problem that now arises is how to identify the rows to be updated in the view. Recall that when the result relation is a table, a special CTID entry is added to the target list to identify the physical locations of the rows to be updated. This does not work if the result relation is a view, because a view does not have any CTID, since its rows do not have actual physical locations. Instead, for an UPDATE or DELETE operation, a special wholerow entry is added to the target list, which expands to include all columns from the view. The executor uses this value to supply the "old" row to the INSTEAD OF trigger. It is up to the trigger to work out what to update based on the old and new row values.

Another possibility is for the user to define INSTEAD rules that specify substitute actions for INSERT, UPDATE, and DELETE commands on a view. These rules will rewrite the command, typically into a command that updates one or more tables, rather than views. That is the topic of the next section.

Note that rules are evaluated first, rewriting the original query before it is planned and executed. Therefore, if a view has INSTEAD OF triggers as well as rules on INSERT, UPDATE, or DELETE, then the rules will be evaluated first, and depending on the result, the triggers may not be used at all.

Automatic rewriting of an INSERT, UPDATE, or DELETE query on a simple view is always tried last. Therefore, if a view has rules or triggers, they will override the default behavior of automatically updatable views.

If there are no INSTEAD rules or INSTEAD OF triggers for the view, and the rewriter cannot automatically rewrite the query as an update on the underlying base relation, an error will be thrown because the executor cannot update a view as such.

39.3. Materialized Views

Materialized views in PostgreSQL use the rule system like views do, but persist the results in a table-like form. The main differences between:

```
CREATE MATERIALIZED VIEW mymatview AS SELECT * FROM mytab;
```

and:

```
CREATE TABLE mymatview AS SELECT * FROM mytab;
```

are that the materialized view cannot subsequently be directly updated and that the query used to create the materialized view is stored in exactly the same way that a view's query is stored, so that fresh data can be generated for the materialized view with:

```
REFRESH MATERIALIZED VIEW mymatview;
```

The information about a materialized view in the PostgreSQL system catalogs is exactly the same as it is for a table or view. So for the parser, a materialized view is a relation, just like a table or a view. When a materialized view is referenced in a query, the data is returned directly from the materialized view, like from a table; the rule is only used for populating the materialized view.

While access to the data stored in a materialized view is often much faster than accessing the underlying tables directly or through a view, the data is not always current; yet sometimes current data is not needed. Consider a table which records sales:

```
CREATE TABLE invoice (
    invoice_no    integer         PRIMARY KEY,
    seller_no     integer,        -- ID of salesperson
    invoice_date  date,           -- date of sale
    invoice_amt   numeric(13,2)   -- amount of sale
);
```

If people want to be able to quickly graph historical sales data, they might want to summarize, and they may not care about the incomplete data for the current date:

```
CREATE MATERIALIZED VIEW sales_summary AS
  SELECT
      seller_no,
      invoice_date,
      sum(invoice_amt)::numeric(13,2) as sales_amt
    FROM invoice
    WHERE invoice_date < CURRENT_DATE
    GROUP BY
      seller_no,
      invoice_date
    ORDER BY
      seller_no,
      invoice_date;

CREATE UNIQUE INDEX sales_summary_seller
  ON sales_summary (seller_no, invoice_date);
```

This materialized view might be useful for displaying a graph in the dashboard created for salespeople. A job could be scheduled to update the statistics each night using this SQL statement:

```
REFRESH MATERIALIZED VIEW sales_summary;
```

Another use for a materialized view is to allow faster access to data brought across from a remote system through a foreign data wrapper. A simple example using `file_fdw` is below, with timings, but since this is using cache on the local system the performance difference compared to access to a remote system would usually be greater than shown here. Notice we are also exploiting the ability to put an index on the materialized view, whereas `file_fdw` does not support indexes; this advantage might not apply for other sorts of foreign data access.

Setup:

```
CREATE EXTENSION file_fdw;
CREATE SERVER local_file FOREIGN DATA WRAPPER file_fdw;
CREATE FOREIGN TABLE words (word text NOT NULL)
  SERVER local_file
  OPTIONS (filename '/usr/share/dict/words');
CREATE MATERIALIZED VIEW wrd AS SELECT * FROM words;
CREATE UNIQUE INDEX wrd_word ON wrd (word);
CREATE EXTENSION pg_trgm;
CREATE INDEX wrd_trgm ON wrd USING gist (word gist_trgm_ops);
VACUUM ANALYZE wrd;
```

Now let's spell-check a word. Using `file_fdw` directly:

```
SELECT count(*) FROM words WHERE word = 'caterpiler';

 count
-------
     0
(1 row)
```

With EXPLAIN ANALYZE, we see:

```
 Aggregate  (cost=21763.99..21764.00 rows=1 width=0) (actual time=188.180..188.181 r
   ->  Foreign Scan on words  (cost=0.00..21761.41 rows=1032 width=0) (actual time=1
         Filter: (word = 'caterpiler'::text)
         Rows Removed by Filter: 479829
         Foreign File: /usr/share/dict/words
         Foreign File Size: 4953699
 Planning time: 0.118 ms
 Execution time: 188.273 ms
```

If the materialized view is used instead, the query is much faster:

```
 Aggregate  (cost=4.44..4.45 rows=1 width=0) (actual time=0.042..0.042 rows=1 loops=
   ->  Index Only Scan using wrd_word on wrd  (cost=0.42..4.44 rows=1 width=0) (actu
         Index Cond: (word = 'caterpiler'::text)
         Heap Fetches: 0
 Planning time: 0.164 ms
 Execution time: 0.117 ms
```

Either way, the word is spelled wrong, so let's look for what we might have wanted. Again using `file_fdw`:

```
SELECT word FROM words ORDER BY word <-> 'caterpiler' LIMIT 10;
```

```
        word
---------------
 cater
 caterpillar
 Caterpillar
 caterpillars
 caterpillar's
 Caterpillar's
 caterer
 caterer's
 caters
 catered
(10 rows)
```

```
 Limit  (cost=11583.61..11583.64 rows=10 width=32) (actual time=1431.591..1431.594 r
   ->  Sort  (cost=11583.61..11804.76 rows=88459 width=32) (actual time=1431.589..14
         Sort Key: ((word <-> 'caterpiler'::text))
         Sort Method: top-N heapsort  Memory: 25kB
         ->  Foreign Scan on words  (cost=0.00..9672.05 rows=88459 width=32) (actual
               Foreign File: /usr/share/dict/words
               Foreign File Size: 4953699
 Planning time: 0.128 ms
 Execution time: 1431.679 ms
```

Using the materialized view:

```
 Limit  (cost=0.29..1.06 rows=10 width=10) (actual time=187.222..188.257 rows=10 loo
   ->  Index Scan using wrd_trgm on wrd  (cost=0.29..37020.87 rows=479829 width=10)
         Order By: (word <-> 'caterpiler'::text)
 Planning time: 0.196 ms
 Execution time: 198.640 ms
```

If you can tolerate periodic update of the remote data to the local database, the performance benefit can be substantial.

39.4. Rules on INSERT, UPDATE, and DELETE

Rules that are defined on INSERT, UPDATE, and DELETE are significantly different from the view rules described in the previous section. First, their CREATE RULE command allows more:

- They are allowed to have no action.

- They can have multiple actions.

- They can be INSTEAD or ALSO (the default).

- The pseudorelations NEW and OLD become useful.

- They can have rule qualifications.

Second, they don't modify the query tree in place. Instead they create zero or more new query trees and can throw away the original one.

> ## **Caution**
>
> In many cases, tasks that could be performed by rules on INSERT/UPDATE/DELETE are better done with triggers. Triggers are notationally a bit more complicated, but their semantics are much simpler to understand. Rules tend to have surprising results when the original query contains volatile functions: volatile functions may get executed more times than expected in the process of carrying out the rules.
>
> Also, there are some cases that are not supported by these types of rules at all, notably including WITH clauses in the original query and multiple-assignment sub-SELECTs in the SET list of UPDATE queries. This is because copying these constructs into a rule query would result in multiple evaluations of the sub-query, contrary to the express intent of the query's author.

39.4.1. How Update Rules Work

Keep the syntax:

```
CREATE [ OR REPLACE ] RULE name AS ON event
    TO table [ WHERE condition ]
    DO [ ALSO | INSTEAD ] { NOTHING | command | ( command ; command ... ) }
```

in mind. In the following, *update rules* means rules that are defined on INSERT, UPDATE, or DELETE.

Update rules get applied by the rule system when the result relation and the command type of a query tree are equal to the object and event given in the CREATE RULE command. For update rules, the rule system creates a list of query trees. Initially the query-tree list is empty. There can be zero (NOTHING key word), one, or multiple actions. To simplify, we will look at a rule with one action. This rule can have a qualification or not and it can be INSTEAD or ALSO (the default).

What is a rule qualification? It is a restriction that tells when the actions of the rule should be done and when not. This qualification can only reference the pseudorelations NEW and/or OLD, which basically represent the relation that was given as object (but with a special meaning).

So we have three cases that produce the following query trees for a one-action rule.

No qualification, with either ALSO or INSTEAD

the query tree from the rule action with the original query tree's qualification added

Qualification given and ALSO

the query tree from the rule action with the rule qualification and the original query tree's qualification added

Qualification given and INSTEAD

the query tree from the rule action with the rule qualification and the original query tree's qualification; and the original query tree with the negated rule qualification added

Finally, if the rule is ALSO, the unchanged original query tree is added to the list. Since only qualified INSTEAD rules already add the original query tree, we end up with either one or two output query trees for a rule with one action.

For `ON INSERT` rules, the original query (if not suppressed by `INSTEAD`) is done before any actions added by rules. This allows the actions to see the inserted row(s). But for `ON UPDATE` and `ON DELETE` rules, the original query is done after the actions added by rules. This ensures that the actions can see the to-be-updated or to-be-deleted rows; otherwise, the actions might do nothing because they find no rows matching their qualifications.

The query trees generated from rule actions are thrown into the rewrite system again, and maybe more rules get applied resulting in more or less query trees. So a rule's actions must have either a different command type or a different result relation than the rule itself is on, otherwise this recursive process will end up in an infinite loop. (Recursive expansion of a rule will be detected and reported as an error.)

The query trees found in the actions of the `pg_rewrite` system catalog are only templates. Since they can reference the range-table entries for `NEW` and `OLD`, some substitutions have to be made before they can be used. For any reference to `NEW`, the target list of the original query is searched for a corresponding entry. If found, that entry's expression replaces the reference. Otherwise, `NEW` means the same as `OLD` (for an `UPDATE`) or is replaced by a null value (for an `INSERT`). Any reference to `OLD` is replaced by a reference to the range-table entry that is the result relation.

After the system is done applying update rules, it applies view rules to the produced query tree(s). Views cannot insert new update actions so there is no need to apply update rules to the output of view rewriting.

39.4.1.1. A First Rule Step by Step

Say we want to trace changes to the `sl_avail` column in the `shoelace_data` relation. So we set up a log table and a rule that conditionally writes a log entry when an `UPDATE` is performed on `shoelace_data`.

```
CREATE TABLE shoelace_log (
    sl_name     text,           -- shoelace changed
    sl_avail    integer,        -- new available value
    log_who     text,           -- who did it
    log_when    timestamp       -- when
);

CREATE RULE log_shoelace AS ON UPDATE TO shoelace_data
    WHERE NEW.sl_avail <> OLD.sl_avail
    DO INSERT INTO shoelace_log VALUES (
                                NEW.sl_name,
                                NEW.sl_avail,
                                current_user,
                                current_timestamp
                        );
```

Now someone does:

```
UPDATE shoelace_data SET sl_avail = 6 WHERE sl_name = 'sl7';
```

and we look at the log table:

```
SELECT * FROM shoelace_log;

 sl_name | sl_avail | log_who | log_when
```

```
---------+----------+---------+---------------------------------
 sl7     |        6 | Al      | Tue Oct 20 16:14:45 1998 MET DST
(1 row)
```

That's what we expected. What happened in the background is the following. The parser created the query tree:

```
UPDATE shoelace_data SET sl_avail = 6
  FROM shoelace_data shoelace_data
 WHERE shoelace_data.sl_name = 'sl7';
```

There is a rule log_shoelace that is ON UPDATE with the rule qualification expression:

```
NEW.sl_avail <> OLD.sl_avail
```

and the action:

```
INSERT INTO shoelace_log VALUES (
       new.sl_name, new.sl_avail,
       current_user, current_timestamp )
  FROM shoelace_data new, shoelace_data old;
```

(This looks a little strange since you cannot normally write INSERT ... VALUES ... FROM. The FROM clause here is just to indicate that there are range-table entries in the query tree for new and old. These are needed so that they can be referenced by variables in the INSERT command's query tree.)

The rule is a qualified ALSO rule, so the rule system has to return two query trees: the modified rule action and the original query tree. In step 1, the range table of the original query is incorporated into the rule's action query tree. This results in:

```
INSERT INTO shoelace_log VALUES (
       new.sl_name, new.sl_avail,
       current_user, current_timestamp )
  FROM shoelace_data new, shoelace_data old,
       shoelace_data shoelace_data;
```

In step 2, the rule qualification is added to it, so the result set is restricted to rows where sl_avail changes:

```
INSERT INTO shoelace_log VALUES (
       new.sl_name, new.sl_avail,
       current_user, current_timestamp )
  FROM shoelace_data new, shoelace_data old,
       shoelace_data shoelace_data
 WHERE new.sl_avail <> old.sl_avail;
```

(This looks even stranger, since INSERT ... VALUES doesn't have a WHERE clause either, but the planner and executor will have no difficulty with it. They need to support this same functionality anyway for INSERT ... SELECT.)

In step 3, the original query tree's qualification is added, restricting the result set further to only the rows that would have been touched by the original query:

```
INSERT INTO shoelace_log VALUES (
       new.sl_name, new.sl_avail,
       current_user, current_timestamp )
  FROM shoelace_data new, shoelace_data old,
       shoelace_data shoelace_data
 WHERE new.sl_avail <> old.sl_avail
   AND shoelace_data.sl_name = 'sl7';
```

Step 4 replaces references to NEW by the target list entries from the original query tree or by the matching variable references from the result relation:

```
INSERT INTO shoelace_log VALUES (
       shoelace_data.sl_name, 6,
       current_user, current_timestamp )
  FROM shoelace_data new, shoelace_data old,
       shoelace_data shoelace_data
 WHERE 6 <> old.sl_avail
   AND shoelace_data.sl_name = 'sl7';
```

Step 5 changes OLD references into result relation references:

```
INSERT INTO shoelace_log VALUES (
       shoelace_data.sl_name, 6,
       current_user, current_timestamp )
  FROM shoelace_data new, shoelace_data old,
       shoelace_data shoelace_data
 WHERE 6 <> shoelace_data.sl_avail
   AND shoelace_data.sl_name = 'sl7';
```

That's it. Since the rule is ALSO, we also output the original query tree. In short, the output from the rule system is a list of two query trees that correspond to these statements:

```
INSERT INTO shoelace_log VALUES (
       shoelace_data.sl_name, 6,
       current_user, current_timestamp )
  FROM shoelace_data
 WHERE 6 <> shoelace_data.sl_avail
   AND shoelace_data.sl_name = 'sl7';

UPDATE shoelace_data SET sl_avail = 6
 WHERE sl_name = 'sl7';
```

These are executed in this order, and that is exactly what the rule was meant to do.

The substitutions and the added qualifications ensure that, if the original query would be, say:

```
UPDATE shoelace_data SET sl_color = 'green'
 WHERE sl_name = 'sl7';
```

no log entry would get written. In that case, the original query tree does not contain a target list entry for `sl_avail`, so `NEW.sl_avail` will get replaced by `shoelace_data.sl_avail`. Thus, the extra command generated by the rule is:

```
INSERT INTO shoelace_log VALUES (
       shoelace_data.sl_name, shoelace_data.sl_avail,
       current_user, current_timestamp )
  FROM shoelace_data
 WHERE shoelace_data.sl_avail <> shoelace_data.sl_avail
   AND shoelace_data.sl_name = 'sl7';
```

and that qualification will never be true.

It will also work if the original query modifies multiple rows. So if someone issued the command:

```
UPDATE shoelace_data SET sl_avail = 0
 WHERE sl_color = 'black';
```

four rows in fact get updated (`sl1`, `sl2`, `sl3`, and `sl4`). But `sl3` already has `sl_avail = 0`. In this case, the original query trees qualification is different and that results in the extra query tree:

```
INSERT INTO shoelace_log
SELECT shoelace_data.sl_name, 0,
       current_user, current_timestamp
  FROM shoelace_data
 WHERE 0 <> shoelace_data.sl_avail
   AND shoelace_data.sl_color = 'black';
```

being generated by the rule. This query tree will surely insert three new log entries. And that's absolutely correct.

Here we can see why it is important that the original query tree is executed last. If the UPDATE had been executed first, all the rows would have already been set to zero, so the logging INSERT would not find any row where `0 <> shoelace_data.sl_avail`.

39.4.2. Cooperation with Views

A simple way to protect view relations from the mentioned possibility that someone can try to run INSERT, UPDATE, or DELETE on them is to let those query trees get thrown away. So we could create the rules:

```
CREATE RULE shoe_ins_protect AS ON INSERT TO shoe
    DO INSTEAD NOTHING;
CREATE RULE shoe_upd_protect AS ON UPDATE TO shoe
    DO INSTEAD NOTHING;
CREATE RULE shoe_del_protect AS ON DELETE TO shoe
    DO INSTEAD NOTHING;
```

If someone now tries to do any of these operations on the view relation `shoe`, the rule system will apply these rules. Since the rules have no actions and are INSTEAD, the resulting list of query trees will be empty and the whole query will become nothing because there is nothing left to be optimized or executed after the rule system is done with it.

A more sophisticated way to use the rule system is to create rules that rewrite the query tree into one that does the right operation on the real tables. To do that on the shoelace view, we create the following rules:

```
CREATE RULE shoelace_ins AS ON INSERT TO shoelace
    DO INSTEAD
    INSERT INTO shoelace_data VALUES (
            NEW.sl_name,
            NEW.sl_avail,
            NEW.sl_color,
            NEW.sl_len,
            NEW.sl_unit
    );

CREATE RULE shoelace_upd AS ON UPDATE TO shoelace
    DO INSTEAD
    UPDATE shoelace_data
        SET sl_name = NEW.sl_name,
            sl_avail = NEW.sl_avail,
            sl_color = NEW.sl_color,
            sl_len = NEW.sl_len,
            sl_unit = NEW.sl_unit
     WHERE sl_name = OLD.sl_name;

CREATE RULE shoelace_del AS ON DELETE TO shoelace
    DO INSTEAD
    DELETE FROM shoelace_data
     WHERE sl_name = OLD.sl_name;
```

If you want to support RETURNING queries on the view, you need to make the rules include RETURNING clauses that compute the view rows. This is usually pretty trivial for views on a single table, but it's a bit tedious for join views such as shoelace. An example for the insert case is:

```
CREATE RULE shoelace_ins AS ON INSERT TO shoelace
    DO INSTEAD
    INSERT INTO shoelace_data VALUES (
            NEW.sl_name,
            NEW.sl_avail,
            NEW.sl_color,
            NEW.sl_len,
            NEW.sl_unit
    )
    RETURNING
            shoelace_data.*,
            (SELECT shoelace_data.sl_len * u.un_fact
             FROM unit u WHERE shoelace_data.sl_unit = u.un_name);
```

Note that this one rule supports both INSERT and INSERT RETURNING queries on the view — the RETURNING clause is simply ignored for INSERT.

Now assume that once in a while, a pack of shoelaces arrives at the shop and a big parts list along with it. But you don't want to manually update the shoelace view every time. Instead we set up two little tables:

one where you can insert the items from the part list, and one with a special trick. The creation commands for these are:

```
CREATE TABLE shoelace_arrive (
    arr_name    text,
    arr_quant   integer
);

CREATE TABLE shoelace_ok (
    ok_name     text,
    ok_quant    integer
);

CREATE RULE shoelace_ok_ins AS ON INSERT TO shoelace_ok
    DO INSTEAD
    UPDATE shoelace
       SET sl_avail = sl_avail + NEW.ok_quant
     WHERE sl_name = NEW.ok_name;
```

Now you can fill the table `shoelace_arrive` with the data from the parts list:

```
SELECT * FROM shoelace_arrive;
```

```
 arr_name | arr_quant
----------+-----------
 sl3      |        10
 sl6      |        20
 sl8      |        20
(3 rows)
```

Take a quick look at the current data:

```
SELECT * FROM shoelace;
```

```
 sl_name | sl_avail | sl_color | sl_len | sl_unit | sl_len_cm
---------+----------+----------+--------+---------+-----------
 sl1     |        5 | black    |     80 | cm      |        80
 sl2     |        6 | black    |    100 | cm      |       100
 sl7     |        6 | brown    |     60 | cm      |        60
 sl3     |        0 | black    |     35 | inch    |      88.9
 sl4     |        8 | black    |     40 | inch    |     101.6
 sl8     |        1 | brown    |     40 | inch    |     101.6
 sl5     |        4 | brown    |      1 | m       |       100
 sl6     |        0 | brown    |    0.9 | m       |        90
(8 rows)
```

Now move the arrived shoelaces in:

```
INSERT INTO shoelace_ok SELECT * FROM shoelace_arrive;
```

and check the results:

```
SELECT * FROM shoelace ORDER BY sl_name;
```

```
sl_name  | sl_avail | sl_color | sl_len | sl_unit | sl_len_cm
---------+----------+----------+--------+---------+-----------
 sl1     |        5 | black    |     80 | cm      |        80
 sl2     |        6 | black    |    100 | cm      |       100
 sl7     |        6 | brown    |     60 | cm      |        60
 sl4     |        8 | black    |     40 | inch    |     101.6
 sl3     |       10 | black    |     35 | inch    |      88.9
 sl8     |       21 | brown    |     40 | inch    |     101.6
 sl5     |        4 | brown    |      1 | m       |       100
 sl6     |       20 | brown    |    0.9 | m       |        90
(8 rows)
```

```
SELECT * FROM shoelace_log;
```

```
sl_name  | sl_avail | log_who| log_when
---------+----------+--------+--------------------------------
 sl7     |        6 | Al     | Tue Oct 20 19:14:45 1998 MET DST
 sl3     |       10 | Al     | Tue Oct 20 19:25:16 1998 MET DST
 sl6     |       20 | Al     | Tue Oct 20 19:25:16 1998 MET DST
 sl8     |       21 | Al     | Tue Oct 20 19:25:16 1998 MET DST
(4 rows)
```

It's a long way from the one INSERT ... SELECT to these results. And the description of the query-tree transformation will be the last in this chapter. First, there is the parser's output:

```
INSERT INTO shoelace_ok
SELECT shoelace_arrive.arr_name, shoelace_arrive.arr_quant
  FROM shoelace_arrive shoelace_arrive, shoelace_ok shoelace_ok;
```

Now the first rule shoelace_ok_ins is applied and turns this into:

```
UPDATE shoelace
   SET sl_avail = shoelace.sl_avail + shoelace_arrive.arr_quant
  FROM shoelace_arrive shoelace_arrive, shoelace_ok shoelace_ok,
       shoelace_ok old, shoelace_ok new,
       shoelace shoelace
 WHERE shoelace.sl_name = shoelace_arrive.arr_name;
```

and throws away the original INSERT on shoelace_ok. This rewritten query is passed to the rule system again, and the second applied rule shoelace_upd produces:

```
UPDATE shoelace_data
   SET sl_name = shoelace.sl_name,
       sl_avail = shoelace.sl_avail + shoelace_arrive.arr_quant,
       sl_color = shoelace.sl_color,
       sl_len = shoelace.sl_len,
       sl_unit = shoelace.sl_unit
  FROM shoelace_arrive shoelace_arrive, shoelace_ok shoelace_ok,
       shoelace_ok old, shoelace_ok new,
       shoelace shoelace, shoelace old,
       shoelace new, shoelace_data shoelace_data
 WHERE shoelace.sl_name = shoelace_arrive.arr_name
```

```
    AND shoelace_data.sl_name = shoelace.sl_name;
```

Again it's an INSTEAD rule and the previous query tree is trashed. Note that this query still uses the view shoelace. But the rule system isn't finished with this step, so it continues and applies the _RETURN rule on it, and we get:

```
UPDATE shoelace_data
   SET sl_name = s.sl_name,
       sl_avail = s.sl_avail + shoelace_arrive.arr_quant,
       sl_color = s.sl_color,
       sl_len = s.sl_len,
       sl_unit = s.sl_unit
  FROM shoelace_arrive shoelace_arrive, shoelace_ok shoelace_ok,
       shoelace_ok old, shoelace_ok new,
       shoelace shoelace, shoelace old,
       shoelace new, shoelace_data shoelace_data,
       shoelace old, shoelace new,
       shoelace_data s, unit u
 WHERE s.sl_name = shoelace_arrive.arr_name
   AND shoelace_data.sl_name = s.sl_name;
```

Finally, the rule log_shoelace gets applied, producing the extra query tree:

```
INSERT INTO shoelace_log
SELECT s.sl_name,
       s.sl_avail + shoelace_arrive.arr_quant,
       current_user,
       current_timestamp
  FROM shoelace_arrive shoelace_arrive, shoelace_ok shoelace_ok,
       shoelace_ok old, shoelace_ok new,
       shoelace shoelace, shoelace old,
       shoelace new, shoelace_data shoelace_data,
       shoelace old, shoelace new,
       shoelace_data s, unit u,
       shoelace_data old, shoelace_data new
       shoelace_log shoelace_log
 WHERE s.sl_name = shoelace_arrive.arr_name
   AND shoelace_data.sl_name = s.sl_name
   AND (s.sl_avail + shoelace_arrive.arr_quant) <> s.sl_avail;
```

After that the rule system runs out of rules and returns the generated query trees.

So we end up with two final query trees that are equivalent to the SQL statements:

```
INSERT INTO shoelace_log
SELECT s.sl_name,
       s.sl_avail + shoelace_arrive.arr_quant,
       current_user,
       current_timestamp
  FROM shoelace_arrive shoelace_arrive, shoelace_data shoelace_data,
       shoelace_data s
 WHERE s.sl_name = shoelace_arrive.arr_name
   AND shoelace_data.sl_name = s.sl_name
   AND s.sl_avail + shoelace_arrive.arr_quant <> s.sl_avail;
```

```
UPDATE shoelace_data
   SET sl_avail = shoelace_data.sl_avail + shoelace_arrive.arr_quant
  FROM shoelace_arrive shoelace_arrive,
       shoelace_data shoelace_data,
       shoelace_data s
 WHERE s.sl_name = shoelace_arrive.sl_name
   AND shoelace_data.sl_name = s.sl_name;
```

The result is that data coming from one relation inserted into another, changed into updates on a third, changed into updating a fourth plus logging that final update in a fifth gets reduced into two queries.

There is a little detail that's a bit ugly. Looking at the two queries, it turns out that the shoelace_data relation appears twice in the range table where it could definitely be reduced to one. The planner does not handle it and so the execution plan for the rule systems output of the INSERT will be

```
Nested Loop
  -> Merge Join
       -> Seq Scan
            -> Sort
                 -> Seq Scan on s
       -> Seq Scan
            -> Sort
                 -> Seq Scan on shoelace_arrive
  -> Seq Scan on shoelace_data
```

while omitting the extra range table entry would result in a

```
Merge Join
  -> Seq Scan
       -> Sort
            -> Seq Scan on s
  -> Seq Scan
       -> Sort
            -> Seq Scan on shoelace_arrive
```

which produces exactly the same entries in the log table. Thus, the rule system caused one extra scan on the table shoelace_data that is absolutely not necessary. And the same redundant scan is done once more in the UPDATE. But it was a really hard job to make that all possible at all.

Now we make a final demonstration of the PostgreSQL rule system and its power. Say you add some shoelaces with extraordinary colors to your database:

```
INSERT INTO shoelace VALUES ('sl9', 0, 'pink', 35.0, 'inch', 0.0);
INSERT INTO shoelace VALUES ('sl10', 1000, 'magenta', 40.0, 'inch', 0.0);
```

We would like to make a view to check which shoelace entries do not fit any shoe in color. The view for this is:

```
CREATE VIEW shoelace_mismatch AS
    SELECT * FROM shoelace WHERE NOT EXISTS
        (SELECT shoename FROM shoe WHERE slcolor = sl_color);
```

Its output is:

```
SELECT * FROM shoelace_mismatch;
```

```
 sl_name | sl_avail | sl_color | sl_len | sl_unit | sl_len_cm
---------+----------+----------+--------+---------+-----------
 sl9     |        0 | pink     |     35 | inch    |      88.9
 sl10    |     1000 | magenta  |     40 | inch    |     101.6
```

Now we want to set it up so that mismatching shoelaces that are not in stock are deleted from the database. To make it a little harder for PostgreSQL, we don't delete it directly. Instead we create one more view:

```
CREATE VIEW shoelace_can_delete AS
    SELECT * FROM shoelace_mismatch WHERE sl_avail = 0;
```

and do it this way:

```
DELETE FROM shoelace WHERE EXISTS
    (SELECT * FROM shoelace_can_delete
            WHERE sl_name = shoelace.sl_name);
```

Voilà:

```
SELECT * FROM shoelace;
```

```
 sl_name | sl_avail | sl_color | sl_len | sl_unit | sl_len_cm
---------+----------+----------+--------+---------+-----------
 sl1     |        5 | black    |     80 | cm      |        80
 sl2     |        6 | black    |    100 | cm      |       100
 sl7     |        6 | brown    |     60 | cm      |        60
 sl4     |        8 | black    |     40 | inch    |     101.6
 sl3     |       10 | black    |     35 | inch    |      88.9
 sl8     |       21 | brown    |     40 | inch    |     101.6
 sl10    |     1000 | magenta  |     40 | inch    |     101.6
 sl5     |        4 | brown    |      1 | m       |       100
 sl6     |       20 | brown    |    0.9 | m       |        90
(9 rows)
```

A DELETE on a view, with a subquery qualification that in total uses 4 nesting/joined views, where one of them itself has a subquery qualification containing a view and where calculated view columns are used, gets rewritten into one single query tree that deletes the requested data from a real table.

There are probably only a few situations out in the real world where such a construct is necessary. But it makes you feel comfortable that it works.

39.5. Rules and Privileges

Due to rewriting of queries by the PostgreSQL rule system, other tables/views than those used in the original query get accessed. When update rules are used, this can include write access to tables.

Rewrite rules don't have a separate owner. The owner of a relation (table or view) is automatically the owner of the rewrite rules that are defined for it. The PostgreSQL rule system changes the behavior of the default access control system. Relations that are used due to rules get checked against the privileges of the rule owner, not the user invoking the rule. This means that users only need the required privileges for the tables/views that are explicitly named in their queries.

For example: A user has a list of phone numbers where some of them are private, the others are of interest for the assistant of the office. The user can construct the following:

```
CREATE TABLE phone_data (person text, phone text, private boolean);
CREATE VIEW phone_number AS
    SELECT person, CASE WHEN NOT private THEN phone END AS phone
    FROM phone_data;
GRANT SELECT ON phone_number TO assistant;
```

Nobody except that user (and the database superusers) can access the phone_data table. But because of the GRANT, the assistant can run a SELECT on the phone_number view. The rule system will rewrite the SELECT from phone_number into a SELECT from phone_data. Since the user is the owner of phone_number and therefore the owner of the rule, the read access to phone_data is now checked against the user's privileges and the query is permitted. The check for accessing phone_number is also performed, but this is done against the invoking user, so nobody but the user and the assistant can use it.

The privileges are checked rule by rule. So the assistant is for now the only one who can see the public phone numbers. But the assistant can set up another view and grant access to that to the public. Then, anyone can see the phone_number data through the assistant's view. What the assistant cannot do is to create a view that directly accesses phone_data. (Actually the assistant can, but it will not work since every access will be denied during the permission checks.) And as soon as the user notices that the assistant opened their phone_number view, the user can revoke the assistant's access. Immediately, any access to the assistant's view would fail.

One might think that this rule-by-rule checking is a security hole, but in fact it isn't. But if it did not work this way, the assistant could set up a table with the same columns as phone_number and copy the data to there once per day. Then it's the assistant's own data and the assistant can grant access to everyone they want. A GRANT command means, "I trust you". If someone you trust does the thing above, it's time to think it over and then use REVOKE.

Note that while views can be used to hide the contents of certain columns using the technique shown above, they cannot be used to reliably conceal the data in unseen rows unless the security_barrier flag has been set. For example, the following view is insecure:

```
CREATE VIEW phone_number AS
    SELECT person, phone FROM phone_data WHERE phone NOT LIKE '412%';
```

This view might seem secure, since the rule system will rewrite any SELECT from phone_number into a SELECT from phone_data and add the qualification that only entries where phone does not begin with 412 are wanted. But if the user can create their own functions, it is not difficult to convince the planner to execute the user-defined function prior to the NOT LIKE expression. For example:

```
CREATE FUNCTION tricky(text, text) RETURNS bool AS $$
BEGIN
    RAISE NOTICE '% => %', $1, $2;
    RETURN true;
END
```

```
$$ LANGUAGE plpgsql COST 0.000000000000000000000001;

SELECT * FROM phone_number WHERE tricky(person, phone);
```

Every person and phone number in the `phone_data` table will be printed as a NOTICE, because the planner will choose to execute the inexpensive `tricky` function before the more expensive NOT LIKE. Even if the user is prevented from defining new functions, built-in functions can be used in similar attacks. (For example, most casting functions include their input values in the error messages they produce.)

Similar considerations apply to update rules. In the examples of the previous section, the owner of the tables in the example database could grant the privileges SELECT, INSERT, UPDATE, and DELETE on the `shoelace` view to someone else, but only SELECT on `shoelace_log`. The rule action to write log entries will still be executed successfully, and that other user could see the log entries. But they could not create fake entries, nor could they manipulate or remove existing ones. In this case, there is no possibility of subverting the rules by convincing the planner to alter the order of operations, because the only rule which references `shoelace_log` is an unqualified INSERT. This might not be true in more complex scenarios.

When it is necessary for a view to provide row level security, the `security_barrier` attribute should be applied to the view. This prevents maliciously-chosen functions and operators from being passed values from rows until after the view has done its work. For example, if the view shown above had been created like this, it would be secure:

```
CREATE VIEW phone_number WITH (security_barrier) AS
    SELECT person, phone FROM phone_data WHERE phone NOT LIKE '412%';
```

Views created with the `security_barrier` may perform far worse than views created without this option. In general, there is no way to avoid this: the fastest possible plan must be rejected if it may compromise security. For this reason, this option is not enabled by default.

The query planner has more flexibility when dealing with functions that have no side effects. Such functions are referred to as LEAKPROOF, and include many simple, commonly used operators, such as many equality operators. The query planner can safely allow such functions to be evaluated at any point in the query execution process, since invoking them on rows invisible to the user will not leak any information about the unseen rows. Further, functions which do not take arguments or which are not passed any arguments from the security barrier view do not have to be marked as LEAKPROOF to be pushed down, as they never receive data from the view. In contrast, a function that might throw an error depending on the values received as arguments (such as one that throws an error in the event of overflow or division by zero) is not leak-proof, and could provide significant information about the unseen rows if applied before the security view's row filters.

It is important to understand that even a view created with the `security_barrier` option is intended to be secure only in the limited sense that the contents of the invisible tuples will not be passed to possibly-insecure functions. The user may well have other means of making inferences about the unseen data; for example, they can see the query plan using EXPLAIN, or measure the run time of queries against the view. A malicious attacker might be able to infer something about the amount of unseen data, or even gain some information about the data distribution or most common values (since these things may affect the run time of the plan; or even, since they are also reflected in the optimizer statistics, the choice of plan). If these types of "covert channel" attacks are of concern, it is probably unwise to grant any access to the data at all.

39.6. Rules and Command Status

The PostgreSQL server returns a command status string, such as INSERT 149592 1, for each command it receives. This is simple enough when there are no rules involved, but what happens when the query is rewritten by rules?

Rules affect the command status as follows:

- If there is no unconditional INSTEAD rule for the query, then the originally given query will be executed, and its command status will be returned as usual. (But note that if there were any conditional INSTEAD rules, the negation of their qualifications will have been added to the original query. This might reduce the number of rows it processes, and if so the reported status will be affected.)

- If there is any unconditional INSTEAD rule for the query, then the original query will not be executed at all. In this case, the server will return the command status for the last query that was inserted by an INSTEAD rule (conditional or unconditional) and is of the same command type (INSERT, UPDATE, or DELETE) as the original query. If no query meeting those requirements is added by any rule, then the returned command status shows the original query type and zeroes for the row-count and OID fields.

The programmer can ensure that any desired INSTEAD rule is the one that sets the command status in the second case, by giving it the alphabetically last rule name among the active rules, so that it gets applied last.

39.7. Rules Versus Triggers

Many things that can be done using triggers can also be implemented using the PostgreSQL rule system. One of the things that cannot be implemented by rules are some kinds of constraints, especially foreign keys. It is possible to place a qualified rule that rewrites a command to NOTHING if the value of a column does not appear in another table. But then the data is silently thrown away and that's not a good idea. If checks for valid values are required, and in the case of an invalid value an error message should be generated, it must be done by a trigger.

In this chapter, we focused on using rules to update views. All of the update rule examples in this chapter can also be implemented using INSTEAD OF triggers on the views. Writing such triggers is often easier than writing rules, particularly if complex logic is required to perform the update.

For the things that can be implemented by both, which is best depends on the usage of the database. A trigger is fired once for each affected row. A rule modifies the query or generates an additional query. So if many rows are affected in one statement, a rule issuing one extra command is likely to be faster than a trigger that is called for every single row and must re-determine what to do many times. However, the trigger approach is conceptually far simpler than the rule approach, and is easier for novices to get right.

Here we show an example of how the choice of rules versus triggers plays out in one situation. There are two tables:

```
CREATE TABLE computer (
    hostname        text,       -- indexed
    manufacturer    text        -- indexed
);
```

```
CREATE TABLE software (
    software        text,    -- indexed
    hostname        text     -- indexed
);
```

Both tables have many thousands of rows and the indexes on `hostname` are unique. The rule or trigger should implement a constraint that deletes rows from `software` that reference a deleted computer. The trigger would use this command:

```
DELETE FROM software WHERE hostname = $1;
```

Since the trigger is called for each individual row deleted from `computer`, it can prepare and save the plan for this command and pass the `hostname` value in the parameter. The rule would be written as:

```
CREATE RULE computer_del AS ON DELETE TO computer
    DO DELETE FROM software WHERE hostname = OLD.hostname;
```

Now we look at different types of deletes. In the case of a:

```
DELETE FROM computer WHERE hostname = 'mypc.local.net';
```

the table `computer` is scanned by index (fast), and the command issued by the trigger would also use an index scan (also fast). The extra command from the rule would be:

```
DELETE FROM software WHERE computer.hostname = 'mypc.local.net'
                    AND software.hostname = computer.hostname;
```

Since there are appropriate indexes set up, the planner will create a plan of

```
Nestloop
  -> Index Scan using comp_hostidx on computer
  -> Index Scan using soft_hostidx on software
```

So there would be not that much difference in speed between the trigger and the rule implementation.

With the next delete we want to get rid of all the 2000 computers where the `hostname` starts with `old`. There are two possible commands to do that. One is:

```
DELETE FROM computer WHERE hostname >= 'old'
                    AND hostname <  'ole'
```

The command added by the rule will be:

```
DELETE FROM software WHERE computer.hostname >= 'old' AND computer.hostname < 'ole'
                    AND software.hostname = computer.hostname;
```

with the plan

```
Hash Join
  -> Seq Scan on software
  -> Hash
    -> Index Scan using comp_hostidx on computer
```

The other possible command is:

```
DELETE FROM computer WHERE hostname ~ '^old';
```

which results in the following executing plan for the command added by the rule:

```
Nestloop
   ->  Index Scan using comp_hostidx on computer
   ->  Index Scan using soft_hostidx on software
```

This shows, that the planner does not realize that the qualification for `hostname` in `computer` could also be used for an index scan on `software` when there are multiple qualification expressions combined with `AND`, which is what it does in the regular-expression version of the command. The trigger will get invoked once for each of the 2000 old computers that have to be deleted, and that will result in one index scan over `computer` and 2000 index scans over `software`. The rule implementation will do it with two commands that use indexes. And it depends on the overall size of the table `software` whether the rule will still be faster in the sequential scan situation. 2000 command executions from the trigger over the SPI manager take some time, even if all the index blocks will soon be in the cache.

The last command we look at is:

```
DELETE FROM computer WHERE manufacturer = 'bim';
```

Again this could result in many rows to be deleted from `computer`. So the trigger will again run many commands through the executor. The command generated by the rule will be:

```
DELETE FROM software WHERE computer.manufacturer = 'bim'
                    AND software.hostname = computer.hostname;
```

The plan for that command will again be the nested loop over two index scans, only using a different index on `computer`:

```
Nestloop
   ->  Index Scan using comp_manufidx on computer
   ->  Index Scan using soft_hostidx on software
```

In any of these cases, the extra commands from the rule system will be more or less independent from the number of affected rows in a command.

The summary is, rules will only be significantly slower than triggers if their actions result in large and badly qualified joins, a situation where the planner fails.

Chapter 40. Procedural Languages

PostgreSQL allows user-defined functions to be written in other languages besides SQL and C. These other languages are generically called *procedural languages* (PLs). For a function written in a procedural language, the database server has no built-in knowledge about how to interpret the function's source text. Instead, the task is passed to a special handler that knows the details of the language. The handler could either do all the work of parsing, syntax analysis, execution, etc. itself, or it could serve as "glue" between PostgreSQL and an existing implementation of a programming language. The handler itself is a C language function compiled into a shared object and loaded on demand, just like any other C function.

There are currently four procedural languages available in the standard PostgreSQL distribution: PL/pgSQL (Chapter 41), PL/Tcl (Chapter 42), PL/Perl (Chapter 43), and PL/Python (Chapter 44). There are additional procedural languages available that are not included in the core distribution. Appendix H has information about finding them. In addition other languages can be defined by users; the basics of developing a new procedural language are covered in Chapter 54.

40.1. Installing Procedural Languages

A procedural language must be "installed" into each database where it is to be used. But procedural languages installed in the database `template1` are automatically available in all subsequently created databases, since their entries in `template1` will be copied by `CREATE DATABASE`. So the database administrator can decide which languages are available in which databases and can make some languages available by default if desired.

For the languages supplied with the standard distribution, it is only necessary to execute `CREATE EXTENSION` *language_name* to install the language into the current database. Alternatively, the program createlang can be used to do this from the shell command line. For example, to install the language PL/Perl into the database `template1`, use:

```
createlang plperl template1
```

The manual procedure described below is only recommended for installing languages that have not been packaged as extensions.

Manual Procedural Language Installation

A procedural language is installed in a database in five steps, which must be carried out by a database superuser. In most cases the required SQL commands should be packaged as the installation script of an "extension", so that `CREATE EXTENSION` can be used to execute them.

1. The shared object for the language handler must be compiled and installed into an appropriate library directory. This works in the same way as building and installing modules with regular user-defined C functions does; see Section 36.9.6. Often, the language handler will depend on an external library that provides the actual programming language engine; if so, that must be installed as well.

2. The handler must be declared with the command

```
CREATE FUNCTION handler_function_name()
    RETURNS language_handler
    AS 'path-to-shared-object'
```

```
LANGUAGE C;
```

The special return type of `language_handler` tells the database system that this function does not return one of the defined SQL data types and is not directly usable in SQL statements.

3. Optionally, the language handler can provide an "inline" handler function that executes anonymous code blocks (DO commands) written in this language. If an inline handler function is provided by the language, declare it with a command like

```
CREATE FUNCTION inline_function_name(internal)
    RETURNS void
    AS 'path-to-shared-object'
    LANGUAGE C;
```

4. Optionally, the language handler can provide a "validator" function that checks a function definition for correctness without actually executing it. The validator function is called by `CREATE FUNCTION` if it exists. If a validator function is provided by the language, declare it with a command like

```
CREATE FUNCTION validator_function_name(oid)
    RETURNS void
    AS 'path-to-shared-object'
    LANGUAGE C STRICT;
```

5. Finally, the PL must be declared with the command

```
CREATE [TRUSTED] [PROCEDURAL] LANGUAGE language-name
    HANDLER handler_function_name
    [INLINE inline_function_name]
    [VALIDATOR validator_function_name] ;
```

The optional key word `TRUSTED` specifies that the language does not grant access to data that the user would not otherwise have. Trusted languages are designed for ordinary database users (those without superuser privilege) and allows them to safely create functions and trigger procedures. Since PL functions are executed inside the database server, the `TRUSTED` flag should only be given for languages that do not allow access to database server internals or the file system. The languages PL/pgSQL, PL/Tcl, and PL/Perl are considered trusted; the languages PL/TclU, PL/PerlU, and PL/PythonU are designed to provide unlimited functionality and should *not* be marked trusted.

Example 40-1 shows how the manual installation procedure would work with the language PL/Perl.

Example 40-1. Manual Installation of PL/Perl

The following command tells the database server where to find the shared object for the PL/Perl language's call handler function:

```
CREATE FUNCTION plperl_call_handler() RETURNS language_handler AS
    '$libdir/plperl' LANGUAGE C;
```

PL/Perl has an inline handler function and a validator function, so we declare those too:

```
CREATE FUNCTION plperl_inline_handler(internal) RETURNS void AS
    '$libdir/plperl' LANGUAGE C;

CREATE FUNCTION plperl_validator(oid) RETURNS void AS
    '$libdir/plperl' LANGUAGE C STRICT;
```

The command:

```
CREATE TRUSTED PROCEDURAL LANGUAGE plperl
```

```
HANDLER plperl_call_handler
INLINE plperl_inline_handler
VALIDATOR plperl_validator;
```
then defines that the previously declared functions should be invoked for functions and trigger procedures where the language attribute is `plperl`.

In a default PostgreSQL installation, the handler for the PL/pgSQL language is built and installed into the "library" directory; furthermore, the PL/pgSQL language itself is installed in all databases. If Tcl support is configured in, the handlers for PL/Tcl and PL/TclU are built and installed in the library directory, but the language itself is not installed in any database by default. Likewise, the PL/Perl and PL/PerlU handlers are built and installed if Perl support is configured, and the PL/PythonU handler is installed if Python support is configured, but these languages are not installed by default.

Chapter 41. PL/pgSQL - SQL Procedural Language

41.1. Overview

PL/pgSQL is a loadable procedural language for the PostgreSQL database system. The design goals of PL/pgSQL were to create a loadable procedural language that

- can be used to create functions and trigger procedures,

- adds control structures to the SQL language,

- can perform complex computations,

- inherits all user-defined types, functions, and operators,

- can be defined to be trusted by the server,

- is easy to use.

Functions created with PL/pgSQL can be used anywhere that built-in functions could be used. For example, it is possible to create complex conditional computation functions and later use them to define operators or use them in index expressions.

In PostgreSQL 9.0 and later, PL/pgSQL is installed by default. However it is still a loadable module, so especially security-conscious administrators could choose to remove it.

41.1.1. Advantages of Using PL/pgSQL

SQL is the language PostgreSQL and most other relational databases use as query language. It's portable and easy to learn. But every SQL statement must be executed individually by the database server.

That means that your client application must send each query to the database server, wait for it to be processed, receive and process the results, do some computation, then send further queries to the server. All this incurs interprocess communication and will also incur network overhead if your client is on a different machine than the database server.

With PL/pgSQL you can group a block of computation and a series of queries *inside* the database server, thus having the power of a procedural language and the ease of use of SQL, but with considerable savings of client/server communication overhead.

- Extra round trips between client and server are eliminated

- Intermediate results that the client does not need do not have to be marshaled or transferred between server and client

- Multiple rounds of query parsing can be avoided

This can result in a considerable performance increase as compared to an application that does not use stored functions.

Also, with PL/pgSQL you can use all the data types, operators and functions of SQL.

41.1.2. Supported Argument and Result Data Types

Functions written in PL/pgSQL can accept as arguments any scalar or array data type supported by the server, and they can return a result of any of these types. They can also accept or return any composite type (row type) specified by name. It is also possible to declare a PL/pgSQL function as returning `record`, which means that the result is a row type whose columns are determined by specification in the calling query, as discussed in Section 7.2.1.4.

PL/pgSQL functions can be declared to accept a variable number of arguments by using the `VARIADIC` marker. This works exactly the same way as for SQL functions, as discussed in Section 36.4.5.

PL/pgSQL functions can also be declared to accept and return the polymorphic types `anyelement`, `anyarray`, `anynonarray`, `anyenum`, and `anyrange`. The actual data types handled by a polymorphic function can vary from call to call, as discussed in Section 36.2.5. An example is shown in Section 41.3.1.

PL/pgSQL functions can also be declared to return a "set" (or table) of any data type that can be returned as a single instance. Such a function generates its output by executing `RETURN NEXT` for each desired element of the result set, or by using `RETURN QUERY` to output the result of evaluating a query.

Finally, a PL/pgSQL function can be declared to return `void` if it has no useful return value.

PL/pgSQL functions can also be declared with output parameters in place of an explicit specification of the return type. This does not add any fundamental capability to the language, but it is often convenient, especially for returning multiple values. The `RETURNS TABLE` notation can also be used in place of `RETURNS SETOF`.

Specific examples appear in Section 41.3.1 and Section 41.6.1.

41.2. Structure of PL/pgSQL

PL/pgSQL is a block-structured language. The complete text of a function definition must be a *block*. A block is defined as:

```
[ <<label>> ]
[ DECLARE
    declarations ]
BEGIN
    statements
END [ label ];
```

Each declaration and each statement within a block is terminated by a semicolon. A block that appears within another block must have a semicolon after `END`, as shown above; however the final `END` that concludes a function body does not require a semicolon.

Tip: A common mistake is to write a semicolon immediately after BEGIN. This is incorrect and will result in a syntax error.

A *label* is only needed if you want to identify the block for use in an EXIT statement, or to qualify the names of the variables declared in the block. If a label is given after END, it must match the label at the block's beginning.

All key words are case-insensitive. Identifiers are implicitly converted to lower case unless double-quoted, just as they are in ordinary SQL commands.

Comments work the same way in PL/pgSQL code as in ordinary SQL. A double dash (--) starts a comment that extends to the end of the line. A /* starts a block comment that extends to the matching occurrence of */. Block comments nest.

Any statement in the statement section of a block can be a *subblock*. Subblocks can be used for logical grouping or to localize variables to a small group of statements. Variables declared in a subblock mask any similarly-named variables of outer blocks for the duration of the subblock; but you can access the outer variables anyway if you qualify their names with their block's label. For example:

```
CREATE FUNCTION somefunc() RETURNS integer AS $$
<< outerblock >>
DECLARE
    quantity integer := 30;
BEGIN
    RAISE NOTICE 'Quantity here is %', quantity;   -- Prints 30
    quantity := 50;
    --
    -- Create a subblock
    --
    DECLARE
        quantity integer := 80;
    BEGIN
        RAISE NOTICE 'Quantity here is %', quantity;   -- Prints 80
        RAISE NOTICE 'Outer quantity here is %', outerblock.quantity;   -- Prints 50
    END;

    RAISE NOTICE 'Quantity here is %', quantity;   -- Prints 50

    RETURN quantity;
END;
$$ LANGUAGE plpgsql;
```

Note: There is actually a hidden "outer block" surrounding the body of any PL/pgSQL function. This block provides the declarations of the function's parameters (if any), as well as some special variables such as FOUND (see Section 41.5.5). The outer block is labeled with the function's name, meaning that parameters and special variables can be qualified with the function's name.

It is important not to confuse the use of BEGIN/END for grouping statements in PL/pgSQL with the similarly-named SQL commands for transaction control. PL/pgSQL's BEGIN/END are only for grouping; they do not start or end a transaction. Functions and trigger procedures are always executed within a transaction established by an outer query — they cannot start or commit that transaction, since there would be no context for them to execute in. However, a block containing an EXCEPTION clause effectively forms a subtransaction that can be rolled back without affecting the outer transaction. For more about that see Section 41.6.6.

41.3. Declarations

All variables used in a block must be declared in the declarations section of the block. (The only exceptions are that the loop variable of a FOR loop iterating over a range of integer values is automatically declared as an integer variable, and likewise the loop variable of a FOR loop iterating over a cursor's result is automatically declared as a record variable.)

PL/pgSQL variables can have any SQL data type, such as integer, varchar, and char.

Here are some examples of variable declarations:

```
user_id integer;
quantity numeric(5);
url varchar;
myrow tablename%ROWTYPE;
myfield tablename.columnname%TYPE;
arow RECORD;
```

The general syntax of a variable declaration is:

```
name [ CONSTANT ] type [ COLLATE collation_name ] [ NOT NULL ] [ { DEFAULT | := | = } e
```

The DEFAULT clause, if given, specifies the initial value assigned to the variable when the block is entered. If the DEFAULT clause is not given then the variable is initialized to the SQL null value. The CONSTANT option prevents the variable from being assigned to after initialization, so that its value will remain constant for the duration of the block. The COLLATE option specifies a collation to use for the variable (see Section 41.3.6). If NOT NULL is specified, an assignment of a null value results in a run-time error. All variables declared as NOT NULL must have a nonnull default value specified. Equal (=) can be used instead of PL/SQL-compliant :=.

A variable's default value is evaluated and assigned to the variable each time the block is entered (not just once per function call). So, for example, assigning now() to a variable of type timestamp causes the variable to have the time of the current function call, not the time when the function was precompiled.

Examples:

```
quantity integer DEFAULT 32;
url varchar := 'http://mysite.com';
user_id CONSTANT integer := 10;
```

41.3.1. Declaring Function Parameters

Parameters passed to functions are named with the identifiers $1, $2, etc. Optionally, aliases can be declared for $n parameter names for increased readability. Either the alias or the numeric identifier can then be used to refer to the parameter value.

There are two ways to create an alias. The preferred way is to give a name to the parameter in the CREATE FUNCTION command, for example:

```
CREATE FUNCTION sales_tax(subtotal real) RETURNS real AS $$
BEGIN
    RETURN subtotal * 0.06;
END;
$$ LANGUAGE plpgsql;
```

The other way is to explicitly declare an alias, using the declaration syntax

```
name ALIAS FOR $n;
```

The same example in this style looks like:

```
CREATE FUNCTION sales_tax(real) RETURNS real AS $$
DECLARE
    subtotal ALIAS FOR $1;
BEGIN
    RETURN subtotal * 0.06;
END;
$$ LANGUAGE plpgsql;
```

> **Note:** These two examples are not perfectly equivalent. In the first case, subtotal could be referenced as sales_tax.subtotal, but in the second case it could not. (Had we attached a label to the inner block, subtotal could be qualified with that label, instead.)

Some more examples:

```
CREATE FUNCTION instr(varchar, integer) RETURNS integer AS $$
DECLARE
    v_string ALIAS FOR $1;
    index ALIAS FOR $2;
BEGIN
    -- some computations using v_string and index here
END;
$$ LANGUAGE plpgsql;
```

```
CREATE FUNCTION concat_selected_fields(in_t sometablename) RETURNS text AS $$
BEGIN
    RETURN in_t.f1 || in_t.f3 || in_t.f5 || in_t.f7;
END;
$$ LANGUAGE plpgsql;
```

When a PL/pgSQL function is declared with output parameters, the output parameters are given $n names and optional aliases in just the same way as the normal input parameters. An output parameter is effectively a variable that starts out NULL; it should be assigned to during the execution of the function. The final value of the parameter is what is returned. For instance, the sales-tax example could also be done this way:

```
CREATE FUNCTION sales_tax(subtotal real, OUT tax real) AS $$
BEGIN
    tax := subtotal * 0.06;
END;
$$ LANGUAGE plpgsql;
```

Notice that we omitted RETURNS real — we could have included it, but it would be redundant.

Output parameters are most useful when returning multiple values. A trivial example is:

```
CREATE FUNCTION sum_n_product(x int, y int, OUT sum int, OUT prod int) AS $$
BEGIN
    sum := x + y;
    prod := x * y;
END;
$$ LANGUAGE plpgsql;
```

As discussed in Section 36.4.4, this effectively creates an anonymous record type for the function's results. If a RETURNS clause is given, it must say RETURNS record.

Another way to declare a PL/pgSQL function is with RETURNS TABLE, for example:

```
CREATE FUNCTION extended_sales(p_itemno int)
RETURNS TABLE(quantity int, total numeric) AS $$
BEGIN
    RETURN QUERY SELECT s.quantity, s.quantity * s.price FROM sales AS s
                 WHERE s.itemno = p_itemno;
END;
$$ LANGUAGE plpgsql;
```

This is exactly equivalent to declaring one or more OUT parameters and specifying RETURNS SETOF *sometype*.

When the return type of a PL/pgSQL function is declared as a polymorphic type (anyelement, anyarray, anynonarray, anyenum, or anyrange), a special parameter $0 is created. Its data type is the actual return type of the function, as deduced from the actual input types (see Section 36.2.5). This allows the function to access its actual return type as shown in Section 41.3.3. $0 is initialized to null and can be modified by the function, so it can be used to hold the return value if desired, though that is not required. $0 can also be given an alias. For example, this function works on any data type that has a + operator:

```
CREATE FUNCTION add_three_values(v1 anyelement, v2 anyelement, v3 anyelement)
RETURNS anyelement AS $$
DECLARE
    result ALIAS FOR $0;
BEGIN
```

```
        result := v1 + v2 + v3;
        RETURN result;
END;
$$ LANGUAGE plpgsql;
```

The same effect can be obtained by declaring one or more output parameters as polymorphic types. In this case the special $0 parameter is not used; the output parameters themselves serve the same purpose. For example:

```
CREATE FUNCTION add_three_values(v1 anyelement, v2 anyelement, v3 anyelement,
                                 OUT sum anyelement)
AS $$
BEGIN
    sum := v1 + v2 + v3;
END;
$$ LANGUAGE plpgsql;
```

41.3.2. ALIAS

```
newname ALIAS FOR oldname;
```

The ALIAS syntax is more general than is suggested in the previous section: you can declare an alias for any variable, not just function parameters. The main practical use for this is to assign a different name for variables with predetermined names, such as NEW or OLD within a trigger procedure.

Examples:

```
DECLARE
  prior ALIAS FOR old;
  updated ALIAS FOR new;
```

Since ALIAS creates two different ways to name the same object, unrestricted use can be confusing. It's best to use it only for the purpose of overriding predetermined names.

41.3.3. Copying Types

```
variable%TYPE
```

%TYPE provides the data type of a variable or table column. You can use this to declare variables that will hold database values. For example, let's say you have a column named user_id in your users table. To declare a variable with the same data type as users.user_id you write:

```
user_id users.user_id%TYPE;
```

By using %TYPE you don't need to know the data type of the structure you are referencing, and most importantly, if the data type of the referenced item changes in the future (for instance: you change the type of user_id from integer to real), you might not need to change your function definition.

%TYPE is particularly valuable in polymorphic functions, since the data types needed for internal variables can change from one call to the next. Appropriate variables can be created by applying %TYPE to the function's arguments or result placeholders.

41.3.4. Row Types

```
name table_name%ROWTYPE;
name composite_type_name;
```

A variable of a composite type is called a *row* variable (or *row-type* variable). Such a variable can hold a whole row of a SELECT or FOR query result, so long as that query's column set matches the declared type of the variable. The individual fields of the row value are accessed using the usual dot notation, for example rowvar.field.

A row variable can be declared to have the same type as the rows of an existing table or view, by using the *table_name*%ROWTYPE notation; or it can be declared by giving a composite type's name. (Since every table has an associated composite type of the same name, it actually does not matter in PostgreSQL whether you write %ROWTYPE or not. But the form with %ROWTYPE is more portable.)

Parameters to a function can be composite types (complete table rows). In that case, the corresponding identifier $n will be a row variable, and fields can be selected from it, for example $1.user_id.

Only the user-defined columns of a table row are accessible in a row-type variable, not the OID or other system columns (because the row could be from a view). The fields of the row type inherit the table's field size or precision for data types such as char(n).

Here is an example of using composite types. table1 and table2 are existing tables having at least the mentioned fields:

```
CREATE FUNCTION merge_fields(t_row table1) RETURNS text AS $$
DECLARE
    t2_row table2%ROWTYPE;
BEGIN
    SELECT * INTO t2_row FROM table2 WHERE ... ;
    RETURN t_row.f1 || t2_row.f3 || t_row.f5 || t2_row.f7;
END;
$$ LANGUAGE plpgsql;

SELECT merge_fields(t.*) FROM table1 t WHERE ... ;
```

41.3.5. Record Types

```
name RECORD;
```

Record variables are similar to row-type variables, but they have no predefined structure. They take on the actual row structure of the row they are assigned during a SELECT or FOR command. The substructure of a record variable can change each time it is assigned to. A consequence of this is that until a record variable is first assigned to, it has no substructure, and any attempt to access a field in it will draw a run-time error.

Note that RECORD is not a true data type, only a placeholder. One should also realize that when a PL/pgSQL function is declared to return type record, this is not quite the same concept as a record variable, even though such a function might use a record variable to hold its result. In both cases the actual row structure is unknown when the function is written, but for a function returning record the actual structure is determined when the calling query is parsed, whereas a record variable can change its row structure on-the-fly.

41.3.6. Collation of PL/pgSQL Variables

When a PL/pgSQL function has one or more parameters of collatable data types, a collation is identified for each function call depending on the collations assigned to the actual arguments, as described in Section 23.2. If a collation is successfully identified (i.e., there are no conflicts of implicit collations among the arguments) then all the collatable parameters are treated as having that collation implicitly. This will affect the behavior of collation-sensitive operations within the function. For example, consider

```
CREATE FUNCTION less_than(a text, b text) RETURNS boolean AS $$
BEGIN
    RETURN a < b;
END;
$$ LANGUAGE plpgsql;

SELECT less_than(text_field_1, text_field_2) FROM table1;
SELECT less_than(text_field_1, text_field_2 COLLATE "C") FROM table1;
```

The first use of less_than will use the common collation of text_field_1 and text_field_2 for the comparison, while the second use will use C collation.

Furthermore, the identified collation is also assumed as the collation of any local variables that are of collatable types. Thus this function would not work any differently if it were written as

```
CREATE FUNCTION less_than(a text, b text) RETURNS boolean AS $$
DECLARE
    local_a text := a;
    local_b text := b;
BEGIN
    RETURN local_a < local_b;
END;
$$ LANGUAGE plpgsql;
```

If there are no parameters of collatable data types, or no common collation can be identified for them, then parameters and local variables use the default collation of their data type (which is usually the database's default collation, but could be different for variables of domain types).

A local variable of a collatable data type can have a different collation associated with it by including the COLLATE option in its declaration, for example

```
DECLARE
    local_a text COLLATE "en_US";
```

This option overrides the collation that would otherwise be given to the variable according to the rules above.

Also, of course explicit COLLATE clauses can be written inside a function if it is desired to force a particular collation to be used in a particular operation. For example,

```
CREATE FUNCTION less_than_c(a text, b text) RETURNS boolean AS $$
BEGIN
    RETURN a < b COLLATE "C";
END;
$$ LANGUAGE plpgsql;
```

This overrides the collations associated with the table columns, parameters, or local variables used in the expression, just as would happen in a plain SQL command.

41.4. Expressions

All expressions used in PL/pgSQL statements are processed using the server's main SQL executor. For example, when you write a PL/pgSQL statement like

```
IF expression THEN ...
```

PL/pgSQL will evaluate the expression by feeding a query like

```
SELECT expression
```

to the main SQL engine. While forming the SELECT command, any occurrences of PL/pgSQL variable names are replaced by parameters, as discussed in detail in Section 41.10.1. This allows the query plan for the SELECT to be prepared just once and then reused for subsequent evaluations with different values of the variables. Thus, what really happens on first use of an expression is essentially a PREPARE command. For example, if we have declared two integer variables x and y, and we write

```
IF x < y THEN ...
```

what happens behind the scenes is equivalent to

```
PREPARE statement_name(integer, integer) AS SELECT $1 < $2;
```

and then this prepared statement is EXECUTEd for each execution of the IF statement, with the current values of the PL/pgSQL variables supplied as parameter values. Normally these details are not important to a PL/pgSQL user, but they are useful to know when trying to diagnose a problem. More information appears in Section 41.10.2.

41.5. Basic Statements

In this section and the following ones, we describe all the statement types that are explicitly understood by PL/pgSQL. Anything not recognized as one of these statement types is presumed to be an SQL command and is sent to the main database engine to execute, as described in Section 41.5.2 and Section 41.5.3.

41.5.1. Assignment

An assignment of a value to a PL/pgSQL variable is written as:

```
variable { := | = } expression;
```

As explained previously, the expression in such a statement is evaluated by means of an SQL SELECT command sent to the main database engine. The expression must yield a single value (possibly a row value, if the variable is a row or record variable). The target variable can be a simple variable (optionally qualified with a block name), a field of a row or record variable, or an element of an array that is a simple variable or field. Equal (=) can be used instead of PL/SQL-compliant := .

If the expression's result data type doesn't match the variable's data type, the value will be coerced as though by an assignment cast (see Section 10.4). If no assignment cast is known for the pair of data types involved, the PL/pgSQL interpreter will attempt to convert the result value textually, that is by applying the result type's output function followed by the variable type's input function. Note that this could result in run-time errors generated by the input function, if the string form of the result value is not acceptable to the input function.

Examples:

```
tax := subtotal * 0.06;
my_record.user_id := 20;
```

41.5.2. Executing a Command With No Result

For any SQL command that does not return rows, for example INSERT without a RETURNING clause, you can execute the command within a PL/pgSQL function just by writing the command.

Any PL/pgSQL variable name appearing in the command text is treated as a parameter, and then the current value of the variable is provided as the parameter value at run time. This is exactly like the processing described earlier for expressions; for details see Section 41.10.1.

When executing a SQL command in this way, PL/pgSQL may cache and re-use the execution plan for the command, as discussed in Section 41.10.2.

Sometimes it is useful to evaluate an expression or SELECT query but discard the result, for example when calling a function that has side-effects but no useful result value. To do this in PL/pgSQL, use the PERFORM statement:

```
PERFORM query;
```

This executes *query* and discards the result. Write the *query* the same way you would write an SQL SELECT command, but replace the initial keyword SELECT with PERFORM. For WITH queries, use PERFORM and then place the query in parentheses. (In this case, the query can only return one row.) PL/pgSQL variables will be substituted into the query just as for commands that return no result, and the plan is cached in the same way. Also, the special variable FOUND is set to true if the query produced at least one row, or false if it produced no rows (see Section 41.5.5).

> **Note:** One might expect that writing SELECT directly would accomplish this result, but at present the only accepted way to do it is PERFORM. A SQL command that can return rows, such as SELECT, will be rejected as an error unless it has an INTO clause as discussed in the next section.

An example:

```
PERFORM create_mv('cs_session_page_requests_mv', my_query);
```

41.5.3. Executing a Query with a Single-row Result

The result of a SQL command yielding a single row (possibly of multiple columns) can be assigned to a record variable, row-type variable, or list of scalar variables. This is done by writing the base SQL command and adding an INTO clause. For example,

```
SELECT select_expressions INTO [STRICT] target FROM ...;
INSERT ... RETURNING expressions INTO [STRICT] target;
UPDATE ... RETURNING expressions INTO [STRICT] target;
DELETE ... RETURNING expressions INTO [STRICT] target;
```

where *target* can be a record variable, a row variable, or a comma-separated list of simple variables and record/row fields. PL/pgSQL variables will be substituted into the rest of the query, and the plan is cached, just as described above for commands that do not return rows. This works for SELECT, INSERT/UPDATE/DELETE with RETURNING, and utility commands that return row-set results (such as EXPLAIN). Except for the INTO clause, the SQL command is the same as it would be written outside PL/pgSQL.

> **Tip:** Note that this interpretation of SELECT with INTO is quite different from PostgreSQL's regular SELECT INTO command, wherein the INTO target is a newly created table. If you want to create a table from a SELECT result inside a PL/pgSQL function, use the syntax CREATE TABLE ... AS SELECT.

If a row or a variable list is used as target, the query's result columns must exactly match the structure of the target as to number and data types, or else a run-time error occurs. When a record variable is the target, it automatically configures itself to the row type of the query result columns.

The INTO clause can appear almost anywhere in the SQL command. Customarily it is written either just before or just after the list of *select_expressions* in a SELECT command, or at the end of the command for other command types. It is recommended that you follow this convention in case the PL/pgSQL parser becomes stricter in future versions.

If STRICT is not specified in the INTO clause, then *target* will be set to the first row returned by the query, or to nulls if the query returned no rows. (Note that "the first row" is not well-defined unless you've used ORDER BY.) Any result rows after the first row are discarded. You can check the special FOUND variable (see Section 41.5.5) to determine whether a row was returned:

```
SELECT * INTO myrec FROM emp WHERE empname = myname;
IF NOT FOUND THEN
    RAISE EXCEPTION 'employee % not found', myname;
END IF;
```

If the STRICT option is specified, the query must return exactly one row or a run-time error will be reported, either NO_DATA_FOUND (no rows) or TOO_MANY_ROWS (more than one row). You can use an exception block if you wish to catch the error, for example:

```
BEGIN
    SELECT * INTO STRICT myrec FROM emp WHERE empname = myname;
    EXCEPTION
        WHEN NO_DATA_FOUND THEN
            RAISE EXCEPTION 'employee % not found', myname;
        WHEN TOO_MANY_ROWS THEN
            RAISE EXCEPTION 'employee % not unique', myname;
END;
```

Successful execution of a command with STRICT always sets FOUND to true.

For INSERT/UPDATE/DELETE with RETURNING, PL/pgSQL reports an error for more than one returned row, even when STRICT is not specified. This is because there is no option such as ORDER BY with which to determine which affected row should be returned.

If print_strict_params is enabled for the function, then when an error is thrown because the requirements of STRICT are not met, the DETAIL part of the error message will include information about the parameters passed to the query. You can change the print_strict_params setting for all functions by setting plpgsql.print_strict_params, though only subsequent function compilations will be affected. You can also enable it on a per-function basis by using a compiler option, for example:

```
CREATE FUNCTION get_userid(username text) RETURNS int
AS $$
#print_strict_params on
DECLARE
userid int;
BEGIN
    SELECT users.userid INTO STRICT userid
        FROM users WHERE users.username = get_userid.username;
    RETURN userid;
END
$$ LANGUAGE plpgsql;
```

On failure, this function might produce an error message such as

```
ERROR:  query returned no rows
DETAIL:  parameters: $1 = 'nosuchuser'
CONTEXT:  PL/pgSQL function get_userid(text) line 6 at SQL statement
```

Note: The STRICT option matches the behavior of Oracle PL/SQL's SELECT INTO and related statements.

To handle cases where you need to process multiple result rows from a SQL query, see Section 41.6.4.

41.5.4. Executing Dynamic Commands

Oftentimes you will want to generate dynamic commands inside your PL/pgSQL functions, that is, commands that will involve different tables or different data types each time they are executed. PL/pgSQL's normal attempts to cache plans for commands (as discussed in Section 41.10.2) will not work in such scenarios. To handle this sort of problem, the EXECUTE statement is provided:

```
EXECUTE command-string [ INTO [STRICT] target ] [ USING expression [, ... ] ];
```

where `command-string` is an expression yielding a string (of type text) containing the command to be executed. The optional `target` is a record variable, a row variable, or a comma-separated list of simple variables and record/row fields, into which the results of the command will be stored. The optional USING expressions supply values to be inserted into the command.

No substitution of PL/pgSQL variables is done on the computed command string. Any required variable values must be inserted in the command string as it is constructed; or you can use parameters as described below.

Also, there is no plan caching for commands executed via EXECUTE. Instead, the command is always planned each time the statement is run. Thus the command string can be dynamically created within the function to perform actions on different tables and columns.

The INTO clause specifies where the results of a SQL command returning rows should be assigned. If a row or variable list is provided, it must exactly match the structure of the query's results (when a record variable is used, it will configure itself to match the result structure automatically). If multiple rows are returned, only the first will be assigned to the INTO variable. If no rows are returned, NULL is assigned to the INTO variable(s). If no INTO clause is specified, the query results are discarded.

If the STRICT option is given, an error is reported unless the query produces exactly one row.

The command string can use parameter values, which are referenced in the command as $1, $2, etc. These symbols refer to values supplied in the USING clause. This method is often preferable to inserting data values into the command string as text: it avoids run-time overhead of converting the values to text and back, and it is much less prone to SQL-injection attacks since there is no need for quoting or escaping. An example is:

```
EXECUTE 'SELECT count(*) FROM mytable WHERE inserted_by = $1 AND inserted <= $2'
   INTO c
   USING checked_user, checked_date;
```

Note that parameter symbols can only be used for data values — if you want to use dynamically determined table or column names, you must insert them into the command string textually. For example, if the preceding query needed to be done against a dynamically selected table, you could do this:

```
EXECUTE 'SELECT count(*) FROM '
    || quote_ident(tabname)
    || ' WHERE inserted_by = $1 AND inserted <= $2'
    INTO c
    USING checked_user, checked_date;
```

A cleaner approach is to use `format()`'s `%I` specification for table or column names (strings separated by a newline are concatenated):

```
EXECUTE format('SELECT count(*) FROM %I '
    'WHERE inserted_by = $1 AND inserted <= $2', tabname)
    INTO c
    USING checked_user, checked_date;
```

Another restriction on parameter symbols is that they only work in SELECT, INSERT, UPDATE, and DELETE commands. In other statement types (generically called utility statements), you must insert values textually even if they are just data values.

An EXECUTE with a simple constant command string and some USING parameters, as in the first example above, is functionally equivalent to just writing the command directly in PL/pgSQL and allowing replacement of PL/pgSQL variables to happen automatically. The important difference is that EXECUTE will re-plan the command on each execution, generating a plan that is specific to the current parameter values; whereas PL/pgSQL may otherwise create a generic plan and cache it for re-use. In situations where the best plan depends strongly on the parameter values, it can be helpful to use EXECUTE to positively ensure that a generic plan is not selected.

SELECT INTO is not currently supported within EXECUTE; instead, execute a plain SELECT command and specify INTO as part of the EXECUTE itself.

> **Note:** The PL/pgSQL EXECUTE statement is not related to the EXECUTE SQL statement supported by the PostgreSQL server. The server's EXECUTE statement cannot be used directly within PL/pgSQL functions (and is not needed).

Example 41-1. Quoting Values In Dynamic Queries

When working with dynamic commands you will often have to handle escaping of single quotes. The recommended method for quoting fixed text in your function body is dollar quoting. (If you have legacy code that does not use dollar quoting, please refer to the overview in Section 41.11.1, which can save you some effort when translating said code to a more reasonable scheme.)

Dynamic values require careful handling since they might contain quote characters. An example using `format()` (this assumes that you are dollar quoting the function body so quote marks need not be doubled):

```
EXECUTE format('UPDATE tbl SET %I = $1 '
    'WHERE key = $2', colname) USING newvalue, keyvalue;
```
It is also possible to call the quoting functions directly:
```
EXECUTE 'UPDATE tbl SET '
        || quote_ident(colname)
        || ' = '
        || quote_literal(newvalue)
```

```
        || ' WHERE key = '
        || quote_literal(keyvalue);
```

This example demonstrates the use of the `quote_ident` and `quote_literal` functions (see Section 9.4). For safety, expressions containing column or table identifiers should be passed through `quote_ident` before insertion in a dynamic query. Expressions containing values that should be literal strings in the constructed command should be passed through `quote_literal`. These functions take the appropriate steps to return the input text enclosed in double or single quotes respectively, with any embedded special characters properly escaped.

Because `quote_literal` is labeled `STRICT`, it will always return null when called with a null argument. In the above example, if `newvalue` or `keyvalue` were null, the entire dynamic query string would become null, leading to an error from `EXECUTE`. You can avoid this problem by using the `quote_nullable` function, which works the same as `quote_literal` except that when called with a null argument it returns the string `NULL`. For example,

```
EXECUTE 'UPDATE tbl SET '
        || quote_ident(colname)
        || ' = '
        || quote_nullable(newvalue)
        || ' WHERE key = '
        || quote_nullable(keyvalue);
```

If you are dealing with values that might be null, you should usually use `quote_nullable` in place of `quote_literal`.

As always, care must be taken to ensure that null values in a query do not deliver unintended results. For example the `WHERE` clause

```
'WHERE key = ' || quote_nullable(keyvalue)
```

will never succeed if `keyvalue` is null, because the result of using the equality operator = with a null operand is always null. If you wish null to work like an ordinary key value, you would need to rewrite the above as

```
'WHERE key IS NOT DISTINCT FROM ' || quote_nullable(keyvalue)
```

(At present, `IS NOT DISTINCT FROM` is handled much less efficiently than =, so don't do this unless you must. See Section 9.2 for more information on nulls and `IS DISTINCT`.)

Note that dollar quoting is only useful for quoting fixed text. It would be a very bad idea to try to write this example as:

```
EXECUTE 'UPDATE tbl SET '
        || quote_ident(colname)
        || ' = $$'
        || newvalue
        || '$$ WHERE key = '
        || quote_literal(keyvalue);
```

because it would break if the contents of `newvalue` happened to contain $$. The same objection would apply to any other dollar-quoting delimiter you might pick. So, to safely quote text that is not known in advance, you *must* use `quote_literal`, `quote_nullable`, or `quote_ident`, as appropriate.

Dynamic SQL statements can also be safely constructed using the `format` function (see Section 9.4). For example:

```
EXECUTE format('UPDATE tbl SET %I = %L '
   'WHERE key = %L', colname, newvalue, keyvalue);
```

%I is equivalent to `quote_ident`, and %L is equivalent to `quote_nullable`. The `format` function can be used in conjunction with the USING clause:

```
EXECUTE format('UPDATE tbl SET %I = $1 WHERE key = $2', colname)
    USING newvalue, keyvalue;
```

This form is better because the variables are handled in their native data type format, rather than unconditionally converting them to text and quoting them via %L. It is also more efficient.

A much larger example of a dynamic command and EXECUTE can be seen in Example 41-9, which builds and executes a CREATE FUNCTION command to define a new function.

41.5.5. Obtaining the Result Status

There are several ways to determine the effect of a command. The first method is to use the GET DIAGNOSTICS command, which has the form:

```
GET [ CURRENT ] DIAGNOSTICS variable { = | := } item [ , ... ];
```

This command allows retrieval of system status indicators. CURRENT is a noise word (but see also GET STACKED DIAGNOSTICS in Section 41.6.6.1). Each *item* is a key word identifying a status value to be assigned to the specified *variable* (which should be of the right data type to receive it). The currently available status items are shown in Table 41-1. Colon-equal (:=) can be used instead of the SQL-standard = token. An example:

```
GET DIAGNOSTICS integer_var = ROW_COUNT;
```

Table 41-1. Available Diagnostics Items

Name	Type	Description
ROW_COUNT	bigint	the number of rows processed by the most recent SQL command
RESULT_OID	oid	the OID of the last row inserted by the most recent SQL command (only useful after an INSERT command into a table having OIDs)
PG_CONTEXT	text	line(s) of text describing the current call stack (see Section 41.6.7)

The second method to determine the effects of a command is to check the special variable named FOUND, which is of type `boolean`. FOUND starts out false within each PL/pgSQL function call. It is set by each of the following types of statements:

- A SELECT INTO statement sets FOUND true if a row is assigned, false if no row is returned.

- A PERFORM statement sets FOUND true if it produces (and discards) one or more rows, false if no row is produced.

- UPDATE, INSERT, and DELETE statements set FOUND true if at least one row is affected, false if no row is affected.

- A FETCH statement sets FOUND true if it returns a row, false if no row is returned.

- A MOVE statement sets FOUND true if it successfully repositions the cursor, false otherwise.

- A FOR or FOREACH statement sets FOUND true if it iterates one or more times, else false. FOUND is set this way when the loop exits; inside the execution of the loop, FOUND is not modified by the loop statement, although it might be changed by the execution of other statements within the loop body.

- RETURN QUERY and RETURN QUERY EXECUTE statements set FOUND true if the query returns at least one row, false if no row is returned.

Other PL/pgSQL statements do not change the state of FOUND. Note in particular that EXECUTE changes the output of GET DIAGNOSTICS, but does not change FOUND.

FOUND is a local variable within each PL/pgSQL function; any changes to it affect only the current function.

41.5.6. Doing Nothing At All

Sometimes a placeholder statement that does nothing is useful. For example, it can indicate that one arm of an if/then/else chain is deliberately empty. For this purpose, use the NULL statement:

```
NULL;
```

For example, the following two fragments of code are equivalent:

```
BEGIN
    y := x / 0;
EXCEPTION
    WHEN division_by_zero THEN
        NULL;  -- ignore the error
END;

BEGIN
    y := x / 0;
EXCEPTION
    WHEN division_by_zero THEN  -- ignore the error
END;
```

Which is preferable is a matter of taste.

> **Note:** In Oracle's PL/SQL, empty statement lists are not allowed, and so NULL statements are *required* for situations such as this. PL/pgSQL allows you to just write nothing, instead.

41.6. Control Structures

Control structures are probably the most useful (and important) part of PL/pgSQL. With PL/pgSQL's control structures, you can manipulate PostgreSQL data in a very flexible and powerful way.

41.6.1. Returning From a Function

There are two commands available that allow you to return data from a function: RETURN and RETURN NEXT.

41.6.1.1. RETURN

```
RETURN expression;
```

RETURN with an expression terminates the function and returns the value of *expression* to the caller. This form is used for PL/pgSQL functions that do not return a set.

In a function that returns a scalar type, the expression's result will automatically be cast into the function's return type as described for assignments. But to return a composite (row) value, you must write an expression delivering exactly the requested column set. This may require use of explicit casting.

If you declared the function with output parameters, write just RETURN with no expression. The current values of the output parameter variables will be returned.

If you declared the function to return void, a RETURN statement can be used to exit the function early; but do not write an expression following RETURN.

The return value of a function cannot be left undefined. If control reaches the end of the top-level block of the function without hitting a RETURN statement, a run-time error will occur. This restriction does not apply to functions with output parameters and functions returning void, however. In those cases a RETURN statement is automatically executed if the top-level block finishes.

Some examples:

```
-- functions returning a scalar type
RETURN 1 + 2;
RETURN scalar_var;

-- functions returning a composite type
RETURN composite_type_var;
RETURN (1, 2, 'three'::text);  -- must cast columns to correct types
```

41.6.1.2. RETURN NEXT and RETURN QUERY

```
RETURN NEXT expression;
RETURN QUERY query;
RETURN QUERY EXECUTE command-string [ USING expression [, ... ] ];
```

When a PL/pgSQL function is declared to return SETOF *sometype*, the procedure to follow is slightly different. In that case, the individual items to return are specified by a sequence of RETURN NEXT or RETURN QUERY commands, and then a final RETURN command with no argument is used to indicate that the function has finished executing. RETURN NEXT can be used with both scalar and composite data types; with a composite result type, an entire "table" of results will be returned. RETURN QUERY appends the results of executing a query to the function's result set. RETURN NEXT and RETURN QUERY can be freely intermixed in a single set-returning function, in which case their results will be concatenated.

RETURN NEXT and RETURN QUERY do not actually return from the function — they simply append zero or more rows to the function's result set. Execution then continues with the next statement in the PL/pgSQL function. As successive RETURN NEXT or RETURN QUERY commands are executed, the result set is built up. A final RETURN, which should have no argument, causes control to exit the function (or you can just let control reach the end of the function).

RETURN QUERY has a variant RETURN QUERY EXECUTE, which specifies the query to be executed dynamically. Parameter expressions can be inserted into the computed query string via USING, in just the same way as in the EXECUTE command.

If you declared the function with output parameters, write just RETURN NEXT with no expression. On each execution, the current values of the output parameter variable(s) will be saved for eventual return as a row of the result. Note that you must declare the function as returning SETOF record when there are multiple output parameters, or SETOF *sometype* when there is just one output parameter of type *sometype*, in order to create a set-returning function with output parameters.

Here is an example of a function using RETURN NEXT:

```
CREATE TABLE foo (fooid INT, foosubid INT, fooname TEXT);
INSERT INTO foo VALUES (1, 2, 'three');
INSERT INTO foo VALUES (4, 5, 'six');

CREATE OR REPLACE FUNCTION get_all_foo() RETURNS SETOF foo AS
$BODY$
DECLARE
    r foo%rowtype;
BEGIN
    FOR r IN
        SELECT * FROM foo WHERE fooid > 0
    LOOP
        -- can do some processing here
        RETURN NEXT r; -- return current row of SELECT
    END LOOP;
    RETURN;
END
$BODY$
LANGUAGE plpgsql;

SELECT * FROM get_all_foo();
```

Here is an example of a function using RETURN QUERY:

```
CREATE FUNCTION get_available_flightid(date) RETURNS SETOF integer AS
$BODY$
```

```
BEGIN
    RETURN QUERY SELECT flightid
                   FROM flight
                  WHERE flightdate >= $1
                    AND flightdate < ($1 + 1);

    -- Since execution is not finished, we can check whether rows were returned
    -- and raise exception if not.
    IF NOT FOUND THEN
        RAISE EXCEPTION 'No flight at %.', $1;
    END IF;

    RETURN;
 END
$BODY$
LANGUAGE plpgsql;

-- Returns available flights or raises exception if there are no
-- available flights.
SELECT * FROM get_available_flightid(CURRENT_DATE);
```

> **Note:** The current implementation of RETURN NEXT and RETURN QUERY stores the entire result set before returning from the function, as discussed above. That means that if a PL/pgSQL function produces a very large result set, performance might be poor: data will be written to disk to avoid memory exhaustion, but the function itself will not return until the entire result set has been generated. A future version of PL/pgSQL might allow users to define set-returning functions that do not have this limitation. Currently, the point at which data begins being written to disk is controlled by the work_mem configuration variable. Administrators who have sufficient memory to store larger result sets in memory should consider increasing this parameter.

41.6.2. Conditionals

IF and CASE statements let you execute alternative commands based on certain conditions. PL/pgSQL has three forms of IF:

* IF ... THEN ... END IF

* IF ... THEN ... ELSE ... END IF

* IF ... THEN ... ELSIF ... THEN ... ELSE ... END IF

and two forms of CASE:

* CASE ... WHEN ... THEN ... ELSE ... END CASE

* CASE WHEN ... THEN ... ELSE ... END CASE

41.6.2.1. IF-THEN

```
IF boolean-expression THEN
    statements
END IF;
```

IF-THEN statements are the simplest form of IF. The statements between THEN and END IF will be executed if the condition is true. Otherwise, they are skipped.

Example:

```
IF v_user_id <> 0 THEN
    UPDATE users SET email = v_email WHERE user_id = v_user_id;
END IF;
```

41.6.2.2. IF-THEN-ELSE

```
IF boolean-expression THEN
    statements
ELSE
    statements
END IF;
```

IF-THEN-ELSE statements add to IF-THEN by letting you specify an alternative set of statements that should be executed if the condition is not true. (Note this includes the case where the condition evaluates to NULL.)

Examples:

```
IF parentid IS NULL OR parentid = ''
THEN
    RETURN fullname;
ELSE
    RETURN hp_true_filename(parentid) || '/' || fullname;
END IF;

IF v_count > 0 THEN
    INSERT INTO users_count (count) VALUES (v_count);
    RETURN 't';
ELSE
    RETURN 'f';
END IF;
```

41.6.2.3. `IF-THEN-ELSIF`

```
IF boolean-expression THEN
    statements
[ ELSIF boolean-expression THEN
    statements
[ ELSIF boolean-expression THEN
    statements
    ...]]
[ ELSE
    statements ]
END IF;
```

Sometimes there are more than just two alternatives. `IF-THEN-ELSIF` provides a convenient method of checking several alternatives in turn. The `IF` conditions are tested successively until the first one that is true is found. Then the associated statement(s) are executed, after which control passes to the next statement after `END IF`. (Any subsequent `IF` conditions are *not* tested.) If none of the `IF` conditions is true, then the `ELSE` block (if any) is executed.

Here is an example:

```
IF number = 0 THEN
    result := 'zero';
ELSIF number > 0 THEN
    result := 'positive';
ELSIF number < 0 THEN
    result := 'negative';
ELSE
    -- hmm, the only other possibility is that number is null
    result := 'NULL';
END IF;
```

The key word `ELSIF` can also be spelled `ELSEIF`.

An alternative way of accomplishing the same task is to nest `IF-THEN-ELSE` statements, as in the following example:

```
IF demo_row.sex = 'm' THEN
    pretty_sex := 'man';
ELSE
    IF demo_row.sex = 'f' THEN
        pretty_sex := 'woman';
    END IF;
END IF;
```

However, this method requires writing a matching `END IF` for each `IF`, so it is much more cumbersome than using `ELSIF` when there are many alternatives.

41.6.2.4. Simple CASE

```
CASE search-expression
    WHEN expression [, expression [ ... ]] THEN
        statements
  [ WHEN expression [, expression [ ... ]] THEN
        statements
    ... ]
  [ ELSE
        statements ]
END CASE;
```

The simple form of CASE provides conditional execution based on equality of operands. The *search-expression* is evaluated (once) and successively compared to each *expression* in the WHEN clauses. If a match is found, then the corresponding *statements* are executed, and then control passes to the next statement after END CASE. (Subsequent WHEN expressions are not evaluated.) If no match is found, the ELSE *statements* are executed; but if ELSE is not present, then a CASE_NOT_FOUND exception is raised.

Here is a simple example:

```
CASE x
    WHEN 1, 2 THEN
        msg := 'one or two';
    ELSE
        msg := 'other value than one or two';
END CASE;
```

41.6.2.5. Searched CASE

```
CASE
    WHEN boolean-expression THEN
        statements
  [ WHEN boolean-expression THEN
        statements
    ... ]
  [ ELSE
        statements ]
END CASE;
```

The searched form of CASE provides conditional execution based on truth of Boolean expressions. Each WHEN clause's *boolean-expression* is evaluated in turn, until one is found that yields true. Then the corresponding *statements* are executed, and then control passes to the next statement after END CASE. (Subsequent WHEN expressions are not evaluated.) If no true result is found, the ELSE *statements* are executed; but if ELSE is not present, then a CASE_NOT_FOUND exception is raised.

Here is an example:

```
CASE
    WHEN x BETWEEN 0 AND 10 THEN
```

```
        msg := 'value is between zero and ten';
    WHEN x BETWEEN 11 AND 20 THEN
        msg := 'value is between eleven and twenty';
END CASE;
```

This form of CASE is entirely equivalent to IF-THEN-ELSIF, except for the rule that reaching an omitted ELSE clause results in an error rather than doing nothing.

41.6.3. Simple Loops

With the LOOP, EXIT, CONTINUE, WHILE, FOR, and FOREACH statements, you can arrange for your PL/pgSQL function to repeat a series of commands.

41.6.3.1. LOOP

```
[ <<label>> ]
LOOP
    statements
END LOOP [ label ];
```

LOOP defines an unconditional loop that is repeated indefinitely until terminated by an EXIT or RETURN statement. The optional label can be used by EXIT and CONTINUE statements within nested loops to specify which loop those statements refer to.

41.6.3.2. EXIT

```
EXIT [ label ] [ WHEN boolean-expression ];
```

If no label is given, the innermost loop is terminated and the statement following END LOOP is executed next. If label is given, it must be the label of the current or some outer level of nested loop or block. Then the named loop or block is terminated and control continues with the statement after the loop's/block's corresponding END.

If WHEN is specified, the loop exit occurs only if boolean-expression is true. Otherwise, control passes to the statement after EXIT.

EXIT can be used with all types of loops; it is not limited to use with unconditional loops.

When used with a BEGIN block, EXIT passes control to the next statement after the end of the block. Note that a label must be used for this purpose; an unlabeled EXIT is never considered to match a BEGIN block. (This is a change from pre-8.4 releases of PostgreSQL, which would allow an unlabeled EXIT to match a BEGIN block.)

Examples:

```
LOOP
    -- some computations
    IF count > 0 THEN
```

```
        EXIT;  -- exit loop
    END IF;
END LOOP;


LOOP
    -- some computations
    EXIT WHEN count > 0;  -- same result as previous example
END LOOP;


<<ablock>>
BEGIN
    -- some computations
    IF stocks > 100000 THEN
        EXIT ablock;  -- causes exit from the BEGIN block
    END IF;
    -- computations here will be skipped when stocks > 100000
END;
```

41.6.3.3. CONTINUE

```
CONTINUE [ label ] [ WHEN boolean-expression ];
```

If no `label` is given, the next iteration of the innermost loop is begun. That is, all statements remaining in the loop body are skipped, and control returns to the loop control expression (if any) to determine whether another loop iteration is needed. If `label` is present, it specifies the label of the loop whose execution will be continued.

If WHEN is specified, the next iteration of the loop is begun only if `boolean-expression` is true. Otherwise, control passes to the statement after CONTINUE.

CONTINUE can be used with all types of loops; it is not limited to use with unconditional loops.

Examples:

```
LOOP
    -- some computations
    EXIT WHEN count > 100;
    CONTINUE WHEN count < 50;
    -- some computations for count IN [50 .. 100]
END LOOP;
```

41.6.3.4. WHILE

```
[ <<label>> ]
WHILE boolean-expression LOOP
    statements
END LOOP [ label ];
```

The WHILE statement repeats a sequence of statements so long as the *boolean-expression* evaluates to true. The expression is checked just before each entry to the loop body.

For example:

```
WHILE amount_owed > 0 AND gift_certificate_balance > 0 LOOP
    -- some computations here
END LOOP;

WHILE NOT done LOOP
    -- some computations here
END LOOP;
```

41.6.3.5. FOR **(Integer Variant)**

```
[ <<label>> ]
FOR name IN [ REVERSE ] expression .. expression [ BY expression ] LOOP
    statements
END LOOP [ label ];
```

This form of FOR creates a loop that iterates over a range of integer values. The variable *name* is automatically defined as type integer and exists only inside the loop (any existing definition of the variable name is ignored within the loop). The two expressions giving the lower and upper bound of the range are evaluated once when entering the loop. If the BY clause isn't specified the iteration step is 1, otherwise it's the value specified in the BY clause, which again is evaluated once on loop entry. If REVERSE is specified then the step value is subtracted, rather than added, after each iteration.

Some examples of integer FOR loops:

```
FOR i IN 1..10 LOOP
    -- i will take on the values 1,2,3,4,5,6,7,8,9,10 within the loop
END LOOP;

FOR i IN REVERSE 10..1 LOOP
    -- i will take on the values 10,9,8,7,6,5,4,3,2,1 within the loop
END LOOP;

FOR i IN REVERSE 10..1 BY 2 LOOP
    -- i will take on the values 10,8,6,4,2 within the loop
END LOOP;
```

If the lower bound is greater than the upper bound (or less than, in the REVERSE case), the loop body is not executed at all. No error is raised.

If a *label* is attached to the FOR loop then the integer loop variable can be referenced with a qualified name, using that *label*.

41.6.4. Looping Through Query Results

Using a different type of FOR loop, you can iterate through the results of a query and manipulate that data accordingly. The syntax is:

```
[ <<label>> ]
FOR target IN query LOOP
    statements
END LOOP [ label ];
```

The *target* is a record variable, row variable, or comma-separated list of scalar variables. The *target* is successively assigned each row resulting from the *query* and the loop body is executed for each row. Here is an example:

```
CREATE FUNCTION cs_refresh_mviews() RETURNS integer AS $$
DECLARE
    mviews RECORD;
BEGIN
    RAISE NOTICE 'Refreshing materialized views...';

    FOR mviews IN SELECT * FROM cs_materialized_views ORDER BY sort_key LOOP

        -- Now "mviews" has one record from cs_materialized_views

        RAISE NOTICE 'Refreshing materialized view %s ...', quote_ident(mviews.mv_nai
        EXECUTE format('TRUNCATE TABLE %I', mviews.mv_name);
        EXECUTE format('INSERT INTO %I %s', mviews.mv_name, mviews.mv_query);
    END LOOP;

    RAISE NOTICE 'Done refreshing materialized views.';
    RETURN 1;
END;
$$ LANGUAGE plpgsql;
```

If the loop is terminated by an EXIT statement, the last assigned row value is still accessible after the loop.

The *query* used in this type of FOR statement can be any SQL command that returns rows to the caller: SELECT is the most common case, but you can also use INSERT, UPDATE, or DELETE with a RETURNING clause. Some utility commands such as EXPLAIN will work too.

PL/pgSQL variables are substituted into the query text, and the query plan is cached for possible re-use, as discussed in detail in Section 41.10.1 and Section 41.10.2.

The FOR-IN-EXECUTE statement is another way to iterate over rows:

```
[ <<label>> ]
FOR target IN EXECUTE text_expression [ USING expression [, ... ] ] LOOP
    statements
END LOOP [ label ];
```

This is like the previous form, except that the source query is specified as a string expression, which is evaluated and replanned on each entry to the FOR loop. This allows the programmer to choose the speed of a preplanned query or the flexibility of a dynamic query, just as with a plain EXECUTE statement. As with EXECUTE, parameter values can be inserted into the dynamic command via USING.

Another way to specify the query whose results should be iterated through is to declare it as a cursor. This is described in Section 41.7.4.

41.6.5. Looping Through Arrays

The FOREACH loop is much like a FOR loop, but instead of iterating through the rows returned by a SQL query, it iterates through the elements of an array value. (In general, FOREACH is meant for looping through components of a composite-valued expression; variants for looping through composites besides arrays may be added in future.) The FOREACH statement to loop over an array is:

```
[ <<label>> ]
FOREACH target [ SLICE number ] IN ARRAY expression LOOP
    statements
END LOOP [ label ];
```

Without SLICE, or if SLICE 0 is specified, the loop iterates through individual elements of the array produced by evaluating the *expression*. The *target* variable is assigned each element value in sequence, and the loop body is executed for each element. Here is an example of looping through the elements of an integer array:

```
CREATE FUNCTION sum(int[]) RETURNS int8 AS $$
DECLARE
  s int8 := 0;
  x int;
BEGIN
  FOREACH x IN ARRAY $1
  LOOP
    s := s + x;
  END LOOP;
  RETURN s;
END;
$$ LANGUAGE plpgsql;
```

The elements are visited in storage order, regardless of the number of array dimensions. Although the *target* is usually just a single variable, it can be a list of variables when looping through an array of composite values (records). In that case, for each array element, the variables are assigned from successive columns of the composite value.

With a positive SLICE value, FOREACH iterates through slices of the array rather than single elements. The SLICE value must be an integer constant not larger than the number of dimensions of the array. The *target* variable must be an array, and it receives successive slices of the array value, where each slice is of the number of dimensions specified by SLICE. Here is an example of iterating through one-dimensional slices:

```
CREATE FUNCTION scan_rows(int[]) RETURNS void AS $$
DECLARE
  x int[];
BEGIN
  FOREACH x SLICE 1 IN ARRAY $1
```

```
  LOOP
    RAISE NOTICE 'row = %', x;
  END LOOP;
END;
$$ LANGUAGE plpgsql;

SELECT scan_rows(ARRAY[[1,2,3],[4,5,6],[7,8,9],[10,11,12]]);

NOTICE:  row = {1,2,3}
NOTICE:  row = {4,5,6}
NOTICE:  row = {7,8,9}
NOTICE:  row = {10,11,12}
```

41.6.6. Trapping Errors

By default, any error occurring in a PL/pgSQL function aborts execution of the function, and indeed of the surrounding transaction as well. You can trap errors and recover from them by using a BEGIN block with an EXCEPTION clause. The syntax is an extension of the normal syntax for a BEGIN block:

```
[ <<label>> ]
[ DECLARE
    declarations ]
BEGIN
    statements
EXCEPTION
    WHEN condition [ OR condition ... ] THEN
        handler_statements
    [ WHEN condition [ OR condition ... ] THEN
        handler_statements
    ... ]
END;
```

If no error occurs, this form of block simply executes all the *statements*, and then control passes to the next statement after END. But if an error occurs within the *statements*, further processing of the *statements* is abandoned, and control passes to the EXCEPTION list. The list is searched for the first *condition* matching the error that occurred. If a match is found, the corresponding *handler_statements* are executed, and then control passes to the next statement after END. If no match is found, the error propagates out as though the EXCEPTION clause were not there at all: the error can be caught by an enclosing block with EXCEPTION, or if there is none it aborts processing of the function.

The *condition* names can be any of those shown in Appendix A. A category name matches any error within its category. The special condition name OTHERS matches every error type except QUERY_CANCELED and ASSERT_FAILURE. (It is possible, but often unwise, to trap those two error types by name.) Condition names are not case-sensitive. Also, an error condition can be specified by SQLSTATE code; for example these are equivalent:

```
WHEN division_by_zero THEN ...
WHEN SQLSTATE '22012' THEN ...
```

If a new error occurs within the selected *handler_statements*, it cannot be caught by this EXCEPTION clause, but is propagated out. A surrounding EXCEPTION clause could catch it.

When an error is caught by an EXCEPTION clause, the local variables of the PL/pgSQL function remain as they were when the error occurred, but all changes to persistent database state within the block are rolled back. As an example, consider this fragment:

```
INSERT INTO mytab(firstname, lastname) VALUES('Tom', 'Jones');
BEGIN
    UPDATE mytab SET firstname = 'Joe' WHERE lastname = 'Jones';
    x := x + 1;
    y := x / 0;
EXCEPTION
    WHEN division_by_zero THEN
        RAISE NOTICE 'caught division_by_zero';
        RETURN x;
END;
```

When control reaches the assignment to y, it will fail with a division_by_zero error. This will be caught by the EXCEPTION clause. The value returned in the RETURN statement will be the incremented value of x, but the effects of the UPDATE command will have been rolled back. The INSERT command preceding the block is not rolled back, however, so the end result is that the database contains Tom Jones not Joe Jones.

> **Tip:** A block containing an EXCEPTION clause is significantly more expensive to enter and exit than a block without one. Therefore, don't use EXCEPTION without need.

Example 41-2. Exceptions with UPDATE/INSERT

This example uses exception handling to perform either UPDATE or INSERT, as appropriate. It is recommended that applications use INSERT with ON CONFLICT DO UPDATE rather than actually using this pattern. This example serves primarily to illustrate use of PL/pgSQL control flow structures:

```
CREATE TABLE db (a INT PRIMARY KEY, b TEXT);

CREATE FUNCTION merge_db(key INT, data TEXT) RETURNS VOID AS
$$
BEGIN
    LOOP
        -- first try to update the key
        UPDATE db SET b = data WHERE a = key;
        IF found THEN
            RETURN;
        END IF;
        -- not there, so try to insert the key
        -- if someone else inserts the same key concurrently,
```

```
            -- we could get a unique-key failure
        BEGIN
            INSERT INTO db(a,b) VALUES (key, data);
            RETURN;
        EXCEPTION WHEN unique_violation THEN
            -- Do nothing, and loop to try the UPDATE again.
        END;
    END LOOP;
END;
$$
LANGUAGE plpgsql;

SELECT merge_db(1, 'david');
SELECT merge_db(1, 'dennis');
```

This coding assumes the `unique_violation` error is caused by the `INSERT`, and not by, say, an `INSERT` in a trigger function on the table. It might also misbehave if there is more than one unique index on the table, since it will retry the operation regardless of which index caused the error. More safety could be had by using the features discussed next to check that the trapped error was the one expected.

41.6.6.1. Obtaining Information About an Error

Exception handlers frequently need to identify the specific error that occurred. There are two ways to get information about the current exception in PL/pgSQL: special variables and the `GET STACKED DIAGNOSTICS` command.

Within an exception handler, the special variable `SQLSTATE` contains the error code that corresponds to the exception that was raised (refer to Table A-1 for a list of possible error codes). The special variable `SQLERRM` contains the error message associated with the exception. These variables are undefined outside exception handlers.

Within an exception handler, one may also retrieve information about the current exception by using the `GET STACKED DIAGNOSTICS` command, which has the form:

```
GET STACKED DIAGNOSTICS variable { = | := } item [ , ... ];
```

Each *item* is a key word identifying a status value to be assigned to the specified *variable* (which should be of the right data type to receive it). The currently available status items are shown in Table 41-2.

Table 41-2. Error Diagnostics Items

Name	Type	Description
RETURNED_SQLSTATE	text	the SQLSTATE error code of the exception
COLUMN_NAME	text	the name of the column related to exception
CONSTRAINT_NAME	text	the name of the constraint related to exception

Name	Type	Description
PG_DATATYPE_NAME	text	the name of the data type related to exception
MESSAGE_TEXT	text	the text of the exception's primary message
TABLE_NAME	text	the name of the table related to exception
SCHEMA_NAME	text	the name of the schema related to exception
PG_EXCEPTION_DETAIL	text	the text of the exception's detail message, if any
PG_EXCEPTION_HINT	text	the text of the exception's hint message, if any
PG_EXCEPTION_CONTEXT	text	line(s) of text describing the call stack at the time of the exception (see Section 41.6.7)

If the exception did not set a value for an item, an empty string will be returned.

Here is an example:

```
DECLARE
  text_var1 text;
  text_var2 text;
  text_var3 text;
BEGIN
  -- some processing which might cause an exception
  ...
EXCEPTION WHEN OTHERS THEN
  GET STACKED DIAGNOSTICS text_var1 = MESSAGE_TEXT,
                          text_var2 = PG_EXCEPTION_DETAIL,
                          text_var3 = PG_EXCEPTION_HINT;
END;
```

41.6.7. Obtaining Execution Location Information

The GET DIAGNOSTICS command, previously described in Section 41.5.5, retrieves information about current execution state (whereas the GET STACKED DIAGNOSTICS command discussed above reports information about the execution state as of a previous error). Its PG_CONTEXT status item is useful for identifying the current execution location. PG_CONTEXT returns a text string with line(s) of text describing the call stack. The first line refers to the current function and currently executing GET DIAGNOSTICS command. The second and any subsequent lines refer to calling functions further up the call stack. For example:

```
CREATE OR REPLACE FUNCTION outer_func() RETURNS integer AS $$
```

```
BEGIN
  RETURN inner_func();
END;
$$ LANGUAGE plpgsql;

CREATE OR REPLACE FUNCTION inner_func() RETURNS integer AS $$
DECLARE
  stack text;
BEGIN
  GET DIAGNOSTICS stack = PG_CONTEXT;
  RAISE NOTICE E'--- Call Stack ---\n%', stack;
  RETURN 1;
END;
$$ LANGUAGE plpgsql;

SELECT outer_func();

NOTICE:  --- Call Stack ---
PL/pgSQL function inner_func() line 5 at GET DIAGNOSTICS
PL/pgSQL function outer_func() line 3 at RETURN
CONTEXT:  PL/pgSQL function outer_func() line 3 at RETURN
 outer_func
 -----------
          1
(1 row)
```

GET STACKED DIAGNOSTICS ... PG_EXCEPTION_CONTEXT returns the same sort of stack trace, but describing the location at which an error was detected, rather than the current location.

41.7. Cursors

Rather than executing a whole query at once, it is possible to set up a *cursor* that encapsulates the query, and then read the query result a few rows at a time. One reason for doing this is to avoid memory overrun when the result contains a large number of rows. (However, PL/pgSQL users do not normally need to worry about that, since FOR loops automatically use a cursor internally to avoid memory problems.) A more interesting usage is to return a reference to a cursor that a function has created, allowing the caller to read the rows. This provides an efficient way to return large row sets from functions.

41.7.1. Declaring Cursor Variables

All access to cursors in PL/pgSQL goes through cursor variables, which are always of the special data type refcursor. One way to create a cursor variable is just to declare it as a variable of type refcursor. Another way is to use the cursor declaration syntax, which in general is:

```
name [ [ NO ] SCROLL ] CURSOR [ ( arguments ) ] FOR query;
```

(FOR can be replaced by IS for Oracle compatibility.) If SCROLL is specified, the cursor will be capable of scrolling backward; if NO SCROLL is specified, backward fetches will be rejected; if neither specification appears, it is query-dependent whether backward fetches will be allowed. *arguments*, if specified, is a comma-separated list of pairs *name datatype* that define names to be replaced by parameter values in the given query. The actual values to substitute for these names will be specified later, when the cursor is opened.

Some examples:

```
DECLARE
    curs1 refcursor;
    curs2 CURSOR FOR SELECT * FROM tenk1;
    curs3 CURSOR (key integer) FOR SELECT * FROM tenk1 WHERE unique1 = key;
```

All three of these variables have the data type refcursor, but the first can be used with any query, while the second has a fully specified query already *bound* to it, and the last has a parameterized query bound to it. (key will be replaced by an integer parameter value when the cursor is opened.) The variable curs1 is said to be *unbound* since it is not bound to any particular query.

41.7.2. Opening Cursors

Before a cursor can be used to retrieve rows, it must be *opened*. (This is the equivalent action to the SQL command DECLARE CURSOR.) PL/pgSQL has three forms of the OPEN statement, two of which use unbound cursor variables while the third uses a bound cursor variable.

> **Note:** Bound cursor variables can also be used without explicitly opening the cursor, via the FOR statement described in Section 41.7.4.

41.7.2.1. OPEN FOR *query*

```
OPEN unbound_cursorvar [ [ NO ] SCROLL ] FOR query;
```

The cursor variable is opened and given the specified query to execute. The cursor cannot be open already, and it must have been declared as an unbound cursor variable (that is, as a simple refcursor variable). The query must be a SELECT, or something else that returns rows (such as EXPLAIN). The query is treated in the same way as other SQL commands in PL/pgSQL: PL/pgSQL variable names are substituted, and the query plan is cached for possible reuse. When a PL/pgSQL variable is substituted into the cursor query, the value that is substituted is the one it has at the time of the OPEN; subsequent changes to the variable will not affect the cursor's behavior. The SCROLL and NO SCROLL options have the same meanings as for a bound cursor.

An example:

```
OPEN curs1 FOR SELECT * FROM foo WHERE key = mykey;
```

41.7.2.2. OPEN FOR EXECUTE

```
OPEN unbound_cursorvar [ [ NO ] SCROLL ] FOR EXECUTE query_string
                                    [ USING expression [, ... ] ];
```

The cursor variable is opened and given the specified query to execute. The cursor cannot be open already, and it must have been declared as an unbound cursor variable (that is, as a simple `refcursor` variable). The query is specified as a string expression, in the same way as in the EXECUTE command. As usual, this gives flexibility so the query plan can vary from one run to the next (see Section 41.10.2), and it also means that variable substitution is not done on the command string. As with EXECUTE, parameter values can be inserted into the dynamic command via `format()` and USING. The SCROLL and NO SCROLL options have the same meanings as for a bound cursor.

An example:

```
OPEN curs1 FOR EXECUTE format('SELECT * FROM %I WHERE col1 = $1',tabname) USING keyv.
```

In this example, the table name is inserted into the query via `format()`. The comparison value for `col1` is inserted via a USING parameter, so it needs no quoting.

41.7.2.3. Opening a Bound Cursor

```
OPEN bound_cursorvar [ ( [ argument_name := ] argument_value [, ...] ) ];
```

This form of OPEN is used to open a cursor variable whose query was bound to it when it was declared. The cursor cannot be open already. A list of actual argument value expressions must appear if and only if the cursor was declared to take arguments. These values will be substituted in the query.

The query plan for a bound cursor is always considered cacheable; there is no equivalent of EXECUTE in this case. Notice that SCROLL and NO SCROLL cannot be specified in OPEN, as the cursor's scrolling behavior was already determined.

Argument values can be passed using either *positional* or *named* notation. In positional notation, all arguments are specified in order. In named notation, each argument's name is specified using := to separate it from the argument expression. Similar to calling functions, described in Section 4.3, it is also allowed to mix positional and named notation.

Examples (these use the cursor declaration examples above):

```
OPEN curs2;
OPEN curs3(42);
OPEN curs3(key := 42);
```

Because variable substitution is done on a bound cursor's query, there are really two ways to pass values into the cursor: either with an explicit argument to OPEN, or implicitly by referencing a PL/pgSQL variable in the query. However, only variables declared before the bound cursor was declared will be substituted into it. In either case the value to be passed is determined at the time of the OPEN. For example, another way to get the same effect as the `curs3` example above is

```
DECLARE
    key integer;
```

```
     curs4 CURSOR FOR SELECT * FROM tenk1 WHERE unique1 = key;
BEGIN
     key := 42;
     OPEN curs4;
```

41.7.3. Using Cursors

Once a cursor has been opened, it can be manipulated with the statements described here.

These manipulations need not occur in the same function that opened the cursor to begin with. You can return a `refcursor` value out of a function and let the caller operate on the cursor. (Internally, a `refcursor` value is simply the string name of a so-called portal containing the active query for the cursor. This name can be passed around, assigned to other `refcursor` variables, and so on, without disturbing the portal.)

All portals are implicitly closed at transaction end. Therefore a `refcursor` value is usable to reference an open cursor only until the end of the transaction.

41.7.3.1. FETCH

```
FETCH [ direction { FROM | IN } ] cursor INTO target;
```

FETCH retrieves the next row from the cursor into a target, which might be a row variable, a record variable, or a comma-separated list of simple variables, just like SELECT INTO. If there is no next row, the target is set to NULL(s). As with SELECT INTO, the special variable FOUND can be checked to see whether a row was obtained or not.

The *direction* clause can be any of the variants allowed in the SQL FETCH command except the ones that can fetch more than one row; namely, it can be NEXT, PRIOR, FIRST, LAST, ABSOLUTE *count*, RELATIVE *count*, FORWARD, or BACKWARD. Omitting *direction* is the same as specifying NEXT. *direction* values that require moving backward are likely to fail unless the cursor was declared or opened with the SCROLL option.

cursor must be the name of a `refcursor` variable that references an open cursor portal.

Examples:

```
FETCH curs1 INTO rowvar;
FETCH curs2 INTO foo, bar, baz;
FETCH LAST FROM curs3 INTO x, y;
FETCH RELATIVE -2 FROM curs4 INTO x;
```

41.7.3.2. MOVE

```
MOVE [ direction { FROM | IN } ] cursor;
```

MOVE repositions a cursor without retrieving any data. MOVE works exactly like the FETCH command, except it only repositions the cursor and does not return the row moved to. As with SELECT INTO, the special variable FOUND can be checked to see whether there was a next row to move to.

The *direction* clause can be any of the variants allowed in the SQL FETCH command, namely NEXT, PRIOR, FIRST, LAST, ABSOLUTE *count*, RELATIVE *count*, ALL, FORWARD [*count* | ALL], or BACKWARD [*count* | ALL]. Omitting *direction* is the same as specifying NEXT. *direction* values that require moving backward are likely to fail unless the cursor was declared or opened with the SCROLL option.

Examples:

```
MOVE curs1;
MOVE LAST FROM curs3;
MOVE RELATIVE -2 FROM curs4;
MOVE FORWARD 2 FROM curs4;
```

41.7.3.3. UPDATE/DELETE WHERE CURRENT OF

```
UPDATE table SET ... WHERE CURRENT OF cursor;
DELETE FROM table WHERE CURRENT OF cursor;
```

When a cursor is positioned on a table row, that row can be updated or deleted using the cursor to identify the row. There are restrictions on what the cursor's query can be (in particular, no grouping) and it's best to use FOR UPDATE in the cursor. For more information see the DECLARE reference page.

An example:

```
UPDATE foo SET dataval = myval WHERE CURRENT OF curs1;
```

41.7.3.4. CLOSE

```
CLOSE cursor;
```

CLOSE closes the portal underlying an open cursor. This can be used to release resources earlier than end of transaction, or to free up the cursor variable to be opened again.

An example:

```
CLOSE curs1;
```

41.7.3.5. Returning Cursors

PL/pgSQL functions can return cursors to the caller. This is useful to return multiple rows or columns, especially with very large result sets. To do this, the function opens the cursor and returns the cursor name to the caller (or simply opens the cursor using a portal name specified by or otherwise known to the caller).

The caller can then fetch rows from the cursor. The cursor can be closed by the caller, or it will be closed automatically when the transaction closes.

The portal name used for a cursor can be specified by the programmer or automatically generated. To specify a portal name, simply assign a string to the refcursor variable before opening it. The string value of the refcursor variable will be used by OPEN as the name of the underlying portal. However, if the refcursor variable is null, OPEN automatically generates a name that does not conflict with any existing portal, and assigns it to the refcursor variable.

> **Note:** A bound cursor variable is initialized to the string value representing its name, so that the portal name is the same as the cursor variable name, unless the programmer overrides it by assignment before opening the cursor. But an unbound cursor variable defaults to the null value initially, so it will receive an automatically-generated unique name, unless overridden.

The following example shows one way a cursor name can be supplied by the caller:

```
CREATE TABLE test (col text);
INSERT INTO test VALUES ('123');

CREATE FUNCTION reffunc(refcursor) RETURNS refcursor AS '
BEGIN
    OPEN $1 FOR SELECT col FROM test;
    RETURN $1;
END;
' LANGUAGE plpgsql;

BEGIN;
SELECT reffunc('funccursor');
FETCH ALL IN funccursor;
COMMIT;
```

The following example uses automatic cursor name generation:

```
CREATE FUNCTION reffunc2() RETURNS refcursor AS '
DECLARE
    ref refcursor;
BEGIN
    OPEN ref FOR SELECT col FROM test;
    RETURN ref;
END;
' LANGUAGE plpgsql;

-- need to be in a transaction to use cursors.
BEGIN;
SELECT reffunc2();

      reffunc2
--------------------
 <unnamed cursor 1>
(1 row)
```

```
FETCH ALL IN "<unnamed cursor 1>";
COMMIT;
```

The following example shows one way to return multiple cursors from a single function:

```
CREATE FUNCTION myfunc(refcursor, refcursor) RETURNS SETOF refcursor AS $$
BEGIN
    OPEN $1 FOR SELECT * FROM table_1;
    RETURN NEXT $1;
    OPEN $2 FOR SELECT * FROM table_2;
    RETURN NEXT $2;
END;
$$ LANGUAGE plpgsql;

-- need to be in a transaction to use cursors.
BEGIN;

SELECT * FROM myfunc('a', 'b');

FETCH ALL FROM a;
FETCH ALL FROM b;
COMMIT;
```

41.7.4. Looping Through a Cursor's Result

There is a variant of the FOR statement that allows iterating through the rows returned by a cursor. The syntax is:

```
[ <<label>> ]
FOR recordvar IN bound_cursorvar [ ( [ argument_name := ] argument_value [, ...] ) ] LOOP
    statements
END LOOP [ label ];
```

The cursor variable must have been bound to some query when it was declared, and it *cannot* be open already. The FOR statement automatically opens the cursor, and it closes the cursor again when the loop exits. A list of actual argument value expressions must appear if and only if the cursor was declared to take arguments. These values will be substituted in the query, in just the same way as during an OPEN (see Section 41.7.2.3).

The variable `recordvar` is automatically defined as type `record` and exists only inside the loop (any existing definition of the variable name is ignored within the loop). Each row returned by the cursor is successively assigned to this record variable and the loop body is executed.

41.8. Errors and Messages

41.8.1. Reporting Errors and Messages

Use the RAISE statement to report messages and raise errors.

```
RAISE [ level ] 'format' [, expression [, ... ]] [ USING option = expression [, ... ] ];
RAISE [ level ] condition_name [ USING option = expression [, ... ] ];
RAISE [ level ] SQLSTATE 'sqlstate' [ USING option = expression [, ... ] ];
RAISE [ level ] USING option = expression [, ... ];
RAISE ;
```

The *level* option specifies the error severity. Allowed levels are DEBUG, LOG, INFO, NOTICE, WARNING, and EXCEPTION, with EXCEPTION being the default. EXCEPTION raises an error (which normally aborts the current transaction); the other levels only generate messages of different priority levels. Whether messages of a particular priority are reported to the client, written to the server log, or both is controlled by the log_min_messages and client_min_messages configuration variables. See Chapter 19 for more information.

After *level* if any, you can write a *format* (which must be a simple string literal, not an expression). The format string specifies the error message text to be reported. The format string can be followed by optional argument expressions to be inserted into the message. Inside the format string, % is replaced by the string representation of the next optional argument's value. Write %% to emit a literal %. The number of arguments must match the number of % placeholders in the format string, or an error is raised during the compilation of the function.

In this example, the value of v_job_id will replace the % in the string:

```
RAISE NOTICE 'Calling cs_create_job(%)', v_job_id;
```

You can attach additional information to the error report by writing USING followed by *option* = *expression* items. Each *expression* can be any string-valued expression. The allowed *option* key words are:

MESSAGE

Sets the error message text. This option can't be used in the form of RAISE that includes a format string before USING.

DETAIL

Supplies an error detail message.

HINT

Supplies a hint message.

ERRCODE

Specifies the error code (SQLSTATE) to report, either by condition name, as shown in Appendix A, or directly as a five-character SQLSTATE code.

```
COLUMN
CONSTRAINT
DATATYPE
TABLE
SCHEMA
```

Supplies the name of a related object.

This example will abort the transaction with the given error message and hint:

```
RAISE EXCEPTION 'Nonexistent ID --> %', user_id
    USING HINT = 'Please check your user ID';
```

These two examples show equivalent ways of setting the SQLSTATE:

```
RAISE 'Duplicate user ID: %', user_id USING ERRCODE = 'unique_violation';
RAISE 'Duplicate user ID: %', user_id USING ERRCODE = '23505';
```

There is a second RAISE syntax in which the main argument is the condition name or SQLSTATE to be reported, for example:

```
RAISE division_by_zero;
RAISE SQLSTATE '22012';
```

In this syntax, USING can be used to supply a custom error message, detail, or hint. Another way to do the earlier example is

```
RAISE unique_violation USING MESSAGE = 'Duplicate user ID: ' || user_id;
```

Still another variant is to write RAISE USING or RAISE *level* USING and put everything else into the USING list.

The last variant of RAISE has no parameters at all. This form can only be used inside a BEGIN block's EXCEPTION clause; it causes the error currently being handled to be re-thrown.

> **Note:** Before PostgreSQL 9.1, RAISE without parameters was interpreted as re-throwing the error from the block containing the active exception handler. Thus an EXCEPTION clause nested within that handler could not catch it, even if the RAISE was within the nested EXCEPTION clause's block. This was deemed surprising as well as being incompatible with Oracle's PL/SQL.

If no condition name nor SQLSTATE is specified in a RAISE EXCEPTION command, the default is to use RAISE_EXCEPTION (P0001). If no message text is specified, the default is to use the condition name or SQLSTATE as message text.

> **Note:** When specifying an error code by SQLSTATE code, you are not limited to the predefined error codes, but can select any error code consisting of five digits and/or upper-case ASCII letters, other

than `00000`. It is recommended that you avoid throwing error codes that end in three zeroes, because these are category codes and can only be trapped by trapping the whole category.

41.8.2. Checking Assertions

The `ASSERT` statement is a convenient shorthand for inserting debugging checks into PL/pgSQL functions.

```
ASSERT condition [ , message ];
```

The `condition` is a Boolean expression that is expected to always evaluate to true; if it does, the `ASSERT` statement does nothing further. If the result is false or null, then an `ASSERT_FAILURE` exception is raised. (If an error occurs while evaluating the `condition`, it is reported as a normal error.)

If the optional `message` is provided, it is an expression whose result (if not null) replaces the default error message text "assertion failed", should the `condition` fail. The `message` expression is not evaluated in the normal case where the assertion succeeds.

Testing of assertions can be enabled or disabled via the configuration parameter `plpgsql.check_asserts`, which takes a Boolean value; the default is `on`. If this parameter is `off` then `ASSERT` statements do nothing.

Note that `ASSERT` is meant for detecting program bugs, not for reporting ordinary error conditions. Use the `RAISE` statement, described above, for that.

41.9. Trigger Procedures

PL/pgSQL can be used to define trigger procedures on data changes or database events. A trigger procedure is created with the `CREATE FUNCTION` command, declaring it as a function with no arguments and a return type of `trigger` (for data change triggers) or `event_trigger` (for database event triggers). Special local variables named `PG_something` are automatically defined to describe the condition that triggered the call.

41.9.1. Triggers on Data Changes

A data change trigger is declared as a function with no arguments and a return type of `trigger`. Note that the function must be declared with no arguments even if it expects to receive some arguments specified in `CREATE TRIGGER` — such arguments are passed via `TG_ARGV`, as described below.

When a PL/pgSQL function is called as a trigger, several special variables are created automatically in the top-level block. They are:

NEW

> Data type `RECORD`; variable holding the new database row for `INSERT`/`UPDATE` operations in row-level triggers. This variable is unassigned in statement-level triggers and for `DELETE` operations.

OLD

> Data type `RECORD`; variable holding the old database row for `UPDATE`/`DELETE` operations in row-level triggers. This variable is unassigned in statement-level triggers and for `INSERT` operations.

TG_NAME

> Data type `name`; variable that contains the name of the trigger actually fired.

TG_WHEN

> Data type `text`; a string of `BEFORE`, `AFTER`, or `INSTEAD OF`, depending on the trigger's definition.

TG_LEVEL

> Data type `text`; a string of either `ROW` or `STATEMENT` depending on the trigger's definition.

TG_OP

> Data type `text`; a string of `INSERT`, `UPDATE`, `DELETE`, or `TRUNCATE` telling for which operation the trigger was fired.

TG_RELID

> Data type `oid`; the object ID of the table that caused the trigger invocation.

TG_RELNAME

> Data type `name`; the name of the table that caused the trigger invocation. This is now deprecated, and could disappear in a future release. Use `TG_TABLE_NAME` instead.

TG_TABLE_NAME

> Data type `name`; the name of the table that caused the trigger invocation.

TG_TABLE_SCHEMA

> Data type `name`; the name of the schema of the table that caused the trigger invocation.

TG_NARGS

> Data type `integer`; the number of arguments given to the trigger procedure in the `CREATE TRIGGER` statement.

TG_ARGV[]

> Data type array of `text`; the arguments from the `CREATE TRIGGER` statement. The index counts from 0. Invalid indexes (less than 0 or greater than or equal to `tg_nargs`) result in a null value.

A trigger function must return either `NULL` or a record/row value having exactly the structure of the table the trigger was fired for.

Row-level triggers fired `BEFORE` can return null to signal the trigger manager to skip the rest of the operation for this row (i.e., subsequent triggers are not fired, and the `INSERT`/`UPDATE`/`DELETE` does not occur for this row). If a nonnull value is returned then the operation proceeds with that row value. Returning a row value different from the original value of `NEW` alters the row that will be inserted or updated. Thus, if the trigger function wants the triggering action to succeed normally without altering the row value, `NEW` (or a value equal thereto) has to be returned. To alter the row to be stored, it is possible to replace single values directly in `NEW` and return the modified `NEW`, or to build a complete new record/row to return. In the case of a before-trigger on `DELETE`, the returned value has no direct effect, but it has to be nonnull to allow the trigger action to proceed. Note that NEW is null in DELETE triggers, so returning that is usually not sensible. The usual idiom in DELETE triggers is to return OLD.

INSTEAD OF triggers (which are always row-level triggers, and may only be used on views) can return null to signal that they did not perform any updates, and that the rest of the operation for this row should be skipped (i.e., subsequent triggers are not fired, and the row is not counted in the rows-affected status for the surrounding INSERT/UPDATE/DELETE). Otherwise a nonnull value should be returned, to signal that the trigger performed the requested operation. For INSERT and UPDATE operations, the return value should be NEW, which the trigger function may modify to support INSERT RETURNING and UPDATE RETURNING (this will also affect the row value passed to any subsequent triggers, or passed to a special EXCLUDED alias reference within an INSERT statement with an ON CONFLICT DO UPDATE clause). For DELETE operations, the return value should be OLD.

The return value of a row-level trigger fired AFTER or a statement-level trigger fired BEFORE or AFTER is always ignored; it might as well be null. However, any of these types of triggers might still abort the entire operation by raising an error.

Example 41-3 shows an example of a trigger procedure in PL/pgSQL.

Example 41-3. A PL/pgSQL Trigger Procedure

This example trigger ensures that any time a row is inserted or updated in the table, the current user name and time are stamped into the row. And it checks that an employee's name is given and that the salary is a positive value.

```
CREATE TABLE emp (
    empname text,
    salary integer,
    last_date timestamp,
    last_user text
);

CREATE FUNCTION emp_stamp() RETURNS trigger AS $emp_stamp$
    BEGIN
        -- Check that empname and salary are given
        IF NEW.empname IS NULL THEN
            RAISE EXCEPTION 'empname cannot be null';
        END IF;
        IF NEW.salary IS NULL THEN
            RAISE EXCEPTION '% cannot have null salary', NEW.empname;
        END IF;

        -- Who works for us when they must pay for it?
        IF NEW.salary < 0 THEN
            RAISE EXCEPTION '% cannot have a negative salary', NEW.empname;
        END IF;

        -- Remember who changed the payroll when
        NEW.last_date := current_timestamp;
        NEW.last_user := current_user;
        RETURN NEW;
    END;
$emp_stamp$ LANGUAGE plpgsql;
```

```
CREATE TRIGGER emp_stamp BEFORE INSERT OR UPDATE ON emp
    FOR EACH ROW EXECUTE PROCEDURE emp_stamp();
```

Another way to log changes to a table involves creating a new table that holds a row for each insert, update, or delete that occurs. This approach can be thought of as auditing changes to a table. Example 41-4 shows an example of an audit trigger procedure in PL/pgSQL.

Example 41-4. A PL/pgSQL Trigger Procedure For Auditing

This example trigger ensures that any insert, update or delete of a row in the emp table is recorded (i.e., audited) in the emp_audit table. The current time and user name are stamped into the row, together with the type of operation performed on it.

```
CREATE TABLE emp (
    empname             text NOT NULL,
    salary              integer
);

CREATE TABLE emp_audit(
    operation           char(1)   NOT NULL,
    stamp               timestamp NOT NULL,
    userid              text      NOT NULL,
    empname             text      NOT NULL,
    salary integer
);

CREATE OR REPLACE FUNCTION process_emp_audit() RETURNS TRIGGER AS $emp_audit$
    BEGIN
        --
        -- Create a row in emp_audit to reflect the operation performed on emp,
        -- make use of the special variable TG_OP to work out the operation.
        --
        IF (TG_OP = 'DELETE') THEN
            INSERT INTO emp_audit SELECT 'D', now(), user, OLD.*;
            RETURN OLD;
        ELSIF (TG_OP = 'UPDATE') THEN
            INSERT INTO emp_audit SELECT 'U', now(), user, NEW.*;
            RETURN NEW;
        ELSIF (TG_OP = 'INSERT') THEN
            INSERT INTO emp_audit SELECT 'I', now(), user, NEW.*;
            RETURN NEW;
        END IF;
        RETURN NULL; -- result is ignored since this is an AFTER trigger
    END;
$emp_audit$ LANGUAGE plpgsql;

CREATE TRIGGER emp_audit
AFTER INSERT OR UPDATE OR DELETE ON emp
    FOR EACH ROW EXECUTE PROCEDURE process_emp_audit();
```

A variation of the previous example uses a view joining the main table to the audit table, to show when each entry was last modified. This approach still records the full audit trail of changes to the table, but also presents a simplified view of the audit trail, showing just the last modified timestamp derived from the audit trail for each entry. Example 41-5 shows an example of an audit trigger on a view in PL/pgSQL.

Example 41-5. A PL/pgSQL View Trigger Procedure For Auditing

This example uses a trigger on the view to make it updatable, and ensure that any insert, update or delete of a row in the view is recorded (i.e., audited) in the emp_audit table. The current time and user name are recorded, together with the type of operation performed, and the view displays the last modified time of each row.

```
CREATE TABLE emp (
    empname            text PRIMARY KEY,
    salary             integer
);

CREATE TABLE emp_audit(
    operation          char(1)   NOT NULL,
    userid             text      NOT NULL,
    empname            text      NOT NULL,
    salary             integer,
    stamp              timestamp NOT NULL
);

CREATE VIEW emp_view AS
    SELECT e.empname,
           e.salary,
           max(ea.stamp) AS last_updated
      FROM emp e
      LEFT JOIN emp_audit ea ON ea.empname = e.empname
     GROUP BY 1, 2;

CREATE OR REPLACE FUNCTION update_emp_view() RETURNS TRIGGER AS $$
    BEGIN
        --
        -- Perform the required operation on emp, and create a row in emp_audit
        -- to reflect the change made to emp.
        --
        IF (TG_OP = 'DELETE') THEN
            DELETE FROM emp WHERE empname = OLD.empname;
            IF NOT FOUND THEN RETURN NULL; END IF;

            OLD.last_updated = now();
            INSERT INTO emp_audit VALUES('D', user, OLD.*);
            RETURN OLD;
        ELSIF (TG_OP = 'UPDATE') THEN
            UPDATE emp SET salary = NEW.salary WHERE empname = OLD.empname;
            IF NOT FOUND THEN RETURN NULL; END IF;

            NEW.last_updated = now();
            INSERT INTO emp_audit VALUES('U', user, NEW.*);
            RETURN NEW;
        ELSIF (TG_OP = 'INSERT') THEN
            INSERT INTO emp VALUES(NEW.empname, NEW.salary);
```

```
            NEW.last_updated = now();
            INSERT INTO emp_audit VALUES ('I', user, NEW.*);
            RETURN NEW;
        END IF;
    END;
$$ LANGUAGE plpgsql;

CREATE TRIGGER emp_audit
INSTEAD OF INSERT OR UPDATE OR DELETE ON emp_view
    FOR EACH ROW EXECUTE PROCEDURE update_emp_view();
```

One use of triggers is to maintain a summary table of another table. The resulting summary can be used in place of the original table for certain queries — often with vastly reduced run times. This technique is commonly used in Data Warehousing, where the tables of measured or observed data (called fact tables) might be extremely large. Example 41-6 shows an example of a trigger procedure in PL/pgSQL that maintains a summary table for a fact table in a data warehouse.

Example 41-6. A PL/pgSQL Trigger Procedure For Maintaining A Summary Table

The schema detailed here is partly based on the *Grocery Store* example from *The Data Warehouse Toolkit* by Ralph Kimball.

```
--
-- Main tables - time dimension and sales fact.
--
CREATE TABLE time_dimension (
    time_key                    integer NOT NULL,
    day_of_week                 integer NOT NULL,
    day_of_month                integer NOT NULL,
    month                       integer NOT NULL,
    quarter                     integer NOT NULL,
    year                        integer NOT NULL
);
CREATE UNIQUE INDEX time_dimension_key ON time_dimension(time_key);

CREATE TABLE sales_fact (
    time_key                    integer NOT NULL,
    product_key                 integer NOT NULL,
    store_key                   integer NOT NULL,
    amount_sold                 numeric(12,2) NOT NULL,
    units_sold                  integer NOT NULL,
    amount_cost                 numeric(12,2) NOT NULL
);
CREATE INDEX sales_fact_time ON sales_fact(time_key);


--
-- Summary table - sales by time.
--
CREATE TABLE sales_summary_bytime (
    time_key                    integer NOT NULL,
    amount_sold                 numeric(15,2) NOT NULL,
    units_sold                  numeric(12) NOT NULL,
```

```
        amount_cost                        numeric(15,2) NOT NULL
);
CREATE UNIQUE INDEX sales_summary_bytime_key ON sales_summary_bytime(time_key);


--
-- Function and trigger to amend summarized column(s) on UPDATE, INSERT, DELETE.
--
CREATE OR REPLACE FUNCTION maint_sales_summary_bytime() RETURNS TRIGGER
AS $maint_sales_summary_bytime$
    DECLARE
        delta_time_key              integer;
        delta_amount_sold           numeric(15,2);
        delta_units_sold            numeric(12);
        delta_amount_cost           numeric(15,2);
    BEGIN

        -- Work out the increment/decrement amount(s).
        IF (TG_OP = 'DELETE') THEN

            delta_time_key = OLD.time_key;
            delta_amount_sold = -1 * OLD.amount_sold;
            delta_units_sold = -1 * OLD.units_sold;
            delta_amount_cost = -1 * OLD.amount_cost;

        ELSIF (TG_OP = 'UPDATE') THEN

            -- forbid updates that change the time_key -
            -- (probably not too onerous, as DELETE + INSERT is how most
            -- changes will be made).
            IF ( OLD.time_key != NEW.time_key) THEN
                RAISE EXCEPTION 'Update of time_key : % -> % not allowed',
                                            OLD.time_key, NEW.time_key;
            END IF;

            delta_time_key = OLD.time_key;
            delta_amount_sold = NEW.amount_sold - OLD.amount_sold;
            delta_units_sold = NEW.units_sold - OLD.units_sold;
            delta_amount_cost = NEW.amount_cost - OLD.amount_cost;

        ELSIF (TG_OP = 'INSERT') THEN

            delta_time_key = NEW.time_key;
            delta_amount_sold = NEW.amount_sold;
            delta_units_sold = NEW.units_sold;
            delta_amount_cost = NEW.amount_cost;

        END IF;


        -- Insert or update the summary row with the new values.
        <<insert_update>>
        LOOP
            UPDATE sales_summary_bytime
```

```
                    SET amount_sold = amount_sold + delta_amount_sold,
                        units_sold = units_sold + delta_units_sold,
                        amount_cost = amount_cost + delta_amount_cost
                    WHERE time_key = delta_time_key;

            EXIT insert_update WHEN found;

            BEGIN
                INSERT INTO sales_summary_bytime (
                            time_key,
                            amount_sold,
                            units_sold,
                            amount_cost)
                    VALUES (
                            delta_time_key,
                            delta_amount_sold,
                            delta_units_sold,
                            delta_amount_cost
                            );

                EXIT insert_update;

            EXCEPTION
                WHEN UNIQUE_VIOLATION THEN
                    -- do nothing
            END;
        END LOOP insert_update;

        RETURN NULL;

    END;
$maint_sales_summary_bytime$ LANGUAGE plpgsql;

CREATE TRIGGER maint_sales_summary_bytime
AFTER INSERT OR UPDATE OR DELETE ON sales_fact
    FOR EACH ROW EXECUTE PROCEDURE maint_sales_summary_bytime();

INSERT INTO sales_fact VALUES(1,1,1,10,3,15);
INSERT INTO sales_fact VALUES(1,2,1,20,5,35);
INSERT INTO sales_fact VALUES(2,2,1,40,15,135);
INSERT INTO sales_fact VALUES(2,3,1,10,1,13);
SELECT * FROM sales_summary_bytime;
DELETE FROM sales_fact WHERE product_key = 1;
SELECT * FROM sales_summary_bytime;
UPDATE sales_fact SET units_sold = units_sold * 2;
SELECT * FROM sales_summary_bytime;
```

41.9.2. Triggers on Events

PL/pgSQL can be used to define event triggers. PostgreSQL requires that a procedure that is to be called as an event trigger must be declared as a function with no arguments and a return type of `event_trigger`.

When a PL/pgSQL function is called as an event trigger, several special variables are created automatically in the top-level block. They are:

TG_EVENT

Data type `text`; a string representing the event the trigger is fired for.

TG_TAG

Data type `text`; variable that contains the command tag for which the trigger is fired.

Example 41-7 shows an example of an event trigger procedure in PL/pgSQL.

Example 41-7. A PL/pgSQL Event Trigger Procedure

This example trigger simply raises a `NOTICE` message each time a supported command is executed.

```
CREATE OR REPLACE FUNCTION snitch() RETURNS event_trigger AS $$
BEGIN
    RAISE NOTICE 'snitch: % %', tg_event, tg_tag;
END;
$$ LANGUAGE plpgsql;

CREATE EVENT TRIGGER snitch ON ddl_command_start EXECUTE PROCEDURE snitch();
```

41.10. PL/pgSQL Under the Hood

This section discusses some implementation details that are frequently important for PL/pgSQL users to know.

41.10.1. Variable Substitution

SQL statements and expressions within a PL/pgSQL function can refer to variables and parameters of the function. Behind the scenes, PL/pgSQL substitutes query parameters for such references. Parameters will only be substituted in places where a parameter or column reference is syntactically allowed. As an extreme case, consider this example of poor programming style:

```
INSERT INTO foo (foo) VALUES (foo);
```

The first occurrence of `foo` must syntactically be a table name, so it will not be substituted, even if the function has a variable named `foo`. The second occurrence must be the name of a column of the table, so it will not be substituted either. Only the third occurrence is a candidate to be a reference to the function's variable.

Note: PostgreSQL versions before 9.0 would try to substitute the variable in all three cases, leading to syntax errors.

Since the names of variables are syntactically no different from the names of table columns, there can be ambiguity in statements that also refer to tables: is a given name meant to refer to a table column, or a variable? Let's change the previous example to

```
INSERT INTO dest (col) SELECT foo + bar FROM src;
```

Here, `dest` and `src` must be table names, and `col` must be a column of `dest`, but `foo` and `bar` might reasonably be either variables of the function or columns of `src`.

By default, PL/pgSQL will report an error if a name in a SQL statement could refer to either a variable or a table column. You can fix such a problem by renaming the variable or column, or by qualifying the ambiguous reference, or by telling PL/pgSQL which interpretation to prefer.

The simplest solution is to rename the variable or column. A common coding rule is to use a different naming convention for PL/pgSQL variables than you use for column names. For example, if you consistently name function variables v_*something* while none of your column names start with v_, no conflicts will occur.

Alternatively you can qualify ambiguous references to make them clear. In the above example, `src.foo` would be an unambiguous reference to the table column. To create an unambiguous reference to a variable, declare it in a labeled block and use the block's label (see Section 41.2). For example,

```
<<block>>
DECLARE
    foo int;
BEGIN
    foo := ...;
    INSERT INTO dest (col) SELECT block.foo + bar FROM src;
```

Here `block.foo` means the variable even if there is a column `foo` in `src`. Function parameters, as well as special variables such as `FOUND`, can be qualified by the function's name, because they are implicitly declared in an outer block labeled with the function's name.

Sometimes it is impractical to fix all the ambiguous references in a large body of PL/pgSQL code. In such cases you can specify that PL/pgSQL should resolve ambiguous references as the variable (which is compatible with PL/pgSQL's behavior before PostgreSQL 9.0), or as the table column (which is compatible with some other systems such as Oracle).

To change this behavior on a system-wide basis, set the configuration parameter `plpgsql.variable_conflict` to one of `error`, `use_variable`, or `use_column` (where `error` is the factory default). This parameter affects subsequent compilations of statements in PL/pgSQL functions, but not statements already compiled in the current session. Because changing this setting can cause unexpected changes in the behavior of PL/pgSQL functions, it can only be changed by a superuser.

You can also set the behavior on a function-by-function basis, by inserting one of these special commands at the start of the function text:

```
#variable_conflict error
#variable_conflict use_variable
#variable_conflict use_column
```

These commands affect only the function they are written in, and override the setting of `plpgsql.variable_conflict`. An example is

```
CREATE FUNCTION stamp_user(id int, comment text) RETURNS void AS $$
    #variable_conflict use_variable
    DECLARE
        curtime timestamp := now();
    BEGIN
        UPDATE users SET last_modified = curtime, comment = comment
          WHERE users.id = id;
    END;
$$ LANGUAGE plpgsql;
```

In the `UPDATE` command, `curtime`, `comment`, and `id` will refer to the function's variable and parameters whether or not `users` has columns of those names. Notice that we had to qualify the reference to `users.id` in the `WHERE` clause to make it refer to the table column. But we did not have to qualify the reference to `comment` as a target in the `UPDATE` list, because syntactically that must be a column of `users`. We could write the same function without depending on the `variable_conflict` setting in this way:

```
CREATE FUNCTION stamp_user(id int, comment text) RETURNS void AS $$
    <<fn>>
    DECLARE
        curtime timestamp := now();
    BEGIN
        UPDATE users SET last_modified = fn.curtime, comment = stamp_user.comment
          WHERE users.id = stamp_user.id;
    END;
$$ LANGUAGE plpgsql;
```

Variable substitution does not happen in the command string given to `EXECUTE` or one of its variants. If you need to insert a varying value into such a command, do so as part of constructing the string value, or use `USING`, as illustrated in Section 41.5.4.

Variable substitution currently works only in `SELECT`, `INSERT`, `UPDATE`, and `DELETE` commands, because the main SQL engine allows query parameters only in these commands. To use a non-constant name or value in other statement types (generically called utility statements), you must construct the utility statement as a string and `EXECUTE` it.

41.10.2. Plan Caching

The PL/pgSQL interpreter parses the function's source text and produces an internal binary instruction tree the first time the function is called (within each session). The instruction tree fully translates the PL/pgSQL statement structure, but individual SQL expressions and SQL commands used in the function are not translated immediately.

As each expression and SQL command is first executed in the function, the PL/pgSQL interpreter parses and analyzes the command to create a prepared statement, using the SPI manager's `SPI_prepare` function. Subsequent visits to that expression or command reuse the prepared statement. Thus, a function with conditional code paths that are seldom visited will never incur the overhead of analyzing those commands that are never executed within the current session. A disadvantage is that errors in a specific expression or command cannot be detected until that part of the function is reached in execution. (Trivial syntax errors will be detected during the initial parsing pass, but anything deeper will not be detected until execution.)

PL/pgSQL (or more precisely, the SPI manager) can furthermore attempt to cache the execution plan associated with any particular prepared statement. If a cached plan is not used, then a fresh execution plan is generated on each visit to the statement, and the current parameter values (that is, PL/pgSQL variable values) can be used to optimize the selected plan. If the statement has no parameters, or is executed many times, the SPI manager will consider creating a *generic* plan that is not dependent on specific parameter values, and caching that for re-use. Typically this will happen only if the execution plan is not very sensitive to the values of the PL/pgSQL variables referenced in it. If it is, generating a plan each time is a net win. See PREPARE for more information about the behavior of prepared statements.

Because PL/pgSQL saves prepared statements and sometimes execution plans in this way, SQL commands that appear directly in a PL/pgSQL function must refer to the same tables and columns on every execution; that is, you cannot use a parameter as the name of a table or column in an SQL command. To get around this restriction, you can construct dynamic commands using the PL/pgSQL EXECUTE statement — at the price of performing new parse analysis and constructing a new execution plan on every execution.

The mutable nature of record variables presents another problem in this connection. When fields of a record variable are used in expressions or statements, the data types of the fields must not change from one call of the function to the next, since each expression will be analyzed using the data type that is present when the expression is first reached. EXECUTE can be used to get around this problem when necessary.

If the same function is used as a trigger for more than one table, PL/pgSQL prepares and caches statements independently for each such table — that is, there is a cache for each trigger function and table combination, not just for each function. This alleviates some of the problems with varying data types; for instance, a trigger function will be able to work successfully with a column named key even if it happens to have different types in different tables.

Likewise, functions having polymorphic argument types have a separate statement cache for each combination of actual argument types they have been invoked for, so that data type differences do not cause unexpected failures.

Statement caching can sometimes have surprising effects on the interpretation of time-sensitive values. For example there is a difference between what these two functions do:

```
CREATE FUNCTION logfunc1(logtxt text) RETURNS void AS $$
    BEGIN
        INSERT INTO logtable VALUES (logtxt, 'now');
    END;
$$ LANGUAGE plpgsql;
```

and:

```
CREATE FUNCTION logfunc2(logtxt text) RETURNS void AS $$
    DECLARE
        curtime timestamp;
    BEGIN
        curtime := 'now';
        INSERT INTO logtable VALUES (logtxt, curtime);
    END;
```

```
$$ LANGUAGE plpgsql;
```

In the case of `logfunc1`, the PostgreSQL main parser knows when analyzing the `INSERT` that the string `'now'` should be interpreted as `timestamp`, because the target column of `logtable` is of that type. Thus, `'now'` will be converted to a `timestamp` constant when the `INSERT` is analyzed, and then used in all invocations of `logfunc1` during the lifetime of the session. Needless to say, this isn't what the programmer wanted. A better idea is to use the `now()` or `current_timestamp` function.

In the case of `logfunc2`, the PostgreSQL main parser does not know what type `'now'` should become and therefore it returns a data value of type `text` containing the string `now`. During the ensuing assignment to the local variable `curtime`, the PL/pgSQL interpreter casts this string to the `timestamp` type by calling the `text_out` and `timestamp_in` functions for the conversion. So, the computed time stamp is updated on each execution as the programmer expects. Even though this happens to work as expected, it's not terribly efficient, so use of the `now()` function would still be a better idea.

41.11. Tips for Developing in PL/pgSQL

One good way to develop in PL/pgSQL is to use the text editor of your choice to create your functions, and in another window, use psql to load and test those functions. If you are doing it this way, it is a good idea to write the function using `CREATE OR REPLACE FUNCTION`. That way you can just reload the file to update the function definition. For example:

```
CREATE OR REPLACE FUNCTION testfunc(integer) RETURNS integer AS $$
        ....
$$ LANGUAGE plpgsql;
```

While running psql, you can load or reload such a function definition file with:

```
\i filename.sql
```

and then immediately issue SQL commands to test the function.

Another good way to develop in PL/pgSQL is with a GUI database access tool that facilitates development in a procedural language. One example of such a tool is pgAdmin, although others exist. These tools often provide convenient features such as escaping single quotes and making it easier to recreate and debug functions.

41.11.1. Handling of Quotation Marks

The code of a PL/pgSQL function is specified in `CREATE FUNCTION` as a string literal. If you write the string literal in the ordinary way with surrounding single quotes, then any single quotes inside the function body must be doubled; likewise any backslashes must be doubled (assuming escape string syntax is used). Doubling quotes is at best tedious, and in more complicated cases the code can become downright incomprehensible, because you can easily find yourself needing half a dozen or more adjacent quote marks. It's recommended that you instead write the function body as a "dollar-quoted" string literal (see

Section 4.1.2.4). In the dollar-quoting approach, you never double any quote marks, but instead take care to choose a different dollar-quoting delimiter for each level of nesting you need. For example, you might write the CREATE FUNCTION command as:

```
CREATE OR REPLACE FUNCTION testfunc(integer) RETURNS integer AS $PROC$
        ....
$PROC$ LANGUAGE plpgsql;
```

Within this, you might use quote marks for simple literal strings in SQL commands and $$ to delimit fragments of SQL commands that you are assembling as strings. If you need to quote text that includes $$, you could use Q, and so on.

The following chart shows what you have to do when writing quote marks without dollar quoting. It might be useful when translating pre-dollar quoting code into something more comprehensible.

1 quotation mark

> To begin and end the function body, for example:
>
> ```
> CREATE FUNCTION foo() RETURNS integer AS '
>         ....
> ' LANGUAGE plpgsql;
> ```
> Anywhere within a single-quoted function body, quote marks *must* appear in pairs.

2 quotation marks

> For string literals inside the function body, for example:
>
> ```
> a_output := "Blah";
> SELECT * FROM users WHERE f_name="foobar";
> ```
> In the dollar-quoting approach, you'd just write:
>
> ```
> a_output := 'Blah';
> SELECT * FROM users WHERE f_name='foobar';
> ```
> which is exactly what the PL/pgSQL parser would see in either case.

4 quotation marks

> When you need a single quotation mark in a string constant inside the function body, for example:
>
> ```
> a_output := a_output || " AND name LIKE ""foobar"" AND xyz"
> ```
> The value actually appended to a_output would be: AND name LIKE 'foobar' AND xyz.
>
> In the dollar-quoting approach, you'd write:
>
> ```
> a_output := a_output || $$ AND name LIKE 'foobar' AND xyz$$
> ```
> being careful that any dollar-quote delimiters around this are not just $$.

6 quotation marks

> When a single quotation mark in a string inside the function body is adjacent to the end of that string constant, for example:
>
> ```
> a_output := a_output || " AND name LIKE ""foobar"""
> ```
> The value appended to a_output would then be: AND name LIKE 'foobar'.
>
> In the dollar-quoting approach, this becomes:
>
> ```
> a_output := a_output || $$ AND name LIKE 'foobar'$$
> ```

10 quotation marks

When you want two single quotation marks in a string constant (which accounts for 8 quotation marks) and this is adjacent to the end of that string constant (2 more). You will probably only need that if you are writing a function that generates other functions, as in Example 41-9. For example:

```
a_output := a_output || " if v_" ||
    referrer_keys.kind || " like """""
    || referrer_keys.key_string || """""
    then return """   || referrer_keys.referrer_type
    || """; end if;";
```

The value of a_output would then be:

```
if v_... like "..." then return "..."; end if;
```

In the dollar-quoting approach, this becomes:

```
a_output := a_output || $$ if v_$$ || referrer_keys.kind || $$ like '$$
    || referrer_keys.key_string || $$'
    then return '$$   || referrer_keys.referrer_type
    || $$'; end if;$$;
```

where we assume we only need to put single quote marks into a_output, because it will be re-quoted before use.

41.11.2. Additional Compile-time Checks

To aid the user in finding instances of simple but common problems before they cause harm, PL/PgSQL provides additional *checks*. When enabled, depending on the configuration, they can be used to emit either a WARNING or an ERROR during the compilation of a function. A function which has received a WARNING can be executed without producing further messages, so you are advised to test in a separate development environment.

These additional checks are enabled through the configuration variables plpgsql.extra_warnings for warnings and plpgsql.extra_errors for errors. Both can be set either to a comma-separated list of checks, "none" or "all". The default is "none". Currently the list of available checks includes only one:

shadowed_variables

Checks if a declaration shadows a previously defined variable.

The following example shows the effect of plpgsql.extra_warnings set to shadowed_variables:

```
SET plpgsql.extra_warnings TO 'shadowed_variables';

CREATE FUNCTION foo(f1 int) RETURNS int AS $$
DECLARE
f1 int;
BEGIN
RETURN f1;
END
$$ LANGUAGE plpgsql;
WARNING:  variable "f1" shadows a previously defined variable
LINE 3: f1 int;
```

CREATE FUNCTION

41.12. Porting from Oracle PL/SQL

This section explains differences between PostgreSQL's PL/pgSQL language and Oracle's PL/SQL language, to help developers who port applications from Oracle® to PostgreSQL.

PL/pgSQL is similar to PL/SQL in many aspects. It is a block-structured, imperative language, and all variables have to be declared. Assignments, loops, conditionals are similar. The main differences you should keep in mind when porting from PL/SQL to PL/pgSQL are:

- If a name used in a SQL command could be either a column name of a table or a reference to a variable of the function, PL/SQL treats it as a column name. This corresponds to PL/pgSQL's `plpgsql.variable_conflict = use_column` behavior, which is not the default, as explained in Section 41.10.1. It's often best to avoid such ambiguities in the first place, but if you have to port a large amount of code that depends on this behavior, setting `variable_conflict` may be the best solution.

- In PostgreSQL the function body must be written as a string literal. Therefore you need to use dollar quoting or escape single quotes in the function body. (See Section 41.11.1.)

- Data type names often need translation. For example, in Oracle string values are commonly declared as being of type `varchar2`, which is a non-SQL-standard type. In PostgreSQL, use type `varchar` or `text` instead. Similarly, replace type `number` with `numeric`, or use some other numeric data type if there's a more appropriate one.

- Instead of packages, use schemas to organize your functions into groups.

- Since there are no packages, there are no package-level variables either. This is somewhat annoying. You can keep per-session state in temporary tables instead.

- Integer `FOR` loops with `REVERSE` work differently: PL/SQL counts down from the second number to the first, while PL/pgSQL counts down from the first number to the second, requiring the loop bounds to be swapped when porting. This incompatibility is unfortunate but is unlikely to be changed. (See Section 41.6.3.5.)

- `FOR` loops over queries (other than cursors) also work differently: the target variable(s) must have been declared, whereas PL/SQL always declares them implicitly. An advantage of this is that the variable values are still accessible after the loop exits.

- There are various notational differences for the use of cursor variables.

41.12.1. Porting Examples

Example 41-8 shows how to port a simple function from PL/SQL to PL/pgSQL.

Example 41-8. Porting a Simple Function from PL/SQL to PL/pgSQL

Here is an Oracle PL/SQL function:

```
CREATE OR REPLACE FUNCTION cs_fmt_browser_version(v_name varchar2,
                                                  v_version varchar2)
RETURN varchar2 IS
BEGIN
    IF v_version IS NULL THEN
        RETURN v_name;
    END IF;
    RETURN v_name || '/' || v_version;
END;
/
show errors;
```

Let's go through this function and see the differences compared to PL/pgSQL:

- The type name `varchar2` has to be changed to `varchar` or `text`. In the examples in this section, we'll use `varchar`, but `text` is often a better choice if you do not need specific string length limits.

- The `RETURN` key word in the function prototype (not the function body) becomes `RETURNS` in PostgreSQL. Also, `IS` becomes `AS`, and you need to add a `LANGUAGE` clause because PL/pgSQL is not the only possible function language.

- In PostgreSQL, the function body is considered to be a string literal, so you need to use quote marks or dollar quotes around it. This substitutes for the terminating / in the Oracle approach.

- The `show errors` command does not exist in PostgreSQL, and is not needed since errors are reported automatically.

This is how this function would look when ported to PostgreSQL:

```
CREATE OR REPLACE FUNCTION cs_fmt_browser_version(v_name varchar,
                                                  v_version varchar)
RETURNS varchar AS $$
BEGIN
    IF v_version IS NULL THEN
        RETURN v_name;
    END IF;
    RETURN v_name || '/' || v_version;
END;
$$ LANGUAGE plpgsql;
```

Example 41-9 shows how to port a function that creates another function and how to handle the ensuing quoting problems.

Example 41-9. Porting a Function that Creates Another Function from PL/SQL to PL/pgSQL

The following procedure grabs rows from a `SELECT` statement and builds a large function with the results in `IF` statements, for the sake of efficiency.

This is the Oracle version:

```
CREATE OR REPLACE PROCEDURE cs_update_referrer_type_proc IS
    CURSOR referrer_keys IS
        SELECT * FROM cs_referrer_keys
        ORDER BY try_order;
    func_cmd VARCHAR(4000);
BEGIN
    func_cmd := 'CREATE OR REPLACE FUNCTION cs_find_referrer_type(v_host IN VARCHAR2
                v_domain IN VARCHAR2, v_url IN VARCHAR2) RETURN VARCHAR2 IS BEGIN';

    FOR referrer_key IN referrer_keys LOOP
        func_cmd := func_cmd ||
          ' IF v_' || referrer_key.kind
          || ' LIKE ''' || referrer_key.key_string
          || ''' THEN RETURN ''' || referrer_key.referrer_type
          || '''; END IF;';
    END LOOP;

    func_cmd := func_cmd || ' RETURN NULL; END;';

    EXECUTE IMMEDIATE func_cmd;
END;
/
show errors;
```

Here is how this function would end up in PostgreSQL:

```
CREATE OR REPLACE FUNCTION cs_update_referrer_type_proc() RETURNS void AS $func$
DECLARE
    referrer_keys CURSOR IS
        SELECT * FROM cs_referrer_keys
        ORDER BY try_order;
    func_body text;
    func_cmd text;
BEGIN
    func_body := 'BEGIN';

    FOR referrer_key IN referrer_keys LOOP
        func_body := func_body ||
          ' IF v_' || referrer_key.kind
          || ' LIKE ' || quote_literal(referrer_key.key_string)
          || ' THEN RETURN ' || quote_literal(referrer_key.referrer_type)
          || '; END IF;' ;
    END LOOP;

    func_body := func_body || ' RETURN NULL; END;';

    func_cmd :=
      'CREATE OR REPLACE FUNCTION cs_find_referrer_type(v_host varchar,
                                                        v_domain varchar,
                                                        v_url varchar)
        RETURNS varchar AS '
      || quote_literal(func_body)
      || ' LANGUAGE plpgsql;' ;
```

```
        EXECUTE func_cmd;
END;
$func$ LANGUAGE plpgsql;
```

Notice how the body of the function is built separately and passed through `quote_literal` to double any quote marks in it. This technique is needed because we cannot safely use dollar quoting for defining the new function: we do not know for sure what strings will be interpolated from the `referrer_key.key_string` field. (We are assuming here that `referrer_key.kind` can be trusted to always be `host`, `domain`, or `url`, but `referrer_key.key_string` might be anything, in particular it might contain dollar signs.) This function is actually an improvement on the Oracle original, because it will not generate broken code when `referrer_key.key_string` or `referrer_key.referrer_type` contain quote marks.

Example 41-10 shows how to port a function with `OUT` parameters and string manipulation. PostgreSQL does not have a built-in `instr` function, but you can create one using a combination of other functions. In Section 41.12.3 there is a PL/pgSQL implementation of `instr` that you can use to make your porting easier.

Example 41-10. Porting a Procedure With String Manipulation and OUT Parameters from PL/SQL to PL/pgSQL

The following Oracle PL/SQL procedure is used to parse a URL and return several elements (host, path, and query).

This is the Oracle version:

```
CREATE OR REPLACE PROCEDURE cs_parse_url(
    v_url IN VARCHAR2,
    v_host OUT VARCHAR2,   -- This will be passed back
    v_path OUT VARCHAR2,   -- This one too
    v_query OUT VARCHAR2) -- And this one
IS
    a_pos1 INTEGER;
    a_pos2 INTEGER;
BEGIN
    v_host := NULL;
    v_path := NULL;
    v_query := NULL;
    a_pos1 := instr(v_url, '//');

    IF a_pos1 = 0 THEN
        RETURN;
    END IF;
    a_pos2 := instr(v_url, '/', a_pos1 + 2);
    IF a_pos2 = 0 THEN
        v_host := substr(v_url, a_pos1 + 2);
        v_path := '/';
        RETURN;
    END IF;

    v_host := substr(v_url, a_pos1 + 2, a_pos2 - a_pos1 - 2);
```

```
        a_pos1 := instr(v_url, '?', a_pos2 + 1);

        IF a_pos1 = 0 THEN
            v_path := substr(v_url, a_pos2);
            RETURN;
        END IF;

        v_path := substr(v_url, a_pos2, a_pos1 - a_pos2);
        v_query := substr(v_url, a_pos1 + 1);
END;
/
show errors;
```

Here is a possible translation into PL/pgSQL:

```
CREATE OR REPLACE FUNCTION cs_parse_url(
    v_url IN VARCHAR,
    v_host OUT VARCHAR,  -- This will be passed back
    v_path OUT VARCHAR,  -- This one too
    v_query OUT VARCHAR) -- And this one
AS $$
DECLARE
    a_pos1 INTEGER;
    a_pos2 INTEGER;
BEGIN
    v_host := NULL;
    v_path := NULL;
    v_query := NULL;
    a_pos1 := instr(v_url, '//');

    IF a_pos1 = 0 THEN
        RETURN;
    END IF;
    a_pos2 := instr(v_url, '/', a_pos1 + 2);
    IF a_pos2 = 0 THEN
        v_host := substr(v_url, a_pos1 + 2);
        v_path := '/';
        RETURN;
    END IF;

    v_host := substr(v_url, a_pos1 + 2, a_pos2 - a_pos1 - 2);
    a_pos1 := instr(v_url, '?', a_pos2 + 1);

    IF a_pos1 = 0 THEN
        v_path := substr(v_url, a_pos2);
        RETURN;
    END IF;

    v_path := substr(v_url, a_pos2, a_pos1 - a_pos2);
    v_query := substr(v_url, a_pos1 + 1);
END;
$$ LANGUAGE plpgsql;
```

This function could be used like this:

```
SELECT * FROM cs_parse_url('http://foobar.com/query.cgi?baz');
```

Example 41-11 shows how to port a procedure that uses numerous features that are specific to Oracle.

Example 41-11. Porting a Procedure from PL/SQL to PL/pgSQL

The Oracle version:

```
CREATE OR REPLACE PROCEDURE cs_create_job(v_job_id IN INTEGER) IS
    a_running_job_count INTEGER;
    PRAGMA AUTONOMOUS_TRANSACTION; ❶
BEGIN
    LOCK TABLE cs_jobs IN EXCLUSIVE MODE; ❷

    SELECT count(*) INTO a_running_job_count FROM cs_jobs WHERE end_stamp IS NULL;

    IF a_running_job_count > 0 THEN
        COMMIT; -- free lock❸
        raise_application_error(-20000,
                'Unable to create a new job: a job is currently running.');
    END IF;

    DELETE FROM cs_active_job;
    INSERT INTO cs_active_job(job_id) VALUES (v_job_id);

    BEGIN
        INSERT INTO cs_jobs (job_id, start_stamp) VALUES (v_job_id, sysdate);
    EXCEPTION
        WHEN dup_val_on_index THEN NULL; -- don't worry if it already exists
    END;
    COMMIT;
END;
/
show errors
```

Procedures like this can easily be converted into PostgreSQL functions returning `void`. This procedure in particular is interesting because it can teach us some things:

❶   There is no `PRAGMA` statement in PostgreSQL.

❷   If you do a `LOCK TABLE` in PL/pgSQL, the lock will not be released until the calling transaction is finished.

❸   You cannot issue `COMMIT` in a PL/pgSQL function. The function is running within some outer transaction and so `COMMIT` would imply terminating the function's execution. However, in this particular case it is not necessary anyway, because the lock obtained by the `LOCK TABLE` will be released when we raise an error.

This is how we could port this procedure to PL/pgSQL:

```
CREATE OR REPLACE FUNCTION cs_create_job(v_job_id integer) RETURNS void AS $$
DECLARE
    a_running_job_count integer;
BEGIN
```

```
    LOCK TABLE cs_jobs IN EXCLUSIVE MODE;

    SELECT count(*) INTO a_running_job_count FROM cs_jobs WHERE end_stamp IS NULL;

    IF a_running_job_count > 0 THEN
        RAISE EXCEPTION 'Unable to create a new job: a job is currently running';❶
    END IF;

    DELETE FROM cs_active_job;
    INSERT INTO cs_active_job(job_id) VALUES (v_job_id);

    BEGIN
        INSERT INTO cs_jobs (job_id, start_stamp) VALUES (v_job_id, now());
    EXCEPTION
        WHEN unique_violation THEN ❷
            -- don't worry if it already exists
    END;
END;
$$ LANGUAGE plpgsql;
```

❶   The syntax of RAISE is considerably different from Oracle's statement, although the basic case RAISE *exception_name* works similarly.

❷   The exception names supported by PL/pgSQL are different from Oracle's. The set of built-in exception names is much larger (see Appendix A). There is not currently a way to declare user-defined exception names, although you can throw user-chosen SQLSTATE values instead.

The main functional difference between this procedure and the Oracle equivalent is that the exclusive lock on the cs_jobs table will be held until the calling transaction completes. Also, if the caller later aborts (for example due to an error), the effects of this procedure will be rolled back.

41.12.2. Other Things to Watch For

This section explains a few other things to watch for when porting Oracle PL/SQL functions to PostgreSQL.

41.12.2.1. Implicit Rollback after Exceptions

In PL/pgSQL, when an exception is caught by an EXCEPTION clause, all database changes since the block's BEGIN are automatically rolled back. That is, the behavior is equivalent to what you'd get in Oracle with:

```
BEGIN
    SAVEPOINT s1;
    ... code here ...
EXCEPTION
    WHEN ... THEN
        ROLLBACK TO s1;
        ... code here ...
    WHEN ... THEN
```

```
        ROLLBACK TO s1;
        ... code here ...
END;
```

If you are translating an Oracle procedure that uses SAVEPOINT and ROLLBACK TO in this style, your task is easy: just omit the SAVEPOINT and ROLLBACK TO. If you have a procedure that uses SAVEPOINT and ROLLBACK TO in a different way then some actual thought will be required.

41.12.2.2. EXECUTE

The PL/pgSQL version of EXECUTE works similarly to the PL/SQL version, but you have to remember to use quote_literal and quote_ident as described in Section 41.5.4. Constructs of the type EXECUTE 'SELECT * FROM $1'; will not work reliably unless you use these functions.

41.12.2.3. Optimizing PL/pgSQL Functions

PostgreSQL gives you two function creation modifiers to optimize execution: "volatility" (whether the function always returns the same result when given the same arguments) and "strictness" (whether the function returns null if any argument is null). Consult the CREATE FUNCTION reference page for details.

When making use of these optimization attributes, your CREATE FUNCTION statement might look something like this:

```
CREATE FUNCTION foo(...) RETURNS integer AS $$
...
$$ LANGUAGE plpgsql STRICT IMMUTABLE;
```

41.12.3. Appendix

This section contains the code for a set of Oracle-compatible instr functions that you can use to simplify your porting efforts.

```
--
-- instr functions that mimic Oracle's counterpart
-- Syntax: instr(string1, string2, [n], [m]) where [] denotes optional parameters.
--
-- Searches string1 beginning at the nth character for the mth occurrence
-- of string2.  If n is negative, search backwards.  If m is not passed,
-- assume 1 (search starts at first character).
--

CREATE FUNCTION instr(varchar, varchar) RETURNS integer AS $$
DECLARE
    pos integer;
BEGIN
    pos:= instr($1, $2, 1);
```

```
        RETURN pos;
END;
$$ LANGUAGE plpgsql STRICT IMMUTABLE;


CREATE FUNCTION instr(string varchar, string_to_search varchar, beg_index integer)
RETURNS integer AS $$
DECLARE
    pos integer NOT NULL DEFAULT 0;
    temp_str varchar;
    beg integer;
    length integer;
    ss_length integer;
BEGIN
    IF beg_index > 0 THEN
        temp_str := substring(string FROM beg_index);
        pos := position(string_to_search IN temp_str);

        IF pos = 0 THEN
            RETURN 0;
        ELSE
            RETURN pos + beg_index - 1;
        END IF;
    ELSIF beg_index < 0 THEN
        ss_length := char_length(string_to_search);
        length := char_length(string);
        beg := length + beg_index - ss_length + 2;

        WHILE beg > 0 LOOP
            temp_str := substring(string FROM beg FOR ss_length);
            pos := position(string_to_search IN temp_str);

            IF pos > 0 THEN
                RETURN beg;
            END IF;

            beg := beg - 1;
        END LOOP;

        RETURN 0;
    ELSE
        RETURN 0;
    END IF;
END;
$$ LANGUAGE plpgsql STRICT IMMUTABLE;


CREATE FUNCTION instr(string varchar, string_to_search varchar,
                      beg_index integer, occur_index integer)
RETURNS integer AS $$
DECLARE
    pos integer NOT NULL DEFAULT 0;
    occur_number integer NOT NULL DEFAULT 0;
```

```
        temp_str varchar;
        beg integer;
        i integer;
        length integer;
        ss_length integer;
BEGIN
    IF beg_index > 0 THEN
        beg := beg_index;
        temp_str := substring(string FROM beg_index);

        FOR i IN 1..occur_index LOOP
            pos := position(string_to_search IN temp_str);

            IF i = 1 THEN
                beg := beg + pos - 1;
            ELSE
                beg := beg + pos;
            END IF;

            temp_str := substring(string FROM beg + 1);
        END LOOP;

        IF pos = 0 THEN
            RETURN 0;
        ELSE
            RETURN beg;
        END IF;
    ELSIF beg_index < 0 THEN
        ss_length := char_length(string_to_search);
        length := char_length(string);
        beg := length + beg_index - ss_length + 2;

        WHILE beg > 0 LOOP
            temp_str := substring(string FROM beg FOR ss_length);
            pos := position(string_to_search IN temp_str);

            IF pos > 0 THEN
                occur_number := occur_number + 1;

                IF occur_number = occur_index THEN
                    RETURN beg;
                END IF;
            END IF;

            beg := beg - 1;
        END LOOP;

        RETURN 0;
    ELSE
        RETURN 0;
    END IF;
END;
$$ LANGUAGE plpgsql STRICT IMMUTABLE;
```

Chapter 42. PL/Tcl - Tcl Procedural Language

PL/Tcl is a loadable procedural language for the PostgreSQL database system that enables the Tcl language[1] to be used to write functions and trigger procedures.

42.1. Overview

PL/Tcl offers most of the capabilities a function writer has in the C language, with a few restrictions, and with the addition of the powerful string processing libraries that are available for Tcl.

One compelling *good* restriction is that everything is executed from within the safety of the context of a Tcl interpreter. In addition to the limited command set of safe Tcl, only a few commands are available to access the database via SPI and to raise messages via `elog()`. PL/Tcl provides no way to access internals of the database server or to gain OS-level access under the permissions of the PostgreSQL server process, as a C function can do. Thus, unprivileged database users can be trusted to use this language; it does not give them unlimited authority.

The other notable implementation restriction is that Tcl functions cannot be used to create input/output functions for new data types.

Sometimes it is desirable to write Tcl functions that are not restricted to safe Tcl. For example, one might want a Tcl function that sends email. To handle these cases, there is a variant of PL/Tcl called `PL/TclU` (for untrusted Tcl). This is exactly the same language except that a full Tcl interpreter is used. *If PL/TclU is used, it must be installed as an untrusted procedural language* so that only database superusers can create functions in it. The writer of a PL/TclU function must take care that the function cannot be used to do anything unwanted, since it will be able to do anything that could be done by a user logged in as the database administrator.

The shared object code for the PL/Tcl and PL/TclU call handlers is automatically built and installed in the PostgreSQL library directory if Tcl support is specified in the configuration step of the installation procedure. To install PL/Tcl and/or PL/TclU in a particular database, use the `CREATE EXTENSION` command or the `createlang` program, for example `createlang pltcl` *dbname* or `createlang pltclu` *dbname*.

42.2. PL/Tcl Functions and Arguments

To create a function in the PL/Tcl language, use the standard CREATE FUNCTION syntax:

```
CREATE FUNCTION funcname (argument-types) RETURNS return-type AS $$
    # PL/Tcl function body
$$ LANGUAGE pltcl;
```

PL/TclU is the same, except that the language has to be specified as `pltclu`.

The body of the function is simply a piece of Tcl script. When the function is called, the argument values are passed as variables `$1` ... `$n` to the Tcl script. The result is returned from the Tcl code in the usual way, with a `return` statement.

---

1. http://www.tcl.tk/

For example, a function returning the greater of two integer values could be defined as:

```
CREATE FUNCTION tcl_max(integer, integer) RETURNS integer AS $$
    if {$1 > $2} {return $1}
    return $2
$$ LANGUAGE pltcl STRICT;
```

Note the clause STRICT, which saves us from having to think about null input values: if a null value is passed, the function will not be called at all, but will just return a null result automatically.

In a nonstrict function, if the actual value of an argument is null, the corresponding $n variable will be set to an empty string. To detect whether a particular argument is null, use the function argisnull. For example, suppose that we wanted tcl_max with one null and one nonnull argument to return the nonnull argument, rather than null:

```
CREATE FUNCTION tcl_max(integer, integer) RETURNS integer AS $$
    if {[argisnull 1]} {
        if {[argisnull 2]} { return_null }
        return $2
    }
    if {[argisnull 2]} { return $1 }
    if {$1 > $2} {return $1}
    return $2
$$ LANGUAGE pltcl;
```

As shown above, to return a null value from a PL/Tcl function, execute return_null. This can be done whether the function is strict or not.

Composite-type arguments are passed to the function as Tcl arrays. The element names of the array are the attribute names of the composite type. If an attribute in the passed row has the null value, it will not appear in the array. Here is an example:

```
CREATE TABLE employee (
    name text,
    salary integer,
    age integer
);

CREATE FUNCTION overpaid(employee) RETURNS boolean AS $$
    if {200000.0 < $1(salary)} {
        return "t"
    }
    if {$1(age) < 30 && 100000.0 < $1(salary)} {
        return "t"
    }
    return "f"
$$ LANGUAGE pltcl;
```

There is currently no support for returning a composite-type result value, nor for returning sets.

PL/Tcl does not currently have full support for domain types: it treats a domain the same as the underlying scalar type. This means that constraints associated with the domain will not be enforced. This is not an issue for function arguments, but it is a hazard if you declare a PL/Tcl function as returning a domain type.

42.3. Data Values in PL/Tcl

The argument values supplied to a PL/Tcl function's code are simply the input arguments converted to text form (just as if they had been displayed by a SELECT statement). Conversely, the return command will accept any string that is acceptable input format for the function's declared return type. So, within the PL/Tcl function, all values are just text strings.

42.4. Global Data in PL/Tcl

Sometimes it is useful to have some global data that is held between two calls to a function or is shared between different functions. This is easily done in PL/Tcl, but there are some restrictions that must be understood.

For security reasons, PL/Tcl executes functions called by any one SQL role in a separate Tcl interpreter for that role. This prevents accidental or malicious interference by one user with the behavior of another user's PL/Tcl functions. Each such interpreter will have its own values for any "global" Tcl variables. Thus, two PL/Tcl functions will share the same global variables if and only if they are executed by the same SQL role. In an application wherein a single session executes code under multiple SQL roles (via SECURITY DEFINER functions, use of SET ROLE, etc) you may need to take explicit steps to ensure that PL/Tcl functions can share data. To do that, make sure that functions that should communicate are owned by the same user, and mark them SECURITY DEFINER. You must of course take care that such functions can't be used to do anything unintended.

All PL/TclU functions used in a session execute in the same Tcl interpreter, which of course is distinct from the interpreter(s) used for PL/Tcl functions. So global data is automatically shared between PL/TclU functions. This is not considered a security risk because all PL/TclU functions execute at the same trust level, namely that of a database superuser.

To help protect PL/Tcl functions from unintentionally interfering with each other, a global array is made available to each function via the upvar command. The global name of this variable is the function's internal name, and the local name is GD. It is recommended that GD be used for persistent private data of a function. Use regular Tcl global variables only for values that you specifically intend to be shared among multiple functions. (Note that the GD arrays are only global within a particular interpreter, so they do not bypass the security restrictions mentioned above.)

An example of using GD appears in the spi_execp example below.

42.5. Database Access from PL/Tcl

The following commands are available to access the database from the body of a PL/Tcl function:

`spi_exec ?-count n? ?-array name? command ?loop-body?`

> Executes an SQL command given as a string. An error in the command causes an error to be raised. Otherwise, the return value of `spi_exec` is the number of rows processed (selected, inserted, updated, or deleted) by the command, or zero if the command is a utility statement. In addition, if the command is a SELECT statement, the values of the selected columns are placed in Tcl variables as described below.
>
> The optional `-count` value tells `spi_exec` the maximum number of rows to process in the command. The effect of this is comparable to setting up a query as a cursor and then saying FETCH *n*.
>
> If the command is a SELECT statement, the values of the result columns are placed into Tcl variables named after the columns. If the `-array` option is given, the column values are instead stored into the named associative array, with the column names used as array indexes.
>
> If the command is a SELECT statement and no *loop-body* script is given, then only the first row of results are stored into Tcl variables; remaining rows, if any, are ignored. No storing occurs if the query returns no rows. (This case can be detected by checking the result of `spi_exec`.) For example:
>
> `spi_exec "SELECT count(*) AS cnt FROM pg_proc"`
> will set the Tcl variable `$cnt` to the number of rows in the `pg_proc` system catalog.
>
> If the optional *loop-body* argument is given, it is a piece of Tcl script that is executed once for each row in the query result. (*loop-body* is ignored if the given command is not a SELECT.) The values of the current row's columns are stored into Tcl variables before each iteration. For example:
>
> ```
> spi_exec -array C "SELECT * FROM pg_class" {
>     elog DEBUG "have table $C(relname)"
> }
> ```
> will print a log message for every row of `pg_class`. This feature works similarly to other Tcl looping constructs; in particular `continue` and `break` work in the usual way inside the loop body.
>
> If a column of a query result is null, the target variable for it is "unset" rather than being set.

`spi_prepare query typelist`

> Prepares and saves a query plan for later execution. The saved plan will be retained for the life of the current session.
>
> The query can use parameters, that is, placeholders for values to be supplied whenever the plan is actually executed. In the query string, refer to parameters by the symbols `$1` ... `$n`. If the query uses parameters, the names of the parameter types must be given as a Tcl list. (Write an empty list for *typelist* if no parameters are used.)
>
> The return value from `spi_prepare` is a query ID to be used in subsequent calls to `spi_execp`. See `spi_execp` for an example.

`spi_execp ?-count n? ?-array name? ?-nulls string? queryid ?value-list?`
`?loop-body?`

> Executes a query previously prepared with `spi_prepare`. *queryid* is the ID returned by `spi_prepare`. If the query references parameters, a *value-list* must be supplied. This is a Tcl

list of actual values for the parameters. The list must be the same length as the parameter type list previously given to `spi_prepare`. Omit *value-list* if the query has no parameters.

The optional value for `-nulls` is a string of spaces and ′n′ characters telling `spi_execp` which of the parameters are null values. If given, it must have exactly the same length as the *value-list*. If it is not given, all the parameter values are nonnull.

Except for the way in which the query and its parameters are specified, `spi_execp` works just like `spi_exec`. The -count, -array, and *loop-body* options are the same, and so is the result value.

Here's an example of a PL/Tcl function using a prepared plan:

```
CREATE FUNCTION t1_count(integer, integer) RETURNS integer AS $$
    if {![ info exists GD(plan) ]} {
        # prepare the saved plan on the first call
        set GD(plan) [ spi_prepare \
                "SELECT count(*) AS cnt FROM t1 WHERE num >= \$1 AND num <= \$2" \
                [ list int4 int4 ] ]
    }
    spi_execp -count 1 $GD(plan) [ list $1 $2 ]
    return $cnt
$$ LANGUAGE pltcl;
```

We need backslashes inside the query string given to `spi_prepare` to ensure that the $*n* markers will be passed through to `spi_prepare` as-is, and not replaced by Tcl variable substitution.

`spi_lastoid`

    Returns the OID of the row inserted by the last `spi_exec` or `spi_execp`, if the command was a single-row INSERT and the modified table contained OIDs. (If not, you get zero.)

`quote` *string*

    Doubles all occurrences of single quote and backslash characters in the given string. This can be used to safely quote strings that are to be inserted into SQL commands given to `spi_exec` or `spi_prepare`. For example, think about an SQL command string like:

```
"SELECT '$val' AS ret"
```

where the Tcl variable `val` actually contains `doesn't`. This would result in the final command string:

```
SELECT 'doesn't' AS ret
```

which would cause a parse error during `spi_exec` or `spi_prepare`. To work properly, the submitted command should contain:

```
SELECT 'doesn''t' AS ret
```

which can be formed in PL/Tcl using:

```
"SELECT '[ quote $val ]' AS ret"
```

One advantage of `spi_execp` is that you don't have to quote parameter values like this, since the parameters are never parsed as part of an SQL command string.

`elog` *level msg*

    Emits a log or error message. Possible levels are DEBUG, LOG, INFO, NOTICE, WARNING, ERROR, and FATAL. ERROR raises an error condition; if this is not trapped by the surrounding Tcl code, the error propagates out to the calling query, causing the current transaction or subtransaction to be aborted. This is effectively the same as the Tcl `error` command. FATAL aborts the transaction and causes the current session to shut down. (There is probably no good reason to use this error level in PL/Tcl functions, but it's provided for completeness.) The other levels only generate messages of different priority levels. Whether messages of a particular priority are reported to the client, written to the server log, or both is controlled by the log_min_messages and client_min_messages configuration variables. See Chapter 19 and Section 42.8 for more information.

42.6. Trigger Procedures in PL/Tcl

Trigger procedures can be written in PL/Tcl. PostgreSQL requires that a procedure that is to be called as a trigger must be declared as a function with no arguments and a return type of `trigger`.

The information from the trigger manager is passed to the procedure body in the following variables:

`$TG_name`

> The name of the trigger from the CREATE TRIGGER statement.

`$TG_relid`

> The object ID of the table that caused the trigger procedure to be invoked.

`$TG_table_name`

> The name of the table that caused the trigger procedure to be invoked.

`$TG_table_schema`

> The schema of the table that caused the trigger procedure to be invoked.

`$TG_relatts`

> A Tcl list of the table column names, prefixed with an empty list element. So looking up a column name in the list with Tcl's `lsearch` command returns the element's number starting with 1 for the first column, the same way the columns are customarily numbered in PostgreSQL. (Empty list elements also appear in the positions of columns that have been dropped, so that the attribute numbering is correct for columns to their right.)

`$TG_when`

> The string BEFORE, AFTER, or INSTEAD OF, depending on the type of trigger event.

`$TG_level`

> The string ROW or STATEMENT depending on the type of trigger event.

`$TG_op`

> The string INSERT, UPDATE, DELETE, or TRUNCATE depending on the type of trigger event.

`$NEW`

> An associative array containing the values of the new table row for INSERT or UPDATE actions, or empty for DELETE. The array is indexed by column name. Columns that are null will not appear in the array. This is not set for statement-level triggers.

$OLD

> An associative array containing the values of the old table row for UPDATE or DELETE actions, or
> empty for INSERT. The array is indexed by column name. Columns that are null will not appear in
> the array. This is not set for statement-level triggers.

$args

> A Tcl list of the arguments to the procedure as given in the CREATE TRIGGER statement. These
> arguments are also accessible as $1 ... $n in the procedure body.

The return value from a trigger procedure can be one of the strings OK or SKIP, or a list as returned by the
array get Tcl command. If the return value is OK, the operation (INSERT/UPDATE/DELETE) that fired
the trigger will proceed normally. SKIP tells the trigger manager to silently suppress the operation for
this row. If a list is returned, it tells PL/Tcl to return a modified row to the trigger manager. This is only
meaningful for row-level BEFORE INSERT or UPDATE triggers for which the modified row will be inserted
instead of the one given in $NEW; or for row-level INSTEAD OF INSERT or UPDATE triggers where the
returned row is used to support INSERT RETURNING and UPDATE RETURNING commands. The return
value is ignored for other types of triggers.

Here's a little example trigger procedure that forces an integer value in a table to keep track of the number
of updates that are performed on the row. For new rows inserted, the value is initialized to 0 and then
incremented on every update operation.

```
CREATE FUNCTION trigfunc_modcount() RETURNS trigger AS $$
    switch $TG_op {
        INSERT {
            set NEW($1) 0
        }
        UPDATE {
            set NEW($1) $OLD($1)
            incr NEW($1)
        }
        default {
            return OK
        }
    }
    return [array get NEW]
$$ LANGUAGE pltcl;

CREATE TABLE mytab (num integer, description text, modcnt integer);

CREATE TRIGGER trig_mytab_modcount BEFORE INSERT OR UPDATE ON mytab
    FOR EACH ROW EXECUTE PROCEDURE trigfunc_modcount('modcnt');
```

Notice that the trigger procedure itself does not know the column name; that's supplied from the trigger
arguments. This lets the trigger procedure be reused with different tables.

42.7. Event Trigger Procedures in PL/Tcl

Event trigger procedures can be written in PL/Tcl. PostgreSQL requires that a procedure that is to be called as an event trigger must be declared as a function with no arguments and a return type of `event_trigger`.

The information from the trigger manager is passed to the procedure body in the following variables:

`$TG_event`

> The name of the event the trigger is fired for.

`$TG_tag`

> The command tag for which the trigger is fired.

The return value of the trigger procedure is ignored.

Here's a little example event trigger procedure that simply raises a `NOTICE` message each time a supported command is executed:

```
CREATE OR REPLACE FUNCTION tclsnitch() RETURNS event_trigger AS $$
  elog NOTICE "tclsnitch: $TG_event $TG_tag"
$$ LANGUAGE pltcl;

CREATE EVENT TRIGGER tcl_a_snitch ON ddl_command_start EXECUTE PROCEDURE tclsnitch()
```

42.8. Error Handling in PL/Tcl

Tcl code within or called from a PL/Tcl function can raise an error, either by executing some invalid operation or by generating an error using the Tcl `error` command or PL/Tcl's `elog` command. Such errors can be caught within Tcl using the Tcl `catch` command. If they are not caught but are allowed to propagate out to the top level of execution of the PL/Tcl function, they turn into database errors.

Conversely, database errors that occur within PL/Tcl's `spi_exec`, `spi_prepare`, and `spi_execp` commands are reported as Tcl errors, so they are catchable by Tcl's `catch` command. Again, if they propagate out to the top level without being caught, they turn back into database errors.

Tcl provides an `errorCode` variable that can represent additional information about an error in a form that is easy for Tcl programs to interpret. The contents are in Tcl list format, and the first word identifies the subsystem or library reporting the error; beyond that the contents are left to the individual subsystem or library. For database errors reported by PL/Tcl commands, the first word is `POSTGRES`, the second word is the Postgres version number, and additional words are field name/value pairs providing detailed information about the error. Fields `SQLSTATE`, `condition`, and `message` are always supplied (the first two represent the error code and condition name as shown in Appendix A). Fields that may be present include `detail`, `hint`, `context`, `schema`, `table`, `column`, `datatype`, `constraint`, `statement`, `cursor_position`, `filename`, `lineno`, and `funcname`.

A convenient way to work with PL/Tcl's `errorCode` information is to load it into an array, so that the field names become array subscripts. Code for doing that might look like

```
if {[catch { spi_exec $sql_command }]} {
    if {[lindex $::errorCode 0] == "POSTGRES"} {
        array set errorArray $::errorCode
        if {$errorArray(condition) == "undefined_table"} {
            # deal with missing table
        } else {
            # deal with some other type of SQL error
        }
    }
}
```

(The double colons explicitly specify that errorCode is a global variable.)

42.9. Modules and the unknown Command

PL/Tcl has support for autoloading Tcl code when used. It recognizes a special table, pltcl_modules, which is presumed to contain modules of Tcl code. If this table exists, the module unknown is fetched from the table and loaded into the Tcl interpreter immediately before the first execution of a PL/Tcl function in a database session. (This happens separately for each Tcl interpreter, if more than one is used in a session; see Section 42.4.)

While the unknown module could actually contain any initialization script you need, it normally defines a Tcl unknown procedure that is invoked whenever Tcl does not recognize an invoked procedure name. PL/Tcl's standard version of this procedure tries to find a module in pltcl_modules that will define the required procedure. If one is found, it is loaded into the interpreter, and then execution is allowed to proceed with the originally attempted procedure call. A secondary table pltcl_modfuncs provides an index of which functions are defined by which modules, so that the lookup is reasonably quick.

The PostgreSQL distribution includes support scripts to maintain these tables: pltcl_loadmod, pltcl_listmod, pltcl_delmod, as well as source for the standard unknown module in share/unknown.pltcl. This module must be loaded into each database initially to support the autoloading mechanism.

The tables pltcl_modules and pltcl_modfuncs must be readable by all, but it is wise to make them owned and writable only by the database administrator. As a security precaution, PL/Tcl will ignore pltcl_modules (and thus, not attempt to load the unknown module) unless it is owned by a superuser. But update privileges on this table can be granted to other users, if you trust them sufficiently.

42.10. Tcl Procedure Names

In PostgreSQL, the same function name can be used for different function definitions as long as the number of arguments or their types differ. Tcl, however, requires all procedure names to be distinct. PL/Tcl deals with this by making the internal Tcl procedure names contain the object ID of the function from the system table pg_proc as part of their name. Thus, PostgreSQL functions with the same name and different argument types will be different Tcl procedures, too. This is not normally a concern for a PL/Tcl programmer, but it might be visible when debugging.

Chapter 43. PL/Perl - Perl Procedural Language

PL/Perl is a loadable procedural language that enables you to write PostgreSQL functions in the Perl programming language[1].

The main advantage to using PL/Perl is that this allows use, within stored functions, of the manyfold "string munging" operators and functions available for Perl. Parsing complex strings might be easier using Perl than it is with the string functions and control structures provided in PL/pgSQL.

To install PL/Perl in a particular database, use CREATE EXTENSION plperl, or from the shell command line use createlang plperl *dbname*.

> **Tip:** If a language is installed into `template1`, all subsequently created databases will have the language installed automatically.

> **Note:** Users of source packages must specially enable the build of PL/Perl during the installation process. (Refer to Chapter 16 for more information.) Users of binary packages might find PL/Perl in a separate subpackage.

43.1. PL/Perl Functions and Arguments

To create a function in the PL/Perl language, use the standard CREATE FUNCTION syntax:

```
CREATE FUNCTION funcname (argument-types) RETURNS return-type AS $$
    # PL/Perl function body
$$ LANGUAGE plperl;
```

The body of the function is ordinary Perl code. In fact, the PL/Perl glue code wraps it inside a Perl subroutine. A PL/Perl function is called in a scalar context, so it can't return a list. You can return non-scalar values (arrays, records, and sets) by returning a reference, as discussed below.

PL/Perl also supports anonymous code blocks called with the DO statement:

```
DO $$
    # PL/Perl code
$$ LANGUAGE plperl;
```

An anonymous code block receives no arguments, and whatever value it might return is discarded. Otherwise it behaves just like a function.

> **Note:** The use of named nested subroutines is dangerous in Perl, especially if they refer to lexical variables in the enclosing scope. Because a PL/Perl function is wrapped in a subroutine, any named subroutine you place inside one will be nested. In general, it is far safer to create anonymous subroutines which you call via a coderef. For more information, see the entries for `Variable "%s" will`

---

1. http://www.perl.org

not stay shared and Variable "%s" is not available in the perldiag man page, or search the Internet for "perl nested named subroutine".

The syntax of the CREATE FUNCTION command requires the function body to be written as a string constant. It is usually most convenient to use dollar quoting (see Section 4.1.2.4) for the string constant. If you choose to use escape string syntax E", you must double any single quote marks (') and backslashes (\) used in the body of the function (see Section 4.1.2.1).

Arguments and results are handled as in any other Perl subroutine: arguments are passed in @_, and a result value is returned with return or as the last expression evaluated in the function.

For example, a function returning the greater of two integer values could be defined as:

```
CREATE FUNCTION perl_max (integer, integer) RETURNS integer AS $$
    if ($_[0] > $_[1]) { return $_[0]; }
    return $_[1];
$$ LANGUAGE plperl;
```

> **Note:** Arguments will be converted from the database's encoding to UTF-8 for use inside PL/Perl, and then converted from UTF-8 back to the database encoding upon return.

If an SQL null value is passed to a function, the argument value will appear as "undefined" in Perl. The above function definition will not behave very nicely with null inputs (in fact, it will act as though they are zeroes). We could add STRICT to the function definition to make PostgreSQL do something more reasonable: if a null value is passed, the function will not be called at all, but will just return a null result automatically. Alternatively, we could check for undefined inputs in the function body. For example, suppose that we wanted perl_max with one null and one nonnull argument to return the nonnull argument, rather than a null value:

```
CREATE FUNCTION perl_max (integer, integer) RETURNS integer AS $$
    my ($x, $y) = @_;
    if (not defined $x) {
        return undef if not defined $y;
        return $y;
    }
    return $x if not defined $y;
    return $x if $x > $y;
    return $y;
$$ LANGUAGE plperl;
```

As shown above, to return an SQL null value from a PL/Perl function, return an undefined value. This can be done whether the function is strict or not.

Anything in a function argument that is not a reference is a string, which is in the standard PostgreSQL external text representation for the relevant data type. In the case of ordinary numeric or text types, Perl will just do the right thing and the programmer will normally not have to worry about it. However, in other cases the argument will need to be converted into a form that is more usable in Perl. For example, the decode_bytea function can be used to convert an argument of type bytea into unescaped binary.

Similarly, values passed back to PostgreSQL must be in the external text representation format. For example, the `encode_bytea` function can be used to escape binary data for a return value of type `bytea`.

Perl can return PostgreSQL arrays as references to Perl arrays. Here is an example:

```
CREATE OR REPLACE function returns_array()
RETURNS text[][] AS $$
    return [['a"b','c,d'],['e\\f','g']];
$$ LANGUAGE plperl;

select returns_array();
```

Perl passes PostgreSQL arrays as a blessed `PostgreSQL::InServer::ARRAY` object. This object may be treated as an array reference or a string, allowing for backward compatibility with Perl code written for PostgreSQL versions below 9.1 to run. For example:

```
CREATE OR REPLACE FUNCTION concat_array_elements(text[]) RETURNS TEXT AS $$
    my $arg = shift;
    my $result = "";
    return undef if (!defined $arg);

    # as an array reference
    for (@$arg) {
        $result .= $_;
    }

    # also works as a string
    $result .= $arg;

    return $result;
$$ LANGUAGE plperl;

SELECT concat_array_elements(ARRAY['PL','/','Perl']);
```

> **Note:** Multidimensional arrays are represented as references to lower-dimensional arrays of references in a way common to every Perl programmer.

Composite-type arguments are passed to the function as references to hashes. The keys of the hash are the attribute names of the composite type. Here is an example:

```
CREATE TABLE employee (
    name text,
    basesalary integer,
    bonus integer
);

CREATE FUNCTION empcomp(employee) RETURNS integer AS $$
    my ($emp) = @_;
```

```
        return $emp->{basesalary} + $emp->{bonus};
$$ LANGUAGE plperl;


SELECT name, empcomp(employee.*) FROM employee;
```

A PL/Perl function can return a composite-type result using the same approach: return a reference to a hash that has the required attributes. For example:

```
CREATE TYPE testrowperl AS (f1 integer, f2 text, f3 text);

CREATE OR REPLACE FUNCTION perl_row() RETURNS testrowperl AS $$
    return {f2 => 'hello', f1 => 1, f3 => 'world'};
$$ LANGUAGE plperl;


SELECT * FROM perl_row();
```

Any columns in the declared result data type that are not present in the hash will be returned as null values.

PL/Perl functions can also return sets of either scalar or composite types. Usually you'll want to return rows one at a time, both to speed up startup time and to keep from queuing up the entire result set in memory. You can do this with return_next as illustrated below. Note that after the last return_next, you must put either return or (better) return undef.

```
CREATE OR REPLACE FUNCTION perl_set_int(int)
RETURNS SETOF INTEGER AS $$
    foreach (0..$_[0]) {
        return_next($_);
    }
    return undef;
$$ LANGUAGE plperl;


SELECT * FROM perl_set_int(5);

CREATE OR REPLACE FUNCTION perl_set()
RETURNS SETOF testrowperl AS $$
    return_next({ f1 => 1, f2 => 'Hello', f3 => 'World' });
    return_next({ f1 => 2, f2 => 'Hello', f3 => 'PostgreSQL' });
    return_next({ f1 => 3, f2 => 'Hello', f3 => 'PL/Perl' });
    return undef;
$$ LANGUAGE plperl;
```

For small result sets, you can return a reference to an array that contains either scalars, references to arrays, or references to hashes for simple types, array types, and composite types, respectively. Here are some simple examples of returning the entire result set as an array reference:

```
CREATE OR REPLACE FUNCTION perl_set_int(int) RETURNS SETOF INTEGER AS $$
    return [0..$_[0]];
$$ LANGUAGE plperl;


SELECT * FROM perl_set_int(5);


CREATE OR REPLACE FUNCTION perl_set() RETURNS SETOF testrowperl AS $$
```

```
        return [
            { f1 => 1, f2 => 'Hello', f3 => 'World' },
            { f1 => 2, f2 => 'Hello', f3 => 'PostgreSQL' },
            { f1 => 3, f2 => 'Hello', f3 => 'PL/Perl' }
        ];
$$ LANGUAGE plperl;

SELECT * FROM perl_set();
```

If you wish to use the `strict` pragma with your code you have a few options. For temporary global use you can `SET plperl.use_strict` to true. This will affect subsequent compilations of PL/Perl functions, but not functions already compiled in the current session. For permanent global use you can set `plperl.use_strict` to true in the `postgresql.conf` file.

For permanent use in specific functions you can simply put:

```
use strict;
```

at the top of the function body.

The `feature` pragma is also available to `use` if your Perl is version 5.10.0 or higher.

43.2. Data Values in PL/Perl

The argument values supplied to a PL/Perl function's code are simply the input arguments converted to text form (just as if they had been displayed by a `SELECT` statement). Conversely, the `return` and `return_next` commands will accept any string that is acceptable input format for the function's declared return type.

43.3. Built-in Functions

43.3.1. Database Access from PL/Perl

Access to the database itself from your Perl function can be done via the following functions:

`spi_exec_query(`*query* `[, `*max-rows*`])`

> `spi_exec_query` executes an SQL command and returns the entire row set as a reference to an array of hash references. *You should only use this command when you know that the result set will be relatively small.* Here is an example of a query (`SELECT` command) with the optional maximum number of rows:
>
> `$rv = spi_exec_query('SELECT * FROM my_table', 5);`
> This returns up to 5 rows from the table `my_table`. If `my_table` has a column `my_column`, you can get that value from row `$i` of the result like this:
>
> `$foo = $rv->{rows}[$i]->{my_column};`

The total number of rows returned from a SELECT query can be accessed like this:

```
$nrows = $rv->{processed}
```

Here is an example using a different command type:

```
$query = "INSERT INTO my_table VALUES (1, 'test')";
$rv = spi_exec_query($query);
```

You can then access the command status (e.g., SPI_OK_INSERT) like this:

```
$res = $rv->{status};
```

To get the number of rows affected, do:

```
$nrows = $rv->{processed};
```

Here is a complete example:

```
CREATE TABLE test (
    i int,
    v varchar
);

INSERT INTO test (i, v) VALUES (1, 'first line');
INSERT INTO test (i, v) VALUES (2, 'second line');
INSERT INTO test (i, v) VALUES (3, 'third line');
INSERT INTO test (i, v) VALUES (4, 'immortal');

CREATE OR REPLACE FUNCTION test_munge() RETURNS SETOF test AS $$
    my $rv = spi_exec_query('select i, v from test;');
    my $status = $rv->{status};
    my $nrows = $rv->{processed};
    foreach my $rn (0 .. $nrows - 1) {
        my $row = $rv->{rows}[$rn];
        $row->{i} += 200 if defined($row->{i});
        $row->{v} =~ tr/A-Za-z/a-zA-Z/ if (defined($row->{v}));
        return_next($row);
    }
    return undef;
$$ LANGUAGE plperl;

SELECT * FROM test_munge();
```

```
spi_query(command)
spi_fetchrow(cursor)
spi_cursor_close(cursor)
```

spi_query and spi_fetchrow work together as a pair for row sets which might be large, or for cases where you wish to return rows as they arrive. spi_fetchrow works *only* with spi_query. The following example illustrates how you use them together:

```
CREATE TYPE foo_type AS (the_num INTEGER, the_text TEXT);

CREATE OR REPLACE FUNCTION lotsa_md5 (INTEGER) RETURNS SETOF foo_type AS $$
    use Digest::MD5 qw(md5_hex);
    my $file = '/usr/share/dict/words';
    my $t = localtime;
    elog(NOTICE, "opening file $file at $t" );
    open my $fh, '<', $file # ooh, it's a file access!
```

```
            or elog(ERROR, "cannot open $file for reading: $!");
    my @words = <$fh>;
    close $fh;
    $t = localtime;
    elog(NOTICE, "closed file $file at $t");
    chomp(@words);
    my $row;
    my $sth = spi_query("SELECT * FROM generate_series(1,$_[0]) AS b(a)");
    while (defined ($row = spi_fetchrow($sth))) {
        return_next({
            the_num => $row->{a},
            the_text => md5_hex($words[rand @words])
        });
    }
    return;
$$ LANGUAGE plperlu;


SELECT * from lotsa_md5(500);
```

Normally, `spi_fetchrow` should be repeated until it returns `undef`, indicating that there are no more rows to read. The cursor returned by `spi_query` is automatically freed when `spi_fetchrow` returns `undef`. If you do not wish to read all the rows, instead call `spi_cursor_close` to free the cursor. Failure to do so will result in memory leaks.

```
spi_prepare(command, argument types)
spi_query_prepared(plan, arguments)
spi_exec_prepared(plan [, attributes], arguments)
spi_freeplan(plan)
```

`spi_prepare`, `spi_query_prepared`, `spi_exec_prepared`, and `spi_freeplan` implement the same functionality but for prepared queries. `spi_prepare` accepts a query string with numbered argument placeholders ($1, $2, etc) and a string list of argument types:

```
$plan = spi_prepare('SELECT * FROM test WHERE id > $1 AND name = $2',
                                           'INTEGER', 'TEXT');
```

Once a query plan is prepared by a call to `spi_prepare`, the plan can be used instead of the string query, either in `spi_exec_prepared`, where the result is the same as returned by `spi_exec_query`, or in `spi_query_prepared` which returns a cursor exactly as `spi_query` does, which can be later passed to `spi_fetchrow`. The optional second parameter to `spi_exec_prepared` is a hash reference of attributes; the only attribute currently supported is `limit`, which sets the maximum number of rows returned by a query.

The advantage of prepared queries is that is it possible to use one prepared plan for more than one query execution. After the plan is not needed anymore, it can be freed with `spi_freeplan`:

```
CREATE OR REPLACE FUNCTION init() RETURNS VOID AS $$
        $_SHARED{my_plan} = spi_prepare('SELECT (now() + $1)::date AS now',
                                           'INTERVAL');
$$ LANGUAGE plperl;


CREATE OR REPLACE FUNCTION add_time( INTERVAL ) RETURNS TEXT AS $$
        return spi_exec_prepared(
                $_SHARED{my_plan},
                $_[0]
```

```
        )->{rows}->[0]->{now};
$$ LANGUAGE plperl;

CREATE OR REPLACE FUNCTION done() RETURNS VOID AS $$
        spi_freeplan( $_SHARED{my_plan});
        undef $_SHARED{my_plan};
$$ LANGUAGE plperl;

SELECT init();
SELECT add_time('1 day'), add_time('2 days'), add_time('3 days');
SELECT done();

  add_time  |  add_time  |  add_time
------------+------------+------------
 2005-12-10 | 2005-12-11 | 2005-12-12
```

Note that the parameter subscript in `spi_prepare` is defined via $1, $2, $3, etc, so avoid declaring query strings in double quotes that might easily lead to hard-to-catch bugs.

Another example illustrates usage of an optional parameter in `spi_exec_prepared`:

```
CREATE TABLE hosts AS SELECT id, ('192.168.1.'||id)::inet AS address
                    FROM generate_series(1,3) AS id;

CREATE OR REPLACE FUNCTION init_hosts_query() RETURNS VOID AS $$
        $_SHARED{plan} = spi_prepare('SELECT * FROM hosts
                                        WHERE address << $1', 'inet');
$$ LANGUAGE plperl;

CREATE OR REPLACE FUNCTION query_hosts(inet) RETURNS SETOF hosts AS $$
        return spi_exec_prepared(
                $_SHARED{plan},
                {limit => 2},
                $_[0]
        )->{rows};
$$ LANGUAGE plperl;

CREATE OR REPLACE FUNCTION release_hosts_query() RETURNS VOID AS $$
        spi_freeplan($_SHARED{plan});
        undef $_SHARED{plan};
$$ LANGUAGE plperl;

SELECT init_hosts_query();
SELECT query_hosts('192.168.1.0/30');
SELECT release_hosts_query();

    query_hosts
-----------------
 (1,192.168.1.1)
 (2,192.168.1.2)
(2 rows)
```

43.3.2. Utility Functions in PL/Perl

elog(*level*, *msg*)

> Emit a log or error message. Possible levels are DEBUG, LOG, INFO, NOTICE, WARNING, and ERROR. ERROR raises an error condition; if this is not trapped by the surrounding Perl code, the error propagates out to the calling query, causing the current transaction or subtransaction to be aborted. This is effectively the same as the Perl die command. The other levels only generate messages of different priority levels. Whether messages of a particular priority are reported to the client, written to the server log, or both is controlled by the log_min_messages and client_min_messages configuration variables. See Chapter 19 for more information.

quote_literal(*string*)

> Return the given string suitably quoted to be used as a string literal in an SQL statement string. Embedded single-quotes and backslashes are properly doubled. Note that quote_literal returns undef on undef input; if the argument might be undef, quote_nullable is often more suitable.

quote_nullable(*string*)

> Return the given string suitably quoted to be used as a string literal in an SQL statement string; or, if the argument is undef, return the unquoted string "NULL". Embedded single-quotes and backslashes are properly doubled.

quote_ident(*string*)

> Return the given string suitably quoted to be used as an identifier in an SQL statement string. Quotes are added only if necessary (i.e., if the string contains non-identifier characters or would be case-folded). Embedded quotes are properly doubled.

decode_bytea(*string*)

> Return the unescaped binary data represented by the contents of the given string, which should be bytea encoded.

encode_bytea(*string*)

> Return the bytea encoded form of the binary data contents of the given string.

encode_array_literal(*array*)
encode_array_literal(*array*, *delimiter*)

> Returns the contents of the referenced array as a string in array literal format (see Section 8.15.2). Returns the argument value unaltered if it's not a reference to an array. The delimiter used between elements of the array literal defaults to ", " if a delimiter is not specified or is undef.

encode_typed_literal(*value*, *typename*)

> Converts a Perl variable to the value of the data type passed as a second argument and returns a string representation of this value. Correctly handles nested arrays and values of composite types.

encode_array_constructor(*array*)

> Returns the contents of the referenced array as a string in array constructor format (see Section 4.2.12). Individual values are quoted using quote_nullable. Returns the argument value, quoted using quote_nullable, if it's not a reference to an array.

```
looks_like_number(string)
```

> Returns a true value if the content of the given string looks like a number, according to Perl, returns false otherwise. Returns undef if the argument is undef. Leading and trailing space is ignored. Inf and Infinity are regarded as numbers.

```
is_array_ref(argument)
```

> Returns a true value if the given argument may be treated as an array reference, that is, if ref of the argument is ARRAY or PostgreSQL::InServer::ARRAY. Returns false otherwise.

43.4. Global Values in PL/Perl

You can use the global hash %_SHARED to store data, including code references, between function calls for the lifetime of the current session.

Here is a simple example for shared data:

```
CREATE OR REPLACE FUNCTION set_var(name text, val text) RETURNS text AS $$
    if ($_SHARED{$_[0]} = $_[1]) {
        return 'ok';
    } else {
        return "cannot set shared variable $_[0] to $_[1]";
    }
$$ LANGUAGE plperl;

CREATE OR REPLACE FUNCTION get_var(name text) RETURNS text AS $$
    return $_SHARED{$_[0]};
$$ LANGUAGE plperl;

SELECT set_var('sample', 'Hello, PL/Perl!  How"s tricks?');
SELECT get_var('sample');
```

Here is a slightly more complicated example using a code reference:

```
CREATE OR REPLACE FUNCTION myfuncs() RETURNS void AS $$
    $_SHARED{myquote} = sub {
        my $arg = shift;
        $arg =~ s/(['\\])/\\$1/g;
        return "'$arg'";
    };
$$ LANGUAGE plperl;

SELECT myfuncs(); /* initializes the function */

/* Set up a function that uses the quote function */

CREATE OR REPLACE FUNCTION use_quote(TEXT) RETURNS text AS $$
    my $text_to_quote = shift;
    my $qfunc = $_SHARED{myquote};
```

```
    return &$qfunc($text_to_quote);
$$ LANGUAGE plperl;
```

(You could have replaced the above with the one-liner `return $_SHARED{myquote}->($_[0]);` at the expense of readability.)

For security reasons, PL/Perl executes functions called by any one SQL role in a separate Perl interpreter for that role. This prevents accidental or malicious interference by one user with the behavior of another user's PL/Perl functions. Each such interpreter has its own value of the `%_SHARED` variable and other global state. Thus, two PL/Perl functions will share the same value of `%_SHARED` if and only if they are executed by the same SQL role. In an application wherein a single session executes code under multiple SQL roles (via `SECURITY DEFINER` functions, use of `SET ROLE`, etc) you may need to take explicit steps to ensure that PL/Perl functions can share data via `%_SHARED`. To do that, make sure that functions that should communicate are owned by the same user, and mark them `SECURITY DEFINER`. You must of course take care that such functions can't be used to do anything unintended.

43.5. Trusted and Untrusted PL/Perl

Normally, PL/Perl is installed as a "trusted" programming language named `plperl`. In this setup, certain Perl operations are disabled to preserve security. In general, the operations that are restricted are those that interact with the environment. This includes file handle operations, `require`, and `use` (for external modules). There is no way to access internals of the database server process or to gain OS-level access with the permissions of the server process, as a C function can do. Thus, any unprivileged database user can be permitted to use this language.

Here is an example of a function that will not work because file system operations are not allowed for security reasons:

```
CREATE FUNCTION badfunc() RETURNS integer AS $$
    my $tmpfile = "/tmp/badfile";
    open my $fh, '>', $tmpfile
        or elog(ERROR, qq{could not open the file "$tmpfile": $!});
    print $fh "Testing writing to a file\n";
    close $fh or elog(ERROR, qq{could not close the file "$tmpfile": $!});
    return 1;
$$ LANGUAGE plperl;
```

The creation of this function will fail as its use of a forbidden operation will be caught by the validator.

Sometimes it is desirable to write Perl functions that are not restricted. For example, one might want a Perl function that sends mail. To handle these cases, PL/Perl can also be installed as an "untrusted" language (usually called PL/PerlU). In this case the full Perl language is available. When installing the language, the language name `plperlu` will select the untrusted PL/Perl variant.

The writer of a PL/PerlU function must take care that the function cannot be used to do anything unwanted, since it will be able to do anything that could be done by a user logged in as the database administrator. Note that the database system allows only database superusers to create functions in untrusted languages.

If the above function was created by a superuser using the language `plperlu`, execution would succeed.

In the same way, anonymous code blocks written in Perl can use restricted operations if the language is specified as `plperlu` rather than `plperl`, but the caller must be a superuser.

> **Note:** While PL/Perl functions run in a separate Perl interpreter for each SQL role, all PL/PerlU functions executed in a given session run in a single Perl interpreter (which is not any of the ones used for PL/Perl functions). This allows PL/PerlU functions to share data freely, but no communication can occur between PL/Perl and PL/PerlU functions.

> **Note:** Perl cannot support multiple interpreters within one process unless it was built with the appropriate flags, namely either `usemultiplicity` or `useithreads`. (`usemultiplicity` is preferred unless you actually need to use threads. For more details, see the perlembed man page.) If PL/Perl is used with a copy of Perl that was not built this way, then it is only possible to have one Perl interpreter per session, and so any one session can only execute either PL/PerlU functions, or PL/Perl functions that are all called by the same SQL role.

43.6. PL/Perl Triggers

PL/Perl can be used to write trigger functions. In a trigger function, the hash reference `$_TD` contains information about the current trigger event. `$_TD` is a global variable, which gets a separate local value for each invocation of the trigger. The fields of the `$_TD` hash reference are:

`$_TD->{new}{foo}`

    `NEW` value of column `foo`

`$_TD->{old}{foo}`

    `OLD` value of column `foo`

`$_TD->{name}`

    Name of the trigger being called

`$_TD->{event}`

    Trigger event: `INSERT`, `UPDATE`, `DELETE`, `TRUNCATE`, or `UNKNOWN`

`$_TD->{when}`

    When the trigger was called: `BEFORE`, `AFTER`, `INSTEAD OF`, or `UNKNOWN`

`$_TD->{level}`

    The trigger level: `ROW`, `STATEMENT`, or `UNKNOWN`

`$_TD->{relid}`

    OID of the table on which the trigger fired

`$_TD->{table_name}`

    Name of the table on which the trigger fired

`$_TD->{relname}`

Name of the table on which the trigger fired. This has been deprecated, and could be removed in a future release. Please use $_TD->{table_name} instead.

`$_TD->{table_schema}`

Name of the schema in which the table on which the trigger fired, is

`$_TD->{argc}`

Number of arguments of the trigger function

`@{$_TD->{args}}`

Arguments of the trigger function. Does not exist if `$_TD->{argc}` is 0.

Row-level triggers can return one of the following:

`return;`

Execute the operation

`"SKIP"`

Don't execute the operation

`"MODIFY"`

Indicates that the NEW row was modified by the trigger function

Here is an example of a trigger function, illustrating some of the above:

```
CREATE TABLE test (
    i int,
    v varchar
);

CREATE OR REPLACE FUNCTION valid_id() RETURNS trigger AS $$
    if (($_TD->{new}{i} >= 100) || ($_TD->{new}{i} <= 0)) {
        return "SKIP";    # skip INSERT/UPDATE command
    } elsif ($_TD->{new}{v} ne "immortal") {
        $_TD->{new}{v} .= "(modified by trigger)";
        return "MODIFY";  # modify row and execute INSERT/UPDATE command
    } else {
        return;           # execute INSERT/UPDATE command
    }
$$ LANGUAGE plperl;

CREATE TRIGGER test_valid_id_trig
    BEFORE INSERT OR UPDATE ON test
    FOR EACH ROW EXECUTE PROCEDURE valid_id();
```

43.7. PL/Perl Event Triggers

PL/Perl can be used to write event trigger functions. In an event trigger function, the hash reference `$_TD` contains information about the current trigger event. `$_TD` is a global variable, which gets a separate local value for each invocation of the trigger. The fields of the `$_TD` hash reference are:

`$_TD->{event}`

> The name of the event the trigger is fired for.

`$_TD->{tag}`

> The command tag for which the trigger is fired.

The return value of the trigger procedure is ignored.

Here is an example of an event trigger function, illustrating some of the above:

```
CREATE OR REPLACE FUNCTION perlsnitch() RETURNS event_trigger AS $$
  elog(NOTICE, "perlsnitch: " . $_TD->{event} . " " . $_TD->{tag} . " ");
$$ LANGUAGE plperl;

CREATE EVENT TRIGGER perl_a_snitch
    ON ddl_command_start
    EXECUTE PROCEDURE perlsnitch();
```

43.8. PL/Perl Under the Hood

43.8.1. Configuration

This section lists configuration parameters that affect PL/Perl.

`plperl.on_init (string)`

> Specifies Perl code to be executed when a Perl interpreter is first initialized, before it is specialized for use by `plperl` or `plperlu`. The SPI functions are not available when this code is executed. If the code fails with an error it will abort the initialization of the interpreter and propagate out to the calling query, causing the current transaction or subtransaction to be aborted.
>
> The Perl code is limited to a single string. Longer code can be placed into a module and loaded by the `on_init` string. Examples:
>
> ```
> plperl.on_init = 'require "plperlinit.pl"'
> plperl.on_init = 'use lib "/my/app"; use MyApp::PgInit;'
> ```
>
> Any modules loaded by `plperl.on_init`, either directly or indirectly, will be available for use by `plperl`. This may create a security risk. To see what modules have been loaded you can use:
>
> ```
> DO 'elog(WARNING, join ", ", sort keys %INC)' LANGUAGE plperl;
> ```

Initialization will happen in the postmaster if the plperl library is included in shared_preload_libraries, in which case extra consideration should be given to the risk of destabilizing the postmaster. The principal reason for making use of this feature is that Perl modules loaded by `plperl.on_init` need be loaded only at postmaster start, and will be instantly available without loading overhead in individual database sessions. However, keep in mind that the overhead is avoided only for the first Perl interpreter used by a database session — either PL/PerlU, or PL/Perl for the first SQL role that calls a PL/Perl function. Any additional Perl interpreters created in a database session will have to execute `plperl.on_init` afresh. Also, on Windows there will be no savings whatsoever from preloading, since the Perl interpreter created in the postmaster process does not propagate to child processes.

This parameter can only be set in the `postgresql.conf` file or on the server command line.

`plperl.on_plperl_init` (string)
`plperl.on_plperlu_init` (string)

These parameters specify Perl code to be executed when a Perl interpreter is specialized for `plperl` or `plperlu` respectively. This will happen when a PL/Perl or PL/PerlU function is first executed in a database session, or when an additional interpreter has to be created because the other language is called or a PL/Perl function is called by a new SQL role. This follows any initialization done by `plperl.on_init`. The SPI functions are not available when this code is executed. The Perl code in `plperl.on_plperl_init` is executed after "locking down" the interpreter, and thus it can only perform trusted operations.

If the code fails with an error it will abort the initialization and propagate out to the calling query, causing the current transaction or subtransaction to be aborted. Any actions already done within Perl won't be undone; however, that interpreter won't be used again. If the language is used again the initialization will be attempted again within a fresh Perl interpreter.

Only superusers can change these settings. Although these settings can be changed within a session, such changes will not affect Perl interpreters that have already been used to execute functions.

`plperl.use_strict` (boolean)

When set true subsequent compilations of PL/Perl functions will have the `strict` pragma enabled. This parameter does not affect functions already compiled in the current session.

43.8.2. Limitations and Missing Features

The following features are currently missing from PL/Perl, but they would make welcome contributions.

- PL/Perl functions cannot call each other directly.

- SPI is not yet fully implemented.

- If you are fetching very large data sets using `spi_exec_query`, you should be aware that these will all go into memory. You can avoid this by using `spi_query`/`spi_fetchrow` as illustrated earlier.

A similar problem occurs if a set-returning function passes a large set of rows back to PostgreSQL via `return`. You can avoid this problem too by instead using `return_next` for each row returned, as shown previously.

- When a session ends normally, not due to a fatal error, any END blocks that have been defined are executed. Currently no other actions are performed. Specifically, file handles are not automatically flushed and objects are not automatically destroyed.

Chapter 44. PL/Python - Python Procedural Language

The PL/Python procedural language allows PostgreSQL functions to be written in the Python language[1].

To install PL/Python in a particular database, use `CREATE EXTENSION plpythonu`, or from the shell command line use `createlang plpythonu` *dbname* (but see also Section 44.1).

> **Tip:** If a language is installed into `template1`, all subsequently created databases will have the language installed automatically.

PL/Python is only available as an "untrusted" language, meaning it does not offer any way of restricting what users can do in it and is therefore named `plpythonu`. A trusted variant `plpython` might become available in the future if a secure execution mechanism is developed in Python. The writer of a function in untrusted PL/Python must take care that the function cannot be used to do anything unwanted, since it will be able to do anything that could be done by a user logged in as the database administrator. Only superusers can create functions in untrusted languages such as `plpythonu`.

> **Note:** Users of source packages must specially enable the build of PL/Python during the installation process. (Refer to the installation instructions for more information.) Users of binary packages might find PL/Python in a separate subpackage.

44.1. Python 2 vs. Python 3

PL/Python supports both the Python 2 and Python 3 language variants. (The PostgreSQL installation instructions might contain more precise information about the exact supported minor versions of Python.) Because the Python 2 and Python 3 language variants are incompatible in some important aspects, the following naming and transitioning scheme is used by PL/Python to avoid mixing them:

- The PostgreSQL language named `plpython2u` implements PL/Python based on the Python 2 language variant.

- The PostgreSQL language named `plpython3u` implements PL/Python based on the Python 3 language variant.

- The language named `plpythonu` implements PL/Python based on the default Python language variant, which is currently Python 2. (This default is independent of what any local Python installations might consider to be their "default", for example, what `/usr/bin/python` might be.) The default will probably be changed to Python 3 in a distant future release of PostgreSQL, depending on the progress of the migration to Python 3 in the Python community.

---

1.   http://www.python.org

This scheme is analogous to the recommendations in PEP 394[2] regarding the naming and transitioning of the python command.

It depends on the build configuration or the installed packages whether PL/Python for Python 2 or Python 3 or both are available.

> **Tip:** The built variant depends on which Python version was found during the installation or which version was explicitly set using the PYTHON environment variable; see Section 16.4. To make both variants of PL/Python available in one installation, the source tree has to be configured and built twice.

This results in the following usage and migration strategy:

• Existing users and users who are currently not interested in Python 3 use the language name plpythonu and don't have to change anything for the foreseeable future. It is recommended to gradually "future-proof" the code via migration to Python 2.6/2.7 to simplify the eventual migration to Python 3.

  In practice, many PL/Python functions will migrate to Python 3 with few or no changes.

• Users who know that they have heavily Python 2 dependent code and don't plan to ever change it can make use of the plpython2u language name. This will continue to work into the very distant future, until Python 2 support might be completely dropped by PostgreSQL.

• Users who want to dive into Python 3 can use the plpython3u language name, which will keep working forever by today's standards. In the distant future, when Python 3 might become the default, they might like to remove the "3" for aesthetic reasons.

• Daredevils, who want to build a Python-3-only operating system environment, can change the contents of pg_pltemplate to make plpythonu be equivalent to plpython3u, keeping in mind that this would make their installation incompatible with most of the rest of the world.

See also the document What's New In Python 3.0[3] for more information about porting to Python 3.

It is not allowed to use PL/Python based on Python 2 and PL/Python based on Python 3 in the same session, because the symbols in the dynamic modules would clash, which could result in crashes of the PostgreSQL server process. There is a check that prevents mixing Python major versions in a session, which will abort the session if a mismatch is detected. It is possible, however, to use both PL/Python variants in the same database, from separate sessions.

44.2. PL/Python Functions

Functions in PL/Python are declared via the standard CREATE FUNCTION syntax:

```
CREATE FUNCTION funcname (argument-list)
  RETURNS return-type
```

---

2.   http://www.python.org/dev/peps/pep-0394/
3.   http://docs.python.org/py3k/whatsnew/3.0.html

```
AS $$
  # PL/Python function body
$$ LANGUAGE plpythonu;
```

The body of a function is simply a Python script. When the function is called, its arguments are passed as elements of the list `args`; named arguments are also passed as ordinary variables to the Python script. Use of named arguments is usually more readable. The result is returned from the Python code in the usual way, with `return` or `yield` (in case of a result-set statement). If you do not provide a return value, Python returns the default `None`. PL/Python translates Python's `None` into the SQL null value.

For example, a function to return the greater of two integers can be defined as:

```
CREATE FUNCTION pymax (a integer, b integer)
  RETURNS integer
AS $$
  if a > b:
    return a
  return b
$$ LANGUAGE plpythonu;
```

The Python code that is given as the body of the function definition is transformed into a Python function. For example, the above results in:

```
def __plpython_procedure_pymax_23456():
  if a > b:
    return a
  return b
```

assuming that 23456 is the OID assigned to the function by PostgreSQL.

The arguments are set as global variables. Because of the scoping rules of Python, this has the subtle consequence that an argument variable cannot be reassigned inside the function to the value of an expression that involves the variable name itself, unless the variable is redeclared as global in the block. For example, the following won't work:

```
CREATE FUNCTION pystrip(x text)
  RETURNS text
AS $$
  x = x.strip()  # error
  return x
$$ LANGUAGE plpythonu;
```

because assigning to x makes x a local variable for the entire block, and so the x on the right-hand side of the assignment refers to a not-yet-assigned local variable x, not the PL/Python function parameter. Using the `global` statement, this can be made to work:

```
CREATE FUNCTION pystrip(x text)
  RETURNS text
AS $$
  global x
  x = x.strip()  # ok now
  return x
```

```
$$ LANGUAGE plpythonu;
```

But it is advisable not to rely on this implementation detail of PL/Python. It is better to treat the function parameters as read-only.

44.3. Data Values

Generally speaking, the aim of PL/Python is to provide a "natural" mapping between the PostgreSQL and the Python worlds. This informs the data mapping rules described below.

44.3.1. Data Type Mapping

When a PL/Python function is called, its arguments are converted from their PostgreSQL data type to a corresponding Python type:

- PostgreSQL `boolean` is converted to Python `bool`.

- PostgreSQL `smallint` and `int` are converted to Python `int`. PostgreSQL `bigint` and `oid` are converted to `long` in Python 2 and to `int` in Python 3.

- PostgreSQL `real` and `double` are converted to Python `float`.

- PostgreSQL `numeric` is converted to Python `Decimal`. This type is imported from the `cdecimal` package if that is available. Otherwise, `decimal.Decimal` from the standard library will be used. `cdecimal` is significantly faster than `decimal`. In Python 3.3 and up, however, `cdecimal` has been integrated into the standard library under the name `decimal`, so there is no longer any difference.

- PostgreSQL `bytea` is converted to Python `str` in Python 2 and to `bytes` in Python 3. In Python 2, the string should be treated as a byte sequence without any character encoding.

- All other data types, including the PostgreSQL character string types, are converted to a Python `str`. In Python 2, this string will be in the PostgreSQL server encoding; in Python 3, it will be a Unicode string like all strings.

- For nonscalar data types, see below.

When a PL/Python function returns, its return value is converted to the function's declared PostgreSQL return data type as follows:

- When the PostgreSQL return type is `boolean`, the return value will be evaluated for truth according to the *Python* rules. That is, 0 and empty string are false, but notably `'f'` is true.

- When the PostgreSQL return type is `bytea`, the return value will be converted to a string (Python 2) or bytes (Python 3) using the respective Python built-ins, with the result being converted to `bytea`.

- For all other PostgreSQL return types, the return value is converted to a string using the Python built-in `str`, and the result is passed to the input function of the PostgreSQL data type. (If the Python value is a `float`, it is converted using the `repr` built-in instead of `str`, to avoid loss of precision.)

Strings in Python 2 are required to be in the PostgreSQL server encoding when they are passed to PostgreSQL. Strings that are not valid in the current server encoding will raise an error, but not all encoding mismatches can be detected, so garbage data can still result when this is not done correctly. Unicode strings are converted to the correct encoding automatically, so it can be safer and more convenient to use those. In Python 3, all strings are Unicode strings.

- For nonscalar data types, see below.

Note that logical mismatches between the declared PostgreSQL return type and the Python data type of the actual return object are not flagged; the value will be converted in any case.

44.3.2. Null, None

If an SQL null value is passed to a function, the argument value will appear as None in Python. For example, the function definition of pymax shown in Section 44.2 will return the wrong answer for null inputs. We could add STRICT to the function definition to make PostgreSQL do something more reasonable: if a null value is passed, the function will not be called at all, but will just return a null result automatically. Alternatively, we could check for null inputs in the function body:

```
CREATE FUNCTION pymax (a integer, b integer)
  RETURNS integer
AS $$
  if (a is None) or (b is None):
    return None
  if a > b:
    return a
  return b
$$ LANGUAGE plpythonu;
```

As shown above, to return an SQL null value from a PL/Python function, return the value None. This can be done whether the function is strict or not.

44.3.3. Arrays, Lists

SQL array values are passed into PL/Python as a Python list. To return an SQL array value out of a PL/Python function, return a Python sequence, for example a list or tuple:

```
CREATE FUNCTION return_arr()
  RETURNS int[]
AS $$
return (1, 2, 3, 4, 5)
$$ LANGUAGE plpythonu;

SELECT return_arr();
 return_arr
-------------
 {1,2,3,4,5}
(1 row)
```

Note that in Python, strings are sequences, which can have undesirable effects that might be familiar to Python programmers:

```
CREATE FUNCTION return_str_arr()
  RETURNS varchar[]
AS $$
return "hello"
$$ LANGUAGE plpythonu;

SELECT return_str_arr();
 return_str_arr
----------------
 {h,e,l,l,o}
(1 row)
```

44.3.4. Composite Types

Composite-type arguments are passed to the function as Python mappings. The element names of the mapping are the attribute names of the composite type. If an attribute in the passed row has the null value, it has the value None in the mapping. Here is an example:

```
CREATE TABLE employee (
  name text,
  salary integer,
  age integer
);

CREATE FUNCTION overpaid (e employee)
  RETURNS boolean
AS $$
  if e["salary"] > 200000:
    return True
  if (e["age"] < 30) and (e["salary"] > 100000):
    return True
  return False
$$ LANGUAGE plpythonu;
```

There are multiple ways to return row or composite types from a Python function. The following examples assume we have:

```
CREATE TYPE named_value AS (
  name    text,
  value   integer
);
```

A composite result can be returned as a:

Sequence type (a tuple or list, but not a set because it is not indexable)

Returned sequence objects must have the same number of items as the composite result type has fields. The item with index 0 is assigned to the first field of the composite type, 1 to the second and so on. For example:

```
CREATE FUNCTION make_pair (name text, value integer)
  RETURNS named_value
AS $$
  return [ name, value ]
  # or alternatively, as tuple: return ( name, value )
$$ LANGUAGE plpythonu;
```
To return a SQL null for any column, insert None at the corresponding position.

Mapping (dictionary)

The value for each result type column is retrieved from the mapping with the column name as key. Example:

```
CREATE FUNCTION make_pair (name text, value integer)
  RETURNS named_value
AS $$
  return { "name": name, "value": value }
$$ LANGUAGE plpythonu;
```
Any extra dictionary key/value pairs are ignored. Missing keys are treated as errors. To return a SQL null value for any column, insert None with the corresponding column name as the key.

Object (any object providing method __getattr__)

This works the same as a mapping. Example:

```
CREATE FUNCTION make_pair (name text, value integer)
  RETURNS named_value
AS $$
  class named_value:
    def __init__ (self, n, v):
      self.name = n
      self.value = v
  return named_value(name, value)

  # or simply
  class nv: pass
  nv.name = name
  nv.value = value
  return nv
$$ LANGUAGE plpythonu;
```

Functions with OUT parameters are also supported. For example:

```
CREATE FUNCTION multiout_simple(OUT i integer, OUT j integer) AS $$
return (1, 2)
$$ LANGUAGE plpythonu;

SELECT * FROM multiout_simple();
```

44.3.5. Set-returning Functions

A PL/Python function can also return sets of scalar or composite types. There are several ways to achieve this because the returned object is internally turned into an iterator. The following examples assume we have composite type:

```
CREATE TYPE greeting AS (
  how text,
  who text
);
```

A set result can be returned from a:

Sequence type (tuple, list, set)

```
    CREATE FUNCTION greet (how text)
      RETURNS SETOF greeting
    AS $$
      # return tuple containing lists as composite types
      # all other combinations work also
      return ( [ how, "World" ], [ how, "PostgreSQL" ], [ how, "PL/Python" ] )
    $$ LANGUAGE plpythonu;
```

Iterator (any object providing __iter__ and next methods)

```
    CREATE FUNCTION greet (how text)
      RETURNS SETOF greeting
    AS $$
      class producer:
        def __init__ (self, how, who):
          self.how = how
          self.who = who
          self.ndx = -1

        def __iter__ (self):
          return self

        def next (self):
          self.ndx += 1
          if self.ndx == len(self.who):
            raise StopIteration
          return ( self.how, self.who[self.ndx] )

      return producer(how, [ "World", "PostgreSQL", "PL/Python" ])
    $$ LANGUAGE plpythonu;
```

Generator (`yield`)

```
CREATE FUNCTION greet (how text)
  RETURNS SETOF greeting
AS $$
  for who in [ "World", "PostgreSQL", "PL/Python" ]:
    yield ( how, who )
$$ LANGUAGE plpythonu;
```

> **Warning**
>
> Due to Python bug #1483133[4], some debug versions of Python 2.4 (configured and compiled with option `--with-pydebug`) are known to crash the PostgreSQL server when using an iterator to return a set result. Unpatched versions of Fedora 4 contain this bug. It does not happen in production versions of Python or on patched versions of Fedora 4.

Set-returning functions with `OUT` parameters (using `RETURNS SETOF record`) are also supported. For example:

```
CREATE FUNCTION multiout_simple_setof(n integer, OUT integer, OUT integer) RETURNS S
return [(1, 2)] * n
$$ LANGUAGE plpythonu;

SELECT * FROM multiout_simple_setof(3);
```

44.4. Sharing Data

The global dictionary `SD` is available to store data between function calls. This variable is private static data. The global dictionary `GD` is public data, available to all Python functions within a session. Use with care.

Each function gets its own execution environment in the Python interpreter, so that global data and function arguments from `myfunc` are not available to `myfunc2`. The exception is the data in the `GD` dictionary, as mentioned above.

44.5. Anonymous Code Blocks

PL/Python also supports anonymous code blocks called with the DO statement:

```
DO $$
    # PL/Python code
$$ LANGUAGE plpythonu;
```

An anonymous code block receives no arguments, and whatever value it might return is discarded. Otherwise it behaves just like a function.

44.6. Trigger Functions

When a function is used as a trigger, the dictionary `TD` contains trigger-related values:

`TD["event"]`

> contains the event as a string: `INSERT`, `UPDATE`, `DELETE`, or `TRUNCATE`.

`TD["when"]`

> contains one of `BEFORE`, `AFTER`, or `INSTEAD OF`.

`TD["level"]`

> contains `ROW` or `STATEMENT`.

`TD["new"]`
`TD["old"]`

> For a row-level trigger, one or both of these fields contain the respective trigger rows, depending on the trigger event.

`TD["name"]`

> contains the trigger name.

`TD["table_name"]`

> contains the name of the table on which the trigger occurred.

`TD["table_schema"]`

> contains the schema of the table on which the trigger occurred.

`TD["relid"]`

> contains the OID of the table on which the trigger occurred.

`TD["args"]`

> If the `CREATE TRIGGER` command included arguments, they are available in `TD["args"][0]` to `TD["args"][`*n*`-1]`.

If `TD["when"]` is `BEFORE` or `INSTEAD OF` and `TD["level"]` is `ROW`, you can return `None` or `"OK"` from the Python function to indicate the row is unmodified, `"SKIP"` to abort the event, or if `TD["event"]` is `INSERT` or `UPDATE` you can return `"MODIFY"` to indicate you've modified the new row. Otherwise the return value is ignored.

44.7. Database Access

The PL/Python language module automatically imports a Python module called `plpy`. The functions and constants in this module are available to you in the Python code as `plpy.foo`.

44.7.1. Database Access Functions

The `plpy` module provides several functions to execute database commands:

`plpy.execute(query [, max-rows])`

> Calling `plpy.execute` with a query string and an optional row limit argument causes that query to be run and the result to be returned in a result object.
>
> The result object emulates a list or dictionary object. The result object can be accessed by row number and column name. For example:
>
> `rv = plpy.execute("SELECT * FROM my_table", 5)`
> returns up to 5 rows from `my_table`. If `my_table` has a column `my_column`, it would be accessed as:
>
> `foo = rv[i]["my_column"]`
> The number of rows returned can be obtained using the built-in `len` function.
>
> The result object has these additional methods:

`nrows()`

> Returns the number of rows processed by the command. Note that this is not necessarily the same as the number of rows returned. For example, an `UPDATE` command will set this value but won't return any rows (unless `RETURNING` is used).

`status()`

> The `SPI_execute()` return value.

`colnames()`
`coltypes()`
`coltypmods()`

> Return a list of column names, list of column type OIDs, and list of type-specific type modifiers for the columns, respectively.
>
> These methods raise an exception when called on a result object from a command that did not produce a result set, e.g., `UPDATE` without `RETURNING`, or `DROP TABLE`. But it is OK to use these methods on a result set containing zero rows.

`__str__()`

> The standard `__str__` method is defined so that it is possible for example to debug query execution results using `plpy.debug(rv)`.

The result object can be modified.

Note that calling `plpy.execute` will cause the entire result set to be read into memory. Only use that function when you are sure that the result set will be relatively small. If you don't want to risk excessive memory usage when fetching large results, use `plpy.cursor` rather than `plpy.execute`.

`plpy.prepare(query [, argtypes])`

`plpy.execute(plan [, arguments [, max-rows]])`

`plpy.prepare` prepares the execution plan for a query. It is called with a query string and a list of parameter types, if you have parameter references in the query. For example:

`plan = plpy.prepare("SELECT last_name FROM my_users WHERE first_name = $1", ["te>`

`text` is the type of the variable you will be passing for `$1`. The second argument is optional if you don't want to pass any parameters to the query.

After preparing a statement, you use a variant of the function `plpy.execute` to run it:

`rv = plpy.execute(plan, ["name"], 5)`

Pass the plan as the first argument (instead of the query string), and a list of values to substitute into the query as the second argument. The second argument is optional if the query does not expect any parameters. The third argument is the optional row limit as before.

Query parameters and result row fields are converted between PostgreSQL and Python data types as described in Section 44.3.

When you prepare a plan using the PL/Python module it is automatically saved. Read the SPI documentation (Chapter 45) for a description of what this means. In order to make effective use of this across function calls one needs to use one of the persistent storage dictionaries `SD` or `GD` (see Section 44.4). For example:

```
CREATE FUNCTION usesavedplan() RETURNS trigger AS $$
    if "plan" in SD:
        plan = SD["plan"]
    else:
        plan = plpy.prepare("SELECT 1")
        SD["plan"] = plan
    # rest of function
$$ LANGUAGE plpythonu;
```

`plpy.cursor(query)`

`plpy.cursor(plan [, arguments])`

The `plpy.cursor` function accepts the same arguments as `plpy.execute` (except for the row limit) and returns a cursor object, which allows you to process large result sets in smaller chunks. As with `plpy.execute`, either a query string or a plan object along with a list of arguments can be used.

The cursor object provides a `fetch` method that accepts an integer parameter and returns a result object. Each time you call `fetch`, the returned object will contain the next batch of rows, never larger than the parameter value. Once all rows are exhausted, `fetch` starts returning an empty result object. Cursor objects also provide an iterator interface[5], yielding one row at a time until all rows are exhausted. Data fetched that way is not returned as result objects, but rather as dictionaries, each dictionary corresponding to a single result row.

An example of two ways of processing data from a large table is:

---

5.   http://docs.python.org/library/stdtypes.html#iterator-types

```
CREATE FUNCTION count_odd_iterator() RETURNS integer AS $$
odd = 0
for row in plpy.cursor("select num from largetable"):
    if row['num'] % 2:
         odd += 1
return odd
$$ LANGUAGE plpythonu;

CREATE FUNCTION count_odd_fetch(batch_size integer) RETURNS integer AS $$
odd = 0
cursor = plpy.cursor("select num from largetable")
while True:
    rows = cursor.fetch(batch_size)
    if not rows:
        break
    for row in rows:
        if row['num'] % 2:
            odd += 1
return odd
$$ LANGUAGE plpythonu;

CREATE FUNCTION count_odd_prepared() RETURNS integer AS $$
odd = 0
plan = plpy.prepare("select num from largetable where num % $1 <> 0", ["integer"
rows = list(plpy.cursor(plan, [2]))

return len(rows)
$$ LANGUAGE plpythonu;
```

Cursors are automatically disposed of. But if you want to explicitly release all resources held by a cursor, use the `close` method. Once closed, a cursor cannot be fetched from anymore.

> **Tip:** Do not confuse objects created by `plpy.cursor` with DB-API cursors as defined by the Python Database API specification[6]. They don't have anything in common except for the name.

44.7.2. Trapping Errors

Functions accessing the database might encounter errors, which will cause them to abort and raise an exception. Both `plpy.execute` and `plpy.prepare` can raise an instance of a subclass of `plpy.SPIError`, which by default will terminate the function. This error can be handled just like any other Python exception, by using the `try`/`except` construct. For example:

```
CREATE FUNCTION try_adding_joe() RETURNS text AS $$
    try:
        plpy.execute("INSERT INTO users(username) VALUES ('joe')")
    except plpy.SPIError:
```

---

6.   http://www.python.org/dev/peps/pep-0249/

```
        return "something went wrong"
    else:
        return "Joe added"
$$ LANGUAGE plpythonu;
```

The actual class of the exception being raised corresponds to the specific condition that caused the error. Refer to Table A-1 for a list of possible conditions. The module plpy.spiexceptions defines an exception class for each PostgreSQL condition, deriving their names from the condition name. For instance, division_by_zero becomes DivisionByZero, unique_violation becomes UniqueViolation, fdw_error becomes FdwError, and so on. Each of these exception classes inherits from SPIError. This separation makes it easier to handle specific errors, for instance:

```
CREATE FUNCTION insert_fraction(numerator int, denominator int) RETURNS text AS $$
from plpy import spiexceptions
try:
    plan = plpy.prepare("INSERT INTO fractions (frac) VALUES ($1 / $2)", ["int", "in
    plpy.execute(plan, [numerator, denominator])
except spiexceptions.DivisionByZero:
    return "denominator cannot equal zero"
except spiexceptions.UniqueViolation:
    return "already have that fraction"
except plpy.SPIError, e:
    return "other error, SQLSTATE %s" % e.sqlstate
else:
    return "fraction inserted"
$$ LANGUAGE plpythonu;
```

Note that because all exceptions from the plpy.spiexceptions module inherit from SPIError, an except clause handling it will catch any database access error.

As an alternative way of handling different error conditions, you can catch the SPIError exception and determine the specific error condition inside the except block by looking at the sqlstate attribute of the exception object. This attribute is a string value containing the "SQLSTATE" error code. This approach provides approximately the same functionality

44.8. Explicit Subtransactions

Recovering from errors caused by database access as described in Section 44.7.2 can lead to an undesirable situation where some operations succeed before one of them fails, and after recovering from that error the data is left in an inconsistent state. PL/Python offers a solution to this problem in the form of explicit subtransactions.

44.8.1. Subtransaction Context Managers

Consider a function that implements a transfer between two accounts:

```
CREATE FUNCTION transfer_funds() RETURNS void AS $$
```

```
try:
    plpy.execute("UPDATE accounts SET balance = balance - 100 WHERE account_name = '
    plpy.execute("UPDATE accounts SET balance = balance + 100 WHERE account_name = '
except plpy.SPIError, e:
    result = "error transferring funds: %s" % e.args
else:
    result = "funds transferred correctly"
plan = plpy.prepare("INSERT INTO operations (result) VALUES ($1)", ["text"])
plpy.execute(plan, [result])
$$ LANGUAGE plpythonu;
```

If the second UPDATE statement results in an exception being raised, this function will report the error, but the result of the first UPDATE will nevertheless be committed. In other words, the funds will be withdrawn from Joe's account, but will not be transferred to Mary's account.

To avoid such issues, you can wrap your plpy.execute calls in an explicit subtransaction. The plpy module provides a helper object to manage explicit subtransactions that gets created with the plpy.subtransaction() function. Objects created by this function implement the context manager interface[7]. Using explicit subtransactions we can rewrite our function as:

```
CREATE FUNCTION transfer_funds2() RETURNS void AS $$
try:
    with plpy.subtransaction():
        plpy.execute("UPDATE accounts SET balance = balance - 100 WHERE account_name
        plpy.execute("UPDATE accounts SET balance = balance + 100 WHERE account_name
except plpy.SPIError, e:
    result = "error transferring funds: %s" % e.args
else:
    result = "funds transferred correctly"
plan = plpy.prepare("INSERT INTO operations (result) VALUES ($1)", ["text"])
plpy.execute(plan, [result])
$$ LANGUAGE plpythonu;
```

Note that the use of try/catch is still required. Otherwise the exception would propagate to the top of the Python stack and would cause the whole function to abort with a PostgreSQL error, so that the operations table would not have any row inserted into it. The subtransaction context manager does not trap errors, it only assures that all database operations executed inside its scope will be atomically committed or rolled back. A rollback of the subtransaction block occurs on any kind of exception exit, not only ones caused by errors originating from database access. A regular Python exception raised inside an explicit subtransaction block would also cause the subtransaction to be rolled back.

44.8.2. Older Python Versions

Context managers syntax using the with keyword is available by default in Python 2.6. If using PL/Python with an older Python version, it is still possible to use explicit subtransactions, although not as transparently. You can call the subtransaction manager's __enter__ and __exit__ functions using the enter and exit convenience aliases. The example function that transfers funds could be written as:

```
CREATE FUNCTION transfer_funds_old() RETURNS void AS $$
```

---

7.   http://docs.python.org/library/stdtypes.html#context-manager-types

```
try:
    subxact = plpy.subtransaction()
    subxact.enter()
    try:
        plpy.execute("UPDATE accounts SET balance = balance - 100 WHERE account_name
        plpy.execute("UPDATE accounts SET balance = balance + 100 WHERE account_name
    except:
        import sys
        subxact.exit(*sys.exc_info())
        raise
    else:
        subxact.exit(None, None, None)
except plpy.SPIError, e:
    result = "error transferring funds: %s" % e.args
else:
    result = "funds transferred correctly"

plan = plpy.prepare("INSERT INTO operations (result) VALUES ($1)", ["text"])
plpy.execute(plan, [result])
$$ LANGUAGE plpythonu;
```

Note: Although context managers were implemented in Python 2.5, to use the `with` syntax in that version you need to use a future statement[8]. Because of implementation details, however, you cannot use future statements in PL/Python functions.

44.9. Utility Functions

The `plpy` module also provides the functions

```
plpy.debug(msg, **kwargs)
plpy.log(msg, **kwargs)
plpy.info(msg, **kwargs)
plpy.notice(msg, **kwargs)
plpy.warning(msg, **kwargs)
plpy.error(msg, **kwargs)
plpy.fatal(msg, **kwargs)
```

`plpy.error` and `plpy.fatal` actually raise a Python exception which, if uncaught, propagates out to the calling query, causing the current transaction or subtransaction to be aborted. `raise plpy.Error(msg)` and `raise plpy.Fatal(msg)` are equivalent to calling `plpy.error(msg)` and `plpy.fatal(msg)`, respectively but the `raise` form does not allow passing keyword arguments. The other functions only generate messages of different priority levels. Whether messages of a particular priority are reported to the

---

8.   http://docs.python.org/release/2.5/ref/future.html

client, written to the server log, or both is controlled by the log_min_messages and client_min_messages configuration variables. See Chapter 19 for more information.

The *msg* argument is given as a positional argument. For backward compatibility, more than one positional argument can be given. In that case, the string representation of the tuple of positional arguments becomes the message reported to the client.

The following keyword-only arguments are accepted:

```
detail
hint
sqlstate
schema_name
table_name
column_name
datatype_name
constraint_name
```

The string representation of the objects passed as keyword-only arguments is used to enrich the messages reported to the client. For example:

```
CREATE FUNCTION raise_custom_exception() RETURNS void AS $$
plpy.error("custom exception message",
           detail="some info about exception",
           hint="hint for users")
$$ LANGUAGE plpythonu;

=# SELECT raise_custom_exception();
ERROR:  plpy.Error: custom exception message
DETAIL:  some info about exception
HINT:  hint for users
CONTEXT:  Traceback (most recent call last):
  PL/Python function "raise_custom_exception", line 4, in <module>
    hint="hint for users")
PL/Python function "raise_custom_exception"
```

Another set of utility functions are plpy.quote_literal(*string*), plpy.quote_nullable(*string*), and plpy.quote_ident(*string*). They are equivalent to the built-in quoting functions described in Section 9.4. They are useful when constructing ad-hoc queries. A PL/Python equivalent of dynamic SQL from Example 41-1 would be:

```
plpy.execute("UPDATE tbl SET %s = %s WHERE key = %s" % (
    plpy.quote_ident(colname),
    plpy.quote_nullable(newvalue),
    plpy.quote_literal(keyvalue)))
```

44.10. Environment Variables

Some of the environment variables that are accepted by the Python interpreter can also be used to affect PL/Python behavior. They would need to be set in the environment of the main PostgreSQL server process, for example in a start script. The available environment variables depend on the version of Python; see the Python documentation for details. At the time of this writing, the following environment variables have an affect on PL/Python, assuming an adequate Python version:

- `PYTHONHOME`

- `PYTHONPATH`

- `PYTHONY2K`

- `PYTHONOPTIMIZE`

- `PYTHONDEBUG`

- `PYTHONVERBOSE`

- `PYTHONCASEOK`

- `PYTHONDONTWRITEBYTECODE`

- `PYTHONIOENCODING`

- `PYTHONUSERBASE`

- `PYTHONHASHSEED`

(It appears to be a Python implementation detail beyond the control of PL/Python that some of the environment variables listed on the `python` man page are only effective in a command-line interpreter and not an embedded Python interpreter.)

Chapter 45. Server Programming Interface

The *Server Programming Interface* (SPI) gives writers of user-defined C functions the ability to run SQL commands inside their functions. SPI is a set of interface functions to simplify access to the parser, planner, and executor. SPI also does some memory management.

> **Note:** The available procedural languages provide various means to execute SQL commands from procedures. Most of these facilities are based on SPI, so this documentation might be of use for users of those languages as well.

To avoid misunderstanding we'll use the term "function" when we speak of SPI interface functions and "procedure" for a user-defined C-function that is using SPI.

Note that if a command invoked via SPI fails, then control will not be returned to your procedure. Rather, the transaction or subtransaction in which your procedure executes will be rolled back. (This might seem surprising given that the SPI functions mostly have documented error-return conventions. Those conventions only apply for errors detected within the SPI functions themselves, however.) It is possible to recover control after an error by establishing your own subtransaction surrounding SPI calls that might fail. This is not currently documented because the mechanisms required are still in flux.

SPI functions return a nonnegative result on success (either via a returned integer value or in the global variable `SPI_result`, as described below). On error, a negative result or `NULL` will be returned.

Source code files that use SPI must include the header file `executor/spi.h`.

45.1. Interface Functions

SPI_connect

Name

`SPI_connect` — connect a procedure to the SPI manager

Synopsis

```
int SPI_connect(void)
```

Description

`SPI_connect` opens a connection from a procedure invocation to the SPI manager. You must call this function if you want to execute commands through SPI. Some utility SPI functions can be called from unconnected procedures.

If your procedure is already connected, `SPI_connect` will return the error code SPI_ERROR_CONNECT. This could happen if a procedure that has called `SPI_connect` directly calls another procedure that calls `SPI_connect`. While recursive calls to the SPI manager are permitted when an SQL command called through SPI invokes another function that uses SPI, directly nested calls to `SPI_connect` and `SPI_finish` are forbidden. (But see `SPI_push` and `SPI_pop`.)

Return Value

`SPI_OK_CONNECT`

　　on success

`SPI_ERROR_CONNECT`

　　on error

SPI_finish

Name

SPI_finish — disconnect a procedure from the SPI manager

Synopsis

```
int SPI_finish(void)
```

Description

SPI_finish closes an existing connection to the SPI manager. You must call this function after completing the SPI operations needed during your procedure's current invocation. You do not need to worry about making this happen, however, if you abort the transaction via elog(ERROR). In that case SPI will clean itself up automatically.

If SPI_finish is called without having a valid connection, it will return SPI_ERROR_UNCONNECTED. There is no fundamental problem with this; it means that the SPI manager has nothing to do.

Return Value

SPI_OK_FINISH

    if properly disconnected

SPI_ERROR_UNCONNECTED

    if called from an unconnected procedure

SPI_push

Name

SPI_push — push SPI stack to allow recursive SPI usage

Synopsis

```
void SPI_push(void)
```

Description

SPI_push should be called before executing another procedure that might itself wish to use SPI. After SPI_push, SPI is no longer in a "connected" state, and SPI function calls will be rejected unless a fresh SPI_connect is done. This ensures a clean separation between your procedure's SPI state and that of another procedure you call. After the other procedure returns, call SPI_pop to restore access to your own SPI state.

Note that SPI_execute and related functions automatically do the equivalent of SPI_push before passing control back to the SQL execution engine, so it is not necessary for you to worry about this when using those functions. Only when you are directly calling arbitrary code that might contain SPI_connect calls do you need to issue SPI_push and SPI_pop.

SPI_pop

Name

SPI_pop — pop SPI stack to return from recursive SPI usage

Synopsis

```
void SPI_pop(void)
```

Description

SPI_pop pops the previous environment from the SPI call stack. See SPI_push.

SPI_execute

Name

SPI_execute — execute a command

Synopsis

```
int SPI_execute(const char * command, bool read_only, long count)
```

Description

SPI_execute executes the specified SQL command for count rows. If read_only is true, the command must be read-only, and execution overhead is somewhat reduced.

This function can only be called from a connected procedure.

If count is zero then the command is executed for all rows that it applies to. If count is greater than zero, then no more than count rows will be retrieved; execution stops when the count is reached, much like adding a LIMIT clause to the query. For example,

```
SPI_execute("SELECT * FROM foo", true, 5);
```

will retrieve at most 5 rows from the table. Note that such a limit is only effective when the command actually returns rows. For example,

```
SPI_execute("INSERT INTO foo SELECT * FROM bar", false, 5);
```

inserts all rows from bar, ignoring the count parameter. However, with

```
SPI_execute("INSERT INTO foo SELECT * FROM bar RETURNING *", false, 5);
```

at most 5 rows would be inserted, since execution would stop after the fifth RETURNING result row is retrieved.

You can pass multiple commands in one string; SPI_execute returns the result for the command executed last. The count limit applies to each command separately (even though only the last result will actually be returned). The limit is not applied to any hidden commands generated by rules.

When read_only is false, SPI_execute increments the command counter and computes a new *snapshot* before executing each command in the string. The snapshot does not actually change if the current transaction isolation level is SERIALIZABLE or REPEATABLE READ, but in READ COMMITTED mode the snapshot update allows each command to see the results of newly committed transactions from other sessions. This is essential for consistent behavior when the commands are modifying the database.

When read_only is true, SPI_execute does not update either the snapshot or the command counter, and it allows only plain SELECT commands to appear in the command string. The commands are executed using the snapshot previously established for the surrounding query. This execution mode is somewhat faster than the read/write mode due to eliminating per-command overhead. It also allows genuinely *stable* functions to be built: since successive executions will all use the same snapshot, there will be no change in the results.

It is generally unwise to mix read-only and read-write commands within a single function using SPI; that could result in very confusing behavior, since the read-only queries would not see the results of any database updates done by the read-write queries.

The actual number of rows for which the (last) command was executed is returned in the global variable SPI_processed. If the return value of the function is SPI_OK_SELECT, SPI_OK_INSERT_RETURNING, SPI_OK_DELETE_RETURNING, or SPI_OK_UPDATE_RETURNING, then you can use the global pointer SPITupleTable *SPI_tuptable to access the result rows. Some utility commands (such as EXPLAIN) also return row sets, and SPI_tuptable will contain the result in these cases too. Some utility commands (COPY, CREATE TABLE AS) don't return a row set, so SPI_tuptable is NULL, but they still return the number of rows processed in SPI_processed.

The structure SPITupleTable is defined thus:

```
typedef struct
{
    MemoryContext tuptabcxt;    /* memory context of result table */
    uint64      alloced;        /* number of alloced vals */
    uint64      free;           /* number of free vals */
    TupleDesc   tupdesc;        /* row descriptor */
    HeapTuple   *vals;          /* rows */
} SPITupleTable;
```

vals is an array of pointers to rows. (The number of valid entries is given by SPI_processed.) tupdesc is a row descriptor which you can pass to SPI functions dealing with rows. tuptabcxt, alloced, and free are internal fields not intended for use by SPI callers.

SPI_finish frees all SPITupleTables allocated during the current procedure. You can free a particular result table earlier, if you are done with it, by calling SPI_freetuptable.

Arguments

const char * command

   string containing command to execute

bool read_only

   true for read-only execution

long count

   maximum number of rows to return, or 0 for no limit

Return Value

If the execution of the command was successful then one of the following (nonnegative) values will be returned:

SPI_OK_SELECT

> if a SELECT (but not SELECT INTO) was executed

SPI_OK_SELINTO

> if a SELECT INTO was executed

SPI_OK_INSERT

> if an INSERT was executed

SPI_OK_DELETE

> if a DELETE was executed

SPI_OK_UPDATE

> if an UPDATE was executed

SPI_OK_INSERT_RETURNING

> if an INSERT RETURNING was executed

SPI_OK_DELETE_RETURNING

> if a DELETE RETURNING was executed

SPI_OK_UPDATE_RETURNING

> if an UPDATE RETURNING was executed

SPI_OK_UTILITY

> if a utility command (e.g., CREATE TABLE) was executed

SPI_OK_REWRITTEN

> if the command was rewritten into another kind of command (e.g., UPDATE became an INSERT) by a rule.

On error, one of the following negative values is returned:

SPI_ERROR_ARGUMENT

> if command is NULL or count is less than 0

SPI_ERROR_COPY

> if COPY TO stdout or COPY FROM stdin was attempted

SPI_ERROR_TRANSACTION

> if a transaction manipulation command was attempted (BEGIN, COMMIT, ROLLBACK, SAVEPOINT, PREPARE TRANSACTION, COMMIT PREPARED, ROLLBACK PREPARED, or any variant thereof)

SPI_ERROR_OPUNKNOWN

> if the command type is unknown (shouldn't happen)

SPI_ERROR_UNCONNECTED

    if called from an unconnected procedure

Notes

All **SPI** query-execution functions set both SPI_processed and SPI_tuptable (just the pointer, not the contents of the structure). Save these two global variables into local procedure variables if you need to access the result table of SPI_execute or another query-execution function across later calls.

SPI_exec

Name

SPI_exec — execute a read/write command

Synopsis

```
int SPI_exec(const char * command, long count)
```

Description

SPI_exec is the same as SPI_execute, with the latter's read_only parameter always taken as false.

Arguments

const char * command

   string containing command to execute

long count

   maximum number of rows to return, or 0 for no limit

Return Value

See SPI_execute.

SPI_execute_with_args

Name

`SPI_execute_with_args` — execute a command with out-of-line parameters

Synopsis

```
int SPI_execute_with_args(const char *command,
                          int nargs, Oid *argtypes,
                          Datum *values, const char *nulls,
                          bool read_only, long count)
```

Description

`SPI_execute_with_args` executes a command that might include references to externally supplied parameters. The command text refers to a parameter as n, and the call specifies data types and values for each such symbol. `read_only` and `count` have the same interpretation as in `SPI_execute`.

The main advantage of this routine compared to `SPI_execute` is that data values can be inserted into the command without tedious quoting/escaping, and thus with much less risk of SQL-injection attacks.

Similar results can be achieved with `SPI_prepare` followed by `SPI_execute_plan`; however, when using this function the query plan is always customized to the specific parameter values provided. For one-time query execution, this function should be preferred. If the same command is to be executed with many different parameters, either method might be faster, depending on the cost of re-planning versus the benefit of custom plans.

Arguments

`const char * command`

   command string

`int nargs`

   number of input parameters ($1, $2, etc.)

`Oid * argtypes`

   an array of length `nargs`, containing the OIDs of the data types of the parameters

`Datum * values`

   an array of length `nargs`, containing the actual parameter values

`const char * nulls`

   an array of length `nargs`, describing which parameters are null

If `nulls` is `NULL` then `SPI_execute_with_args` assumes that no parameters are null. Otherwise, each entry of the `nulls` array should be `' '` if the corresponding parameter value is non-null, or `'n'` if the corresponding parameter value is null. (In the latter case, the actual value in the corresponding `values` entry doesn't matter.) Note that `nulls` is not a text string, just an array: it does not need a `'\0'` terminator.

`bool read_only`

true for read-only execution

`long count`

maximum number of rows to return, or 0 for no limit

Return Value

The return value is the same as for `SPI_execute`.

`SPI_processed` and `SPI_tuptable` are set as in `SPI_execute` if successful.

SPI_prepare

Name

SPI_prepare — prepare a statement, without executing it yet

Synopsis

```
SPIPlanPtr SPI_prepare(const char * command, int nargs, Oid * argtypes)
```

Description

SPI_prepare creates and returns a prepared statement for the specified command, but doesn't execute the command. The prepared statement can later be executed repeatedly using SPI_execute_plan.

When the same or a similar command is to be executed repeatedly, it is generally advantageous to perform parse analysis only once, and might furthermore be advantageous to re-use an execution plan for the command. SPI_prepare converts a command string into a prepared statement that encapsulates the results of parse analysis. The prepared statement also provides a place for caching an execution plan if it is found that generating a custom plan for each execution is not helpful.

A prepared command can be generalized by writing parameters ($1, $2, etc.) in place of what would be constants in a normal command. The actual values of the parameters are then specified when SPI_execute_plan is called. This allows the prepared command to be used over a wider range of situations than would be possible without parameters.

The statement returned by SPI_prepare can be used only in the current invocation of the procedure, since SPI_finish frees memory allocated for such a statement. But the statement can be saved for longer using the functions SPI_keepplan or SPI_saveplan.

Arguments

const char * command

 command string

int nargs

 number of input parameters ($1, $2, etc.)

Oid * argtypes

 pointer to an array containing the OIDs of the data types of the parameters

Return Value

SPI_prepare returns a non-null pointer to an SPIPlan, which is an opaque struct representing a prepared statement. On error, NULL will be returned, and SPI_result will be set to one of the same error codes used by SPI_execute, except that it is set to SPI_ERROR_ARGUMENT if command is NULL, or if nargs is less than 0, or if nargs is greater than 0 and argtypes is NULL.

Notes

If no parameters are defined, a generic plan will be created at the first use of SPI_execute_plan, and used for all subsequent executions as well. If there are parameters, the first few uses of SPI_execute_plan will generate custom plans that are specific to the supplied parameter values. After enough uses of the same prepared statement, SPI_execute_plan will build a generic plan, and if that is not too much more expensive than the custom plans, it will start using the generic plan instead of re-planning each time. If this default behavior is unsuitable, you can alter it by passing the CURSOR_OPT_GENERIC_PLAN or CURSOR_OPT_CUSTOM_PLAN flag to SPI_prepare_cursor, to force use of generic or custom plans respectively.

Although the main point of a prepared statement is to avoid repeated parse analysis and planning of the statement, PostgreSQL will force re-analysis and re-planning of the statement before using it whenever database objects used in the statement have undergone definitional (DDL) changes since the previous use of the prepared statement. Also, if the value of search_path changes from one use to the next, the statement will be re-parsed using the new search_path. (This latter behavior is new as of PostgreSQL 9.3.) See PREPARE for more information about the behavior of prepared statements.

This function should only be called from a connected procedure.

SPIPlanPtr is declared as a pointer to an opaque struct type in spi.h. It is unwise to try to access its contents directly, as that makes your code much more likely to break in future revisions of PostgreSQL.

The name SPIPlanPtr is somewhat historical, since the data structure no longer necessarily contains an execution plan.

SPI_prepare_cursor

Name

SPI_prepare_cursor — prepare a statement, without executing it yet

Synopsis

```
SPIPlanPtr SPI_prepare_cursor(const char * command, int nargs,
                              Oid * argtypes, int cursorOptions)
```

Description

SPI_prepare_cursor is identical to SPI_prepare, except that it also allows specification of the planner's "cursor options" parameter. This is a bit mask having the values shown in nodes/parsenodes.h for the options field of DeclareCursorStmt. SPI_prepare always takes the cursor options as zero.

Arguments

const char * command

> command string

int nargs

> number of input parameters ($1, $2, etc.)

Oid * argtypes

> pointer to an array containing the OIDs of the data types of the parameters

int cursorOptions

> integer bit mask of cursor options; zero produces default behavior

Return Value

SPI_prepare_cursor has the same return conventions as SPI_prepare.

Notes

Useful bits to set in cursorOptions include CURSOR_OPT_SCROLL, CURSOR_OPT_NO_SCROLL, CURSOR_OPT_FAST_PLAN, CURSOR_OPT_GENERIC_PLAN, and CURSOR_OPT_CUSTOM_PLAN. Note in particular that CURSOR_OPT_HOLD is ignored.

SPI_prepare_params

Name

SPI_prepare_params — prepare a statement, without executing it yet

Synopsis

```
SPIPlanPtr SPI_prepare_params(const char * command,
                              ParserSetupHook parserSetup,
                              void * parserSetupArg,
                              int cursorOptions)
```

Description

SPI_prepare_params creates and returns a prepared statement for the specified command, but doesn't execute the command. This function is equivalent to SPI_prepare_cursor, with the addition that the caller can specify parser hook functions to control the parsing of external parameter references.

Arguments

const char * command

command string

ParserSetupHook parserSetup

Parser hook setup function

void * parserSetupArg

pass-through argument for parserSetup

int cursorOptions

integer bit mask of cursor options; zero produces default behavior

Return Value

SPI_prepare_params has the same return conventions as SPI_prepare.

SPI_getargcount

Name

`SPI_getargcount` — return the number of arguments needed by a statement prepared by `SPI_prepare`

Synopsis

```
int SPI_getargcount(SPIPlanPtr plan)
```

Description

`SPI_getargcount` returns the number of arguments needed to execute a statement prepared by `SPI_prepare`.

Arguments

`SPIPlanPtr plan`

    prepared statement (returned by `SPI_prepare`)

Return Value

The count of expected arguments for the `plan`. If the `plan` is `NULL` or invalid, `SPI_result` is set to `SPI_ERROR_ARGUMENT` and -1 is returned.

SPI_getargtypeid

Name

SPI_getargtypeid — return the data type OID for an argument of a statement prepared by SPI_prepare

Synopsis

```
Oid SPI_getargtypeid(SPIPlanPtr plan, int argIndex)
```

Description

SPI_getargtypeid returns the OID representing the type for the argIndex'th argument of a statement prepared by SPI_prepare. First argument is at index zero.

Arguments

SPIPlanPtr plan

    prepared statement (returned by SPI_prepare)

int argIndex

    zero based index of the argument

Return Value

The type OID of the argument at the given index. If the plan is NULL or invalid, or argIndex is less than 0 or not less than the number of arguments declared for the plan, SPI_result is set to SPI_ERROR_ARGUMENT and InvalidOid is returned.

SPI_is_cursor_plan

Name

SPI_is_cursor_plan — return `true` if a statement prepared by `SPI_prepare` can be used with `SPI_cursor_open`

Synopsis

```
bool SPI_is_cursor_plan(SPIPlanPtr plan)
```

Description

`SPI_is_cursor_plan` returns `true` if a statement prepared by `SPI_prepare` can be passed as an argument to `SPI_cursor_open`, or `false` if that is not the case. The criteria are that the `plan` represents one single command and that this command returns tuples to the caller; for example, `SELECT` is allowed unless it contains an `INTO` clause, and `UPDATE` is allowed only if it contains a `RETURNING` clause.

Arguments

`SPIPlanPtr plan`

> prepared statement (returned by `SPI_prepare`)

Return Value

`true` or `false` to indicate if the `plan` can produce a cursor or not, with `SPI_result` set to zero. If it is not possible to determine the answer (for example, if the `plan` is `NULL` or invalid, or if called when not connected to SPI), then `SPI_result` is set to a suitable error code and `false` is returned.

SPI_execute_plan

Name

SPI_execute_plan — execute a statement prepared by SPI_prepare

Synopsis

```
int SPI_execute_plan(SPIPlanPtr plan, Datum * values, const char * nulls,
                     bool read_only, long count)
```

Description

SPI_execute_plan executes a statement prepared by SPI_prepare or one of its siblings. read_only and count have the same interpretation as in SPI_execute.

Arguments

SPIPlanPtr plan

    prepared statement (returned by SPI_prepare)

Datum * values

    An array of actual parameter values. Must have same length as the statement's number of arguments.

const char * nulls

    An array describing which parameters are null. Must have same length as the statement's number of arguments.

    If nulls is NULL then SPI_execute_plan assumes that no parameters are null. Otherwise, each entry of the nulls array should be ' ' if the corresponding parameter value is non-null, or 'n' if the corresponding parameter value is null. (In the latter case, the actual value in the corresponding values entry doesn't matter.) Note that nulls is not a text string, just an array: it does not need a '\0' terminator.

bool read_only

    true for read-only execution

long count

    maximum number of rows to return, or 0 for no limit

Return Value

The return value is the same as for SPI_execute, with the following additional possible error (negative) results:

SPI_ERROR_ARGUMENT

    if plan is NULL or invalid, or count is less than 0

SPI_ERROR_PARAM

    if values is NULL and plan was prepared with some parameters

SPI_processed and SPI_tuptable are set as in SPI_execute if successful.

SPI_execute_plan_with_paramlist

Name

SPI_execute_plan_with_paramlist — execute a statement prepared by SPI_prepare

Synopsis

```
int SPI_execute_plan_with_paramlist(SPIPlanPtr plan,
                                    ParamListInfo params,
                                    bool read_only,
                                    long count)
```

Description

SPI_execute_plan_with_paramlist executes a statement prepared by SPI_prepare. This function is equivalent to SPI_execute_plan except that information about the parameter values to be passed to the query is presented differently. The ParamListInfo representation can be convenient for passing down values that are already available in that format. It also supports use of dynamic parameter sets via hook functions specified in ParamListInfo.

Arguments

SPIPlanPtr plan

   prepared statement (returned by SPI_prepare)

ParamListInfo params

   data structure containing parameter types and values; NULL if none

bool read_only

   true for read-only execution

long count

   maximum number of rows to return, or 0 for no limit

Return Value

The return value is the same as for SPI_execute_plan.

SPI_processed and SPI_tuptable are set as in SPI_execute_plan if successful.

SPI_execp

Name

SPI_execp — execute a statement in read/write mode

Synopsis

```
int SPI_execp(SPIPlanPtr plan, Datum * values, const char * nulls, long count)
```

Description

SPI_execp is the same as SPI_execute_plan, with the latter's read_only parameter always taken as false.

Arguments

SPIPlanPtr plan

    prepared statement (returned by SPI_prepare)

Datum * values

    An array of actual parameter values. Must have same length as the statement's number of arguments.

const char * nulls

    An array describing which parameters are null. Must have same length as the statement's number of arguments.

    If nulls is NULL then SPI_execp assumes that no parameters are null. Otherwise, each entry of the nulls array should be ' ' if the corresponding parameter value is non-null, or 'n' if the corresponding parameter value is null. (In the latter case, the actual value in the corresponding values entry doesn't matter.) Note that nulls is not a text string, just an array: it does not need a '\0' terminator.

long count

    maximum number of rows to return, or 0 for no limit

Return Value

See SPI_execute_plan.

SPI_processed and SPI_tuptable are set as in SPI_execute if successful.

SPI_cursor_open

Name

SPI_cursor_open — set up a cursor using a statement created with SPI_prepare

Synopsis

```
Portal SPI_cursor_open(const char * name, SPIPlanPtr plan,
                       Datum * values, const char * nulls,
                       bool read_only)
```

Description

SPI_cursor_open sets up a cursor (internally, a portal) that will execute a statement prepared by SPI_prepare. The parameters have the same meanings as the corresponding parameters to SPI_execute_plan.

Using a cursor instead of executing the statement directly has two benefits. First, the result rows can be retrieved a few at a time, avoiding memory overrun for queries that return many rows. Second, a portal can outlive the current procedure (it can, in fact, live to the end of the current transaction). Returning the portal name to the procedure's caller provides a way of returning a row set as result.

The passed-in parameter data will be copied into the cursor's portal, so it can be freed while the cursor still exists.

Arguments

const char * name

> name for portal, or NULL to let the system select a name

SPIPlanPtr plan

> prepared statement (returned by SPI_prepare)

Datum * values

> An array of actual parameter values. Must have same length as the statement's number of arguments.

const char * nulls

> An array describing which parameters are null. Must have same length as the statement's number of arguments.

> If nulls is NULL then SPI_cursor_open assumes that no parameters are null. Otherwise, each entry of the nulls array should be ' ' if the corresponding parameter value is non-null, or 'n' if the corresponding parameter value is null. (In the latter case, the actual value in the corresponding values entry doesn't matter.) Note that nulls is not a text string, just an array: it does not need a '\0' terminator.

`bool read_only`

> `true` for read-only execution

Return Value

Pointer to portal containing the cursor. Note there is no error return convention; any error will be reported via `elog`.

SPI_cursor_open_with_args

Name

SPI_cursor_open_with_args — set up a cursor using a query and parameters

Synopsis

```
Portal SPI_cursor_open_with_args(const char *name,
                                 const char *command,
                                 int nargs, Oid *argtypes,
                                 Datum *values, const char *nulls,
                                 bool read_only, int cursorOptions)
```

Description

SPI_cursor_open_with_args sets up a cursor (internally, a portal) that will execute the specified query. Most of the parameters have the same meanings as the corresponding parameters to SPI_prepare_cursor and SPI_cursor_open.

For one-time query execution, this function should be preferred over SPI_prepare_cursor followed by SPI_cursor_open. If the same command is to be executed with many different parameters, either method might be faster, depending on the cost of re-planning versus the benefit of custom plans.

The passed-in parameter data will be copied into the cursor's portal, so it can be freed while the cursor still exists.

Arguments

const char * name

name for portal, or NULL to let the system select a name

const char * command

command string

int nargs

number of input parameters ($1, $2, etc.)

Oid * argtypes

an array of length nargs, containing the OIDs of the data types of the parameters

Datum * values

an array of length nargs, containing the actual parameter values `const char * nulls`

> an array of length `nargs`, describing which parameters are null

> If `nulls` is `NULL` then `SPI_cursor_open_with_args` assumes that no parameters are null. Otherwise, each entry of the `nulls` array should be `' '` if the corresponding parameter value is non-null, or `'n'` if the corresponding parameter value is null. (In the latter case, the actual value in the corresponding `values` entry doesn't matter.) Note that `nulls` is not a text string, just an array: it does not need a `'\0'` terminator.

`bool read_only`

> `true` for read-only execution

`int cursorOptions`

> integer bit mask of cursor options; zero produces default behavior

Return Value

Pointer to portal containing the cursor. Note there is no error return convention; any error will be reported via `elog`.

SPI_cursor_open_with_paramlist

Name

SPI_cursor_open_with_paramlist — set up a cursor using parameters

Synopsis

```
Portal SPI_cursor_open_with_paramlist(const char *name,
                                      SPIPlanPtr plan,
                                      ParamListInfo params,
                                      bool read_only)
```

Description

SPI_cursor_open_with_paramlist sets up a cursor (internally, a portal) that will execute a statement prepared by SPI_prepare. This function is equivalent to SPI_cursor_open except that information about the parameter values to be passed to the query is presented differently. The ParamListInfo representation can be convenient for passing down values that are already available in that format. It also supports use of dynamic parameter sets via hook functions specified in ParamListInfo.

The passed-in parameter data will be copied into the cursor's portal, so it can be freed while the cursor still exists.

Arguments

const char * name

    name for portal, or NULL to let the system select a name

SPIPlanPtr plan

    prepared statement (returned by SPI_prepare)

ParamListInfo params

    data structure containing parameter types and values; NULL if none

bool read_only

    true for read-only execution

Return Value

Pointer to portal containing the cursor. Note there is no error return convention; any error will be reported via elog.

SPI_cursor_find

Name

SPI_cursor_find — find an existing cursor by name

Synopsis

```
Portal SPI_cursor_find(const char * name)
```

Description

SPI_cursor_find finds an existing portal by name. This is primarily useful to resolve a cursor name returned as text by some other function.

Arguments

`const char * name`

   name of the portal

Return Value

pointer to the portal with the specified name, or NULL if none was found

SPI_cursor_fetch

Name

SPI_cursor_fetch — fetch some rows from a cursor

Synopsis

```
void SPI_cursor_fetch(Portal portal, bool forward, long count)
```

Description

SPI_cursor_fetch fetches some rows from a cursor. This is equivalent to a subset of the SQL command FETCH (see SPI_scroll_cursor_fetch for more functionality).

Arguments

Portal portal

　　portal containing the cursor

bool forward

　　true for fetch forward, false for fetch backward

long count

　　maximum number of rows to fetch

Return Value

SPI_processed and SPI_tuptable are set as in SPI_execute if successful.

Notes

Fetching backward may fail if the cursor's plan was not created with the CURSOR_OPT_SCROLL option.

SPI_cursor_move

Name

SPI_cursor_move — move a cursor

Synopsis

```
void SPI_cursor_move(Portal portal, bool forward, long count)
```

Description

SPI_cursor_move skips over some number of rows in a cursor. This is equivalent to a subset of the SQL command MOVE (see SPI_scroll_cursor_move for more functionality).

Arguments

Portal portal

    portal containing the cursor

bool forward

    true for move forward, false for move backward

long count

    maximum number of rows to move

Notes

Moving backward may fail if the cursor's plan was not created with the CURSOR_OPT_SCROLL option.

SPI_scroll_cursor_fetch

Name

SPI_scroll_cursor_fetch — fetch some rows from a cursor

Synopsis

```
void SPI_scroll_cursor_fetch(Portal portal, FetchDirection direction,
                             long count)
```

Description

SPI_scroll_cursor_fetch fetches some rows from a cursor. This is equivalent to the SQL command FETCH.

Arguments

Portal portal

    portal containing the cursor

FetchDirection direction

    one of FETCH_FORWARD, FETCH_BACKWARD, FETCH_ABSOLUTE or FETCH_RELATIVE

long count

    number of rows to fetch for FETCH_FORWARD or FETCH_BACKWARD; absolute row number to fetch for FETCH_ABSOLUTE; or relative row number to fetch for FETCH_RELATIVE

Return Value

SPI_processed and SPI_tuptable are set as in SPI_execute if successful.

Notes

See the SQL FETCH command for details of the interpretation of the direction and count parameters.

Direction values other than FETCH_FORWARD may fail if the cursor's plan was not created with the CURSOR_OPT_SCROLL option.

SPI_scroll_cursor_move

Name

SPI_scroll_cursor_move — move a cursor

Synopsis

```
void SPI_scroll_cursor_move(Portal portal, FetchDirection direction,
                            long count)
```

Description

SPI_scroll_cursor_move skips over some number of rows in a cursor. This is equivalent to the SQL command MOVE.

Arguments

Portal portal

portal containing the cursor

FetchDirection direction

one of FETCH_FORWARD, FETCH_BACKWARD, FETCH_ABSOLUTE or FETCH_RELATIVE

long count

number of rows to move for FETCH_FORWARD or FETCH_BACKWARD; absolute row number to move to for FETCH_ABSOLUTE; or relative row number to move to for FETCH_RELATIVE

Return Value

SPI_processed is set as in SPI_execute if successful. SPI_tuptable is set to NULL, since no rows are returned by this function.

Notes

See the SQL FETCH command for details of the interpretation of the direction and count parameters.

Direction values other than FETCH_FORWARD may fail if the cursor's plan was not created with the CURSOR_OPT_SCROLL option.

SPI_cursor_close

Name

SPI_cursor_close — close a cursor

Synopsis

```
void SPI_cursor_close(Portal portal)
```

Description

SPI_cursor_close closes a previously created cursor and releases its portal storage.

All open cursors are closed automatically at the end of a transaction. SPI_cursor_close need only be invoked if it is desirable to release resources sooner.

Arguments

Portal portal

> portal containing the cursor

SPI_keepplan

Name

SPI_keepplan — save a prepared statement

Synopsis

```
int SPI_keepplan(SPIPlanPtr plan)
```

Description

SPI_keepplan saves a passed statement (prepared by SPI_prepare) so that it will not be freed by SPI_finish nor by the transaction manager. This gives you the ability to reuse prepared statements in the subsequent invocations of your procedure in the current session.

Arguments

SPIPlanPtr plan

    the prepared statement to be saved

Return Value

0 on success; SPI_ERROR_ARGUMENT if plan is NULL or invalid

Notes

The passed-in statement is relocated to permanent storage by means of pointer adjustment (no data copying is required). If you later wish to delete it, use SPI_freeplan on it.

SPI_saveplan

Name

SPI_saveplan — save a prepared statement

Synopsis

```
SPIPlanPtr SPI_saveplan(SPIPlanPtr plan)
```

Description

SPI_saveplan copies a passed statement (prepared by SPI_prepare) into memory that will not be freed by SPI_finish nor by the transaction manager, and returns a pointer to the copied statement. This gives you the ability to reuse prepared statements in the subsequent invocations of your procedure in the current session.

Arguments

SPIPlanPtr plan

   the prepared statement to be saved

Return Value

Pointer to the copied statement; or NULL if unsuccessful. On error, SPI_result is set thus:

SPI_ERROR_ARGUMENT

   if plan is NULL or invalid

SPI_ERROR_UNCONNECTED

   if called from an unconnected procedure

Notes

The originally passed-in statement is not freed, so you might wish to do SPI_freeplan on it to avoid leaking memory until SPI_finish.

In most cases, SPI_keepplan is preferred to this function, since it accomplishes largely the same result without needing to physically copy the prepared statement's data structures.

45.2. Interface Support Functions

The functions described here provide an interface for extracting information from result sets returned by `SPI_execute` and other SPI functions.

All functions described in this section can be used by both connected and unconnected procedures.

SPI_fname

Name

`SPI_fname` — determine the column name for the specified column number

Synopsis

```
char * SPI_fname(TupleDesc rowdesc, int colnumber)
```

Description

`SPI_fname` returns a copy of the column name of the specified column. (You can use `pfree` to release the copy of the name when you don't need it anymore.)

Arguments

`TupleDesc rowdesc`

　　input row description

`int colnumber`

　　column number (count starts at 1)

Return Value

The column name; `NULL` if `colnumber` is out of range. `SPI_result` set to `SPI_ERROR_NOATTRIBUTE` on error.

SPI_fnumber

Name

SPI_fnumber — determine the column number for the specified column name

Synopsis

```
int SPI_fnumber(TupleDesc rowdesc, const char * colname)
```

Description

SPI_fnumber returns the column number for the column with the specified name.

If colname refers to a system column (e.g., oid) then the appropriate negative column number will be returned. The caller should be careful to test the return value for exact equality to SPI_ERROR_NOATTRIBUTE to detect an error; testing the result for less than or equal to 0 is not correct unless system columns should be rejected.

Arguments

TupleDesc rowdesc

    input row description

const char * colname

    column name

Return Value

Column number (count starts at 1), or SPI_ERROR_NOATTRIBUTE if the named column was not found.

SPI_getvalue

Name

SPI_getvalue — return the string value of the specified column

Synopsis

```
char * SPI_getvalue(HeapTuple row, TupleDesc rowdesc, int colnumber)
```

Description

SPI_getvalue returns the string representation of the value of the specified column.

The result is returned in memory allocated using palloc. (You can use pfree to release the memory when you don't need it anymore.)

Arguments

HeapTuple row

    input row to be examined

TupleDesc rowdesc

    input row description

int colnumber

    column number (count starts at 1)

Return Value

Column value, or NULL if the column is null, colnumber is out of range (SPI_result is set to SPI_ERROR_NOATTRIBUTE), or no output function is available (SPI_result is set to SPI_ERROR_NOOUTFUNC).

SPI_getbinval

Name

SPI_getbinval — return the binary value of the specified column

Synopsis

```
Datum SPI_getbinval(HeapTuple row, TupleDesc rowdesc, int colnumber,
                    bool * isnull)
```

Description

SPI_getbinval returns the value of the specified column in the internal form (as type Datum).

This function does not allocate new space for the datum. In the case of a pass-by-reference data type, the return value will be a pointer into the passed row.

Arguments

HeapTuple row

> input row to be examined

TupleDesc rowdesc

> input row description

int colnumber

> column number (count starts at 1)

bool * isnull

> flag for a null value in the column

Return Value

The binary value of the column is returned. The variable pointed to by isnull is set to true if the column is null, else to false.

SPI_result is set to SPI_ERROR_NOATTRIBUTE on error.

SPI_gettype

Name

SPI_gettype — return the data type name of the specified column

Synopsis

```
char * SPI_gettype(TupleDesc rowdesc, int colnumber)
```

Description

SPI_gettype returns a copy of the data type name of the specified column. (You can use pfree to release the copy of the name when you don't need it anymore.)

Arguments

TupleDesc rowdesc

   input row description

int colnumber

   column number (count starts at 1)

Return Value

The data type name of the specified column, or NULL on error. SPI_result is set to SPI_ERROR_NOATTRIBUTE on error.

SPI_gettypeid

Name

SPI_gettypeid — return the data type OID of the specified column

Synopsis

```
Oid SPI_gettypeid(TupleDesc rowdesc, int colnumber)
```

Description

SPI_gettypeid returns the OID of the data type of the specified column.

Arguments

```
TupleDesc rowdesc
```

    input row description

```
int colnumber
```

    column number (count starts at 1)

Return Value

The OID of the data type of the specified column or InvalidOid on error. On error, SPI_result is set to SPI_ERROR_NOATTRIBUTE.

SPI_getrelname

Name

SPI_getrelname — return the name of the specified relation

Synopsis

```
char * SPI_getrelname(Relation rel)
```

Description

SPI_getrelname returns a copy of the name of the specified relation. (You can use pfree to release the copy of the name when you don't need it anymore.)

Arguments

Relation rel

    input relation

Return Value

The name of the specified relation.

SPI_getnspname

Name

SPI_getnspname — return the namespace of the specified relation

Synopsis

```
char * SPI_getnspname(Relation rel)
```

Description

SPI_getnspname returns a copy of the name of the namespace that the specified Relation belongs to. This is equivalent to the relation's schema. You should pfree the return value of this function when you are finished with it.

Arguments

Relation rel

    input relation

Return Value

The name of the specified relation's namespace.

45.3. Memory Management

PostgreSQL allocates memory within *memory contexts*, which provide a convenient method of managing allocations made in many different places that need to live for differing amounts of time. Destroying a context releases all the memory that was allocated in it. Thus, it is not necessary to keep track of individual objects to avoid memory leaks; instead only a relatively small number of contexts have to be managed. palloc and related functions allocate memory from the "current" context.

SPI_connect creates a new memory context and makes it current. SPI_finish restores the previous current memory context and destroys the context created by SPI_connect. These actions ensure that transient memory allocations made inside your procedure are reclaimed at procedure exit, avoiding memory leakage.

However, if your procedure needs to return an object in allocated memory (such as a value of a pass-by-reference data type), you cannot allocate that memory using palloc, at least not while you are connected to SPI. If you try, the object will be deallocated by SPI_finish, and your procedure will not work reliably. To solve this problem, use SPI_palloc to allocate memory for your return object. SPI_palloc allocates memory in the "upper executor context", that is, the memory context that was current when SPI_connect was called, which is precisely the right context for a value returned from your procedure.

If SPI_palloc is called while the procedure is not connected to SPI, then it acts the same as a normal palloc. Before a procedure connects to the SPI manager, the current memory context is the upper executor context, so all allocations made by the procedure via palloc or by SPI utility functions are made in this context.

When SPI_connect is called, the private context of the procedure, which is created by SPI_connect, is made the current context. All allocations made by palloc, repalloc, or SPI utility functions (except for SPI_copytuple, SPI_returntuple, SPI_modifytuple, and SPI_palloc) are made in this context. When a procedure disconnects from the SPI manager (via SPI_finish) the current context is restored to the upper executor context, and all allocations made in the procedure memory context are freed and cannot be used any more.

All functions described in this section can be used by both connected and unconnected procedures. In an unconnected procedure, they act the same as the underlying ordinary server functions (palloc, etc.).

SPI_palloc

Name

SPI_palloc — allocate memory in the upper executor context

Synopsis

```
void * SPI_palloc(Size size)
```

Description

SPI_palloc allocates memory in the upper executor context.

Arguments

Size size

> size in bytes of storage to allocate

Return Value

pointer to new storage space of the specified size

SPI_repalloc

Name

SPI_repalloc — reallocate memory in the upper executor context

Synopsis

```
void * SPI_repalloc(void * pointer, Size size)
```

Description

SPI_repalloc changes the size of a memory segment previously allocated using SPI_palloc.

This function is no longer different from plain repalloc. It's kept just for backward compatibility of existing code.

Arguments

```
void * pointer
```

pointer to existing storage to change

```
Size size
```

size in bytes of storage to allocate

Return Value

pointer to new storage space of specified size with the contents copied from the existing area

SPI_pfree

Name

SPI_pfree — free memory in the upper executor context

Synopsis

```
void SPI_pfree(void * pointer)
```

Description

SPI_pfree frees memory previously allocated using SPI_palloc or SPI_repalloc.

This function is no longer different from plain pfree. It's kept just for backward compatibility of existing code.

Arguments

void * pointer

   pointer to existing storage to free

SPI_copytuple

Name

SPI_copytuple — make a copy of a row in the upper executor context

Synopsis

```
HeapTuple SPI_copytuple(HeapTuple row)
```

Description

SPI_copytuple makes a copy of a row in the upper executor context. This is normally used to return a modified row from a trigger. In a function declared to return a composite type, use SPI_returntuple instead.

Arguments

HeapTuple row

   row to be copied

Return Value

the copied row; NULL only if tuple is NULL

SPI_returntuple

Name

SPI_returntuple — prepare to return a tuple as a Datum

Synopsis

```
HeapTupleHeader SPI_returntuple(HeapTuple row, TupleDesc rowdesc)
```

Description

SPI_returntuple makes a copy of a row in the upper executor context, returning it in the form of a row type Datum. The returned pointer need only be converted to Datum via PointerGetDatum before returning.

Note that this should be used for functions that are declared to return composite types. It is not used for triggers; use SPI_copytuple for returning a modified row in a trigger.

Arguments

HeapTuple row

    row to be copied

TupleDesc rowdesc

    descriptor for row (pass the same descriptor each time for most effective caching)

Return Value

HeapTupleHeader pointing to copied row; NULL only if row or rowdesc is NULL

SPI_modifytuple

Name

SPI_modifytuple — create a row by replacing selected fields of a given row

Synopsis

```
HeapTuple SPI_modifytuple(Relation rel, HeapTuple row, int ncols,
                     int * colnum, Datum * values, const char * nulls)
```

Description

SPI_modifytuple creates a new row by substituting new values for selected columns, copying the original row's columns at other positions. The input row is not modified.

Arguments

Relation rel

Used only as the source of the row descriptor for the row. (Passing a relation rather than a row descriptor is a misfeature.)

HeapTuple row

row to be modified

int ncols

number of columns to be changed

int * colnum

an array of length ncols, containing the numbers of the columns that are to be changed (column numbers start at 1)

Datum * values

an array of length ncols, containing the new values for the specified columns

const char * nulls

an array of length ncols, describing which new values are null

If nulls is NULL then SPI_modifytuple assumes that no new values are null. Otherwise, each entry of the nulls array should be ' ' if the corresponding new value is non-null, or 'n' if the corresponding new value is null. (In the latter case, the actual value in the corresponding values entry doesn't matter.) Note that nulls is not a text string, just an array: it does not need a '\0' terminator.

Return Value

new row with modifications, allocated in the upper executor context; NULL only if row is NULL

On error, SPI_result is set as follows:

SPI_ERROR_ARGUMENT

> if rel is NULL, or if row is NULL, or if ncols is less than or equal to 0, or if colnum is NULL, or if values is NULL.

SPI_ERROR_NOATTRIBUTE

> if colnum contains an invalid column number (less than or equal to 0 or greater than the number of column in row)

SPI_freetuple

Name

SPI_freetuple — free a row allocated in the upper executor context

Synopsis

```
void SPI_freetuple(HeapTuple row)
```

Description

SPI_freetuple frees a row previously allocated in the upper executor context.

This function is no longer different from plain heap_freetuple. It's kept just for backward compatibility of existing code.

Arguments

HeapTuple row

    row to free

SPI_freetuptable

Name

SPI_freetuptable — free a row set created by SPI_execute or a similar function

Synopsis

```
void SPI_freetuptable(SPITupleTable * tuptable)
```

Description

SPI_freetuptable frees a row set created by a prior SPI command execution function, such as SPI_execute. Therefore, this function is often called with the global variable SPI_tuptable as argument.

This function is useful if a SPI procedure needs to execute multiple commands and does not want to keep the results of earlier commands around until it ends. Note that any unfreed row sets will be freed anyway at SPI_finish. Also, if a subtransaction is started and then aborted within execution of a SPI procedure, SPI automatically frees any row sets created while the subtransaction was running.

Beginning in PostgreSQL 9.3, SPI_freetuptable contains guard logic to protect against duplicate deletion requests for the same row set. In previous releases, duplicate deletions would lead to crashes.

Arguments

SPITupleTable * tuptable

> pointer to row set to free, or NULL to do nothing

SPI_freeplan

Name

SPI_freeplan — free a previously saved prepared statement

Synopsis

```
int SPI_freeplan(SPIPlanPtr plan)
```

Description

SPI_freeplan releases a prepared statement previously returned by SPI_prepare or saved by SPI_keepplan or SPI_saveplan.

Arguments

SPIPlanPtr plan

   pointer to statement to free

Return Value

0 on success; SPI_ERROR_ARGUMENT if plan is NULL or invalid

45.4. Visibility of Data Changes

The following rules govern the visibility of data changes in functions that use SPI (or any other C function):

- During the execution of an SQL command, any data changes made by the command are invisible to the command itself. For example, in:

  ```
  INSERT INTO a SELECT * FROM a;
  ```
  the inserted rows are invisible to the SELECT part.

- Changes made by a command C are visible to all commands that are started after C, no matter whether they are started inside C (during the execution of C) or after C is done.

- Commands executed via SPI inside a function called by an SQL command (either an ordinary function or a trigger) follow one or the other of the above rules depending on the read/write flag passed to SPI. Commands executed in read-only mode follow the first rule: they cannot see changes of the calling command. Commands executed in read-write mode follow the second rule: they can see all changes made so far.

- All standard procedural languages set the SPI read-write mode depending on the volatility attribute of the function. Commands of STABLE and IMMUTABLE functions are done in read-only mode, while commands of VOLATILE functions are done in read-write mode. While authors of C functions are able to violate this convention, it's unlikely to be a good idea to do so.

The next section contains an example that illustrates the application of these rules.

45.5. Examples

This section contains a very simple example of SPI usage. The procedure execq takes an SQL command as its first argument and a row count as its second, executes the command using SPI_exec and returns the number of rows that were processed by the command. You can find more complex examples for SPI in the source tree in src/test/regress/regress.c and in the spi module.

```
#include "postgres.h"

#include "executor/spi.h"
#include "utils/builtins.h"

#ifdef PG_MODULE_MAGIC
PG_MODULE_MAGIC;
#endif

int64 execq(text *sql, int cnt);

int64
execq(text *sql, int cnt)
{
    char *command;
```

```
    int ret;
    uint64 proc;

    /* Convert given text object to a C string */
    command = text_to_cstring(sql);

    SPI_connect();

    ret = SPI_exec(command, cnt);

    proc = SPI_processed;
    /*
     * If some rows were fetched, print them via elog(INFO).
     */
    if (ret > 0 && SPI_tuptable != NULL)
    {
        TupleDesc tupdesc = SPI_tuptable->tupdesc;
        SPITupleTable *tuptable = SPI_tuptable;
        char buf[8192];
        uint64 j;

        for (j = 0; j < proc; j++)
        {
            HeapTuple tuple = tuptable->vals[j];
            int i;

            for (i = 1, buf[0] = 0; i <= tupdesc->natts; i++)
                snprintf(buf + strlen (buf), sizeof(buf) - strlen(buf), " %s%s",
                        SPI_getvalue(tuple, tupdesc, i),
                        (i == tupdesc->natts) ? " " : " |");
            elog(INFO, "EXECQ: %s", buf);
        }
    }

    SPI_finish();
    pfree(command);

    return (proc);
}
```

(This function uses call convention version 0, to make the example easier to understand. In real applications you should use the new version 1 interface.)

This is how you declare the function after having compiled it into a shared library (details are in Section 36.9.6.):

```
CREATE FUNCTION execq(text, integer) RETURNS int8
    AS 'filename'
    LANGUAGE C STRICT;
```

Here is a sample session:

```
=> SELECT execq('CREATE TABLE a (x integer)', 0);
 execq
-------
      0
(1 row)

=> INSERT INTO a VALUES (execq('INSERT INTO a VALUES (0)', 0));
INSERT 0 1
=> SELECT execq('SELECT * FROM a', 0);
INFO:  EXECQ:  0     -- inserted by execq
INFO:  EXECQ:  1     -- returned by execq and inserted by upper INSERT

 execq
-------
      2
(1 row)

=> SELECT execq('INSERT INTO a SELECT x + 2 FROM a', 1);
 execq
-------
      1
(1 row)

=> SELECT execq('SELECT * FROM a', 10);
INFO:  EXECQ:  0
INFO:  EXECQ:  1
INFO:  EXECQ:  2     -- 0 + 2, only one row inserted - as specified

 execq
-------
      3                 -- 10 is the max value only, 3 is the real number of rows
(1 row)

=> DELETE FROM a;
DELETE 3
=> INSERT INTO a VALUES (execq('SELECT * FROM a', 0) + 1);
INSERT 0 1
=> SELECT * FROM a;
 x
---
 1                   -- no rows in a (0) + 1
(1 row)

=> INSERT INTO a VALUES (execq('SELECT * FROM a', 0) + 1);
INFO:  EXECQ:  1
INSERT 0 1
=> SELECT * FROM a;
 x
---
 1
 2                   -- there was one row in a + 1
(2 rows)
```

```
-- This demonstrates the data changes visibility rule:

=> INSERT INTO a SELECT execq('SELECT * FROM a', 0) * x FROM a;
INFO:   EXECQ:   1
INFO:   EXECQ:   2
INFO:   EXECQ:   1
INFO:   EXECQ:   2
INFO:   EXECQ:   2
INSERT 0 2
=> SELECT * FROM a;
 x
---
 1
 2
 2                       -- 2 rows * 1 (x in first row)
 6                       -- 3 rows (2 + 1 just inserted) * 2 (x in second row)
(4 rows)                    ^^^^^^
                        rows visible to execq() in different invocations
```

Chapter 46. Background Worker Processes

PostgreSQL can be extended to run user-supplied code in separate processes. Such processes are started, stopped and monitored by `postgres`, which permits them to have a lifetime closely linked to the server's status. These processes have the option to attach to PostgreSQL's shared memory area and to connect to databases internally; they can also run multiple transactions serially, just like a regular client-connected server process. Also, by linking to libpq they can connect to the server and behave like a regular client application.

Warning

There are considerable robustness and security risks in using background worker processes because, being written in the c language, they have unrestricted access to data. Administrators wishing to enable modules that include background worker process should exercise extreme caution. Only carefully audited modules should be permitted to run background worker processes.

Background workers can be initialized at the time that PostgreSQL is started by including the module name in `shared_preload_libraries`. A module wishing to run a background worker can register it by calling `RegisterBackgroundWorker(BackgroundWorker *worker)` from its `_PG_init()`. Background workers can also be started after the system is up and running by calling the function `RegisterDynamicBackgroundWorker(BackgroundWorker *worker, BackgroundWorkerHandle **handle)`. Unlike `RegisterBackgroundWorker`, which can only be called from within the postmaster, `RegisterDynamicBackgroundWorker` must be called from a regular backend.

The structure `BackgroundWorker` is defined thus:

```
typedef void (*bgworker_main_type)(Datum main_arg);
typedef struct BackgroundWorker
{
    char        bgw_name[BGW_MAXLEN];
    int         bgw_flags;
    BgWorkerStartTime bgw_start_time;
    int         bgw_restart_time;      /* in seconds, or BGW_NEVER_RESTART */
    bgworker_main_type bgw_main;
    char        bgw_library_name[BGW_MAXLEN];   /* only if bgw_main is NULL */
    char        bgw_function_name[BGW_MAXLEN];  /* only if bgw_main is NULL */
    Datum       bgw_main_arg;
    char        bgw_extra[BGW_EXTRALEN];
    int         bgw_notify_pid;
} BackgroundWorker;
```

`bgw_name` is a string to be used in log messages, process listings and similar contexts.

`bgw_flags` is a bitwise-or'd bit mask indicating the capabilities that the module wants. Possible values are:

`BGWORKER_SHMEM_ACCESS`

> Requests shared memory access. Workers without shared memory access cannot access any of PostgreSQL's shared data structures, such as heavyweight or lightweight locks, shared buffers, or any custom data structures which the worker itself may wish to create and use.

`BGWORKER_BACKEND_DATABASE_CONNECTION`

> Requests the ability to establish a database connection through which it can later run transactions and queries. A background worker using `BGWORKER_BACKEND_DATABASE_CONNECTION` to connect to a database must also attach shared memory using `BGWORKER_SHMEM_ACCESS`, or worker start-up will fail.

`bgw_start_time` is the server state during which `postgres` should start the process; it can be one of `BgWorkerStart_PostmasterStart` (start as soon as `postgres` itself has finished its own initialization; processes requesting this are not eligible for database connections), `BgWorkerStart_ConsistentState` (start as soon as a consistent state has been reached in a hot standby, allowing processes to connect to databases and run read-only queries), and `BgWorkerStart_RecoveryFinished` (start as soon as the system has entered normal read-write state). Note the last two values are equivalent in a server that's not a hot standby. Note that this setting only indicates when the processes are to be started; they do not stop when a different state is reached.

`bgw_restart_time` is the interval, in seconds, that `postgres` should wait before restarting the process, in case it crashes. It can be any positive value, or `BGW_NEVER_RESTART`, indicating not to restart the process in case of a crash.

`bgw_main` is a pointer to the function to run when the process is started. This field can only safely be used to launch functions within the core server, because shared libraries may be loaded at different starting addresses in different backend processes. This will happen on all platforms when the library is loaded using any mechanism other than shared_preload_libraries. Even when that mechanism is used, address space layout variations will still occur on Windows, and when `EXEC_BACKEND` is used. Therefore, most users of this API should set this field to NULL. If it is non-NULL, it takes precedence over `bgw_library_name` and `bgw_function_name`.

`bgw_library_name` is the name of a library in which the initial entry point for the background worker should be sought. The named library will be dynamically loaded by the worker process and `bgw_function_name` will be used to identify the function to be called. If loading a function from the core code, `bgw_main` should be set instead.

`bgw_function_name` is the name of a function in a dynamically loaded library which should be used as the initial entry point for a new background worker.

`bgw_main_arg` is the `Datum` argument to the background worker main function. Regardless of whether that function is specified via `bgw_main` or via the combination of `bgw_library_name` and `bgw_function_name`, this main function should take a single argument of type `Datum` and return `void`. `bgw_main_arg` will be passed as the argument. In addition, the global variable `MyBgworkerEntry` points to a copy of the `BackgroundWorker` structure passed at registration time; the worker may find it helpful to examine this structure.

On Windows (and anywhere else where `EXEC_BACKEND` is defined) or in dynamic background workers it is not safe to pass a `Datum` by reference, only by value. If an argument is required, it is safest to pass an int32 or other small value and use that as an index into an array allocated in shared memory. If a value like a `cstring` or `text` is passed then the pointer won't be valid from the new background worker process.

`bgw_extra` can contain extra data to be passed to the background worker. Unlike `bgw_main_arg`, this data is not passed as an argument to the worker's main function, but it can be accessed via `MyBgworkerEntry`, as discussed above.

`bgw_notify_pid` is the PID of a PostgreSQL backend process to which the postmaster should send `SIGUSR1` when the process is started or exits. It should be 0 for workers registered at postmaster startup time, or when the backend registering the worker does not wish to wait for the worker to start up. Otherwise, it should be initialized to `MyProcPid`.

Once running, the process can connect to a database by calling `BackgroundWorkerInitializeConnection(char *dbname, char *username)` or `BackgroundWorkerInitializeConnectionByOid(Oid dboid, Oid useroid)`. This allows the process to run transactions and queries using the `SPI` interface. If dbname is NULL or dboid is `InvalidOid`, the session is not connected to any particular database, but shared catalogs can be accessed. If username is NULL or useroid is `InvalidOid`, the process will run as the superuser created during `initdb`. A background worker can only call one of these two functions, and only once. It is not possible to switch databases.

Signals are initially blocked when control reaches the `bgw_main` function, and must be unblocked by it; this is to allow the process to customize its signal handlers, if necessary. Signals can be unblocked in the new process by calling `BackgroundWorkerUnblockSignals` and blocked by calling `BackgroundWorkerBlockSignals`.

If `bgw_restart_time` for a background worker is configured as `BGW_NEVER_RESTART`, or if it exits with an exit code of 0 or is terminated by `TerminateBackgroundWorker`, it will be automatically unregistered by the postmaster on exit. Otherwise, it will be restarted after the time period configured via `bgw_restart_time`, or immediately if the postmaster reinitializes the cluster due to a backend failure. Backends which need to suspend execution only temporarily should use an interruptible sleep rather than exiting; this can be achieved by calling `WaitLatch()`. Make sure the `WL_POSTMASTER_DEATH` flag is set when calling that function, and verify the return code for a prompt exit in the emergency case that `postgres` itself has terminated.

When a background worker is registered using the `RegisterDynamicBackgroundWorker` function, it is possible for the backend performing the registration to obtain information regarding the status of the worker. Backends wishing to do this should pass the address of a `BackgroundWorkerHandle *` as the second argument to `RegisterDynamicBackgroundWorker`. If the worker is successfully registered, this pointer will be initialized with an opaque handle that can subsequently be passed to `GetBackgroundWorkerPid(BackgroundWorkerHandle *, pid_t *)` or `TerminateBackgroundWorker(BackgroundWorkerHandle *)`. `GetBackgroundWorkerPid` can be used to poll the status of the worker: a return value of `BGWH_NOT_YET_STARTED` indicates that the worker has not yet been started by the postmaster; `BGWH_STOPPED` indicates that it has been started but is no longer running; and `BGWH_STARTED` indicates that it is currently running. In this last case, the PID will also be returned via the second argument. `TerminateBackgroundWorker` causes the postmaster to send `SIGTERM` to the worker if it is running, and to unregister it as soon as it is not.

In some cases, a process which registers a background worker may wish to wait for the worker to start up. This can be accomplished by initializing `bgw_notify_pid` to `MyProcPid` and then passing the `BackgroundWorkerHandle *` obtained at registration time to `WaitForBackgroundWorkerStartup(BackgroundWorkerHandle *handle, pid_t *)` function. This function will block until the postmaster has attempted to start the background worker, or until the postmaster dies. If the background runner is running, the return value will `BGWH_STARTED`, and the

PID will be written to the provided address. Otherwise, the return value will be `BGWH_STOPPED` or `BGWH_POSTMASTER_DIED`.

If a background worker sends asynchronous notifications with the `NOTIFY` command via the Server Programming Interface (SPI), it should call `ProcessCompletedNotifies` explicitly after committing the enclosing transaction so that any notifications can be delivered. If a background worker registers to receive asynchronous notifications with the `LISTEN` through SPI, the worker will log those notifications, but there is no programmatic way for the worker to intercept and respond to those notifications.

The `src/test/modules/worker_spi` module contains a working example, which demonstrates some useful techniques.

The maximum number of registered background workers is limited by max_worker_processes.

Chapter 47. Logical Decoding

PostgreSQL provides infrastructure to stream the modifications performed via SQL to external consumers. This functionality can be used for a variety of purposes, including replication solutions and auditing.

Changes are sent out in streams identified by logical replication slots.

The format in which those changes are streamed is determined by the output plugin used. An example plugin is provided in the PostgreSQL distribution. Additional plugins can be written to extend the choice of available formats without modifying any core code. Every output plugin has access to each individual new row produced by INSERT and the new row version created by UPDATE. Availability of old row versions for UPDATE and DELETE depends on the configured replica identity (see REPLICA IDENTITY).

Changes can be consumed either using the streaming replication protocol (see Section 51.3 and Section 47.3), or by calling functions via SQL (see Section 47.4). It is also possible to write additional methods of consuming the output of a replication slot without modifying core code (see Section 47.7).

47.1. Logical Decoding Examples

The following example demonstrates controlling logical decoding using the SQL interface.

Before you can use logical decoding, you must set wal_level to logical and max_replication_slots to at least 1. Then, you should connect to the target database (in the example below, postgres) as a superuser.

```
postgres=# -- Create a slot named 'regression_slot' using the output plugin 'test_de
postgres=# SELECT * FROM pg_create_logical_replication_slot('regression_slot', 'test
    slot_name     | xlog_position
------------------+---------------
 regression_slot  | 0/16B1970
(1 row)

postgres=# SELECT slot_name, plugin, slot_type, database, active, restart_lsn, confi
    slot_name     |    plugin     | slot_type | database | active | restart_lsn | con
------------------+---------------+-----------+----------+--------+-------------+----
 regression_slot  | test_decoding | logical   | postgres | f      | 0/16A4408   | 0/1
(1 row)

postgres=# -- There are no changes to see yet
postgres=# SELECT * FROM pg_logical_slot_get_changes('regression_slot', NULL, NULL);
 location | xid | data
----------+-----+------
(0 rows)

postgres=# CREATE TABLE data(id serial primary key, data text);
CREATE TABLE

postgres=# -- DDL isn't replicated, so all you'll see is the transaction
postgres=# SELECT * FROM pg_logical_slot_get_changes('regression_slot', NULL, NULL);
 location  | xid |    data
-----------+-----+------------
 0/16D5D48 | 688 | BEGIN 688
```

```
 0/16E0380 | 688 | COMMIT 688
(2 rows)

postgres=# -- Once changes are read, they're consumed and not emitted
postgres=# -- in a subsequent call:
postgres=# SELECT * FROM pg_logical_slot_get_changes('regression_slot', NULL, NULL);
 location | xid | data
----------+-----+------
(0 rows)

postgres=# BEGIN;
postgres=# INSERT INTO data(data) VALUES('1');
postgres=# INSERT INTO data(data) VALUES('2');
postgres=# COMMIT;

postgres=# SELECT * FROM pg_logical_slot_get_changes('regression_slot', NULL, NULL);
 location  | xid |                         data
-----------+-----+--------------------------------------------------
 0/16E0478 | 689 | BEGIN 689
 0/16E0478 | 689 | table public.data: INSERT: id[integer]:1 data[text]:'1'
 0/16E0580 | 689 | table public.data: INSERT: id[integer]:2 data[text]:'2'
 0/16E0650 | 689 | COMMIT 689
(4 rows)

postgres=# INSERT INTO data(data) VALUES('3');

postgres=# -- You can also peek ahead in the change stream without consuming changes
postgres=# SELECT * FROM pg_logical_slot_peek_changes('regression_slot', NULL, NULL)
 location  | xid |                         data
-----------+-----+--------------------------------------------------
 0/16E09C0 | 690 | BEGIN 690
 0/16E09C0 | 690 | table public.data: INSERT: id[integer]:3 data[text]:'3'
 0/16E0B90 | 690 | COMMIT 690
(3 rows)

postgres=# -- The next call to pg_logical_slot_peek_changes() returns the same chang
postgres=# SELECT * FROM pg_logical_slot_peek_changes('regression_slot', NULL, NULL)
 location  | xid |                         data
-----------+-----+--------------------------------------------------
 0/16E09C0 | 690 | BEGIN 690
 0/16E09C0 | 690 | table public.data: INSERT: id[integer]:3 data[text]:'3'
 0/16E0B90 | 690 | COMMIT 690
(3 rows)

postgres=# -- options can be passed to output plugin, to influence the formatting
postgres=# SELECT * FROM pg_logical_slot_peek_changes('regression_slot', NULL, NULL,
 location  | xid |                         data
-----------+-----+--------------------------------------------------
 0/16E09C0 | 690 | BEGIN 690
 0/16E09C0 | 690 | table public.data: INSERT: id[integer]:3 data[text]:'3'
 0/16E0B90 | 690 | COMMIT 690 (at 2014-02-27 16:41:51.863092+01)
(3 rows)
```

```
postgres=# -- Remember to destroy a slot you no longer need to stop it consuming
postgres=# -- server resources:
postgres=# SELECT pg_drop_replication_slot('regression_slot');
 pg_drop_replication_slot
----------------------

(1 row)
```

The following example shows how logical decoding is controlled over the streaming replication protocol, using the program pg_recvlogical included in the PostgreSQL distribution. This requires that client authentication is set up to allow replication connections (see Section 26.2.5.1) and that max_wal_senders is set sufficiently high to allow an additional connection.

```
$ pg_recvlogical -d postgres --slot test --create-slot
$ pg_recvlogical -d postgres --slot test --start -f -
Control+Z
$ psql -d postgres -c "INSERT INTO data(data) VALUES('4');"
$ fg
BEGIN 693
table public.data: INSERT: id[integer]:4 data[text]:'4'
COMMIT 693
Control+C
$ pg_recvlogical -d postgres --slot test --drop-slot
```

47.2. Logical Decoding Concepts

47.2.1. Logical Decoding

Logical decoding is the process of extracting all persistent changes to a database's tables into a coherent, easy to understand format which can be interpreted without detailed knowledge of the database's internal state.

In PostgreSQL, logical decoding is implemented by decoding the contents of the write-ahead log, which describe changes on a storage level, into an application-specific form such as a stream of tuples or SQL statements.

47.2.2. Replication Slots

In the context of logical replication, a slot represents a stream of changes that can be replayed to a client in the order they were made on the origin server. Each slot streams a sequence of changes from a single database.

> **Note:** PostgreSQL also has streaming replication slots (see Section 26.2.5), but they are used somewhat differently there.

A replication slot has an identifier that is unique across all databases in a PostgreSQL cluster. Slots persist independently of the connection using them and are crash-safe.

A logical slot will emit each change just once in normal operation. The current position of each slot is persisted only at checkpoint, so in the case of a crash the slot may return to an earlier LSN, which will then cause recent changes to be resent when the server restarts. Logical decoding clients are responsible for avoiding ill effects from handling the same message more than once. Clients may wish to record the last LSN they saw when decoding and skip over any repeated data or (when using the replication protocol) request that decoding start from that LSN rather than letting the server determine the start point. The Replication Progress Tracking feature is designed for this purpose, refer to replication origins.

Multiple independent slots may exist for a single database. Each slot has its own state, allowing different consumers to receive changes from different points in the database change stream. For most applications, a separate slot will be required for each consumer.

A logical replication slot knows nothing about the state of the receiver(s). It's even possible to have multiple different receivers using the same slot at different times; they'll just get the changes following on from when the last receiver stopped consuming them. Only one receiver may consume changes from a slot at any given time.

> **Note:** Replication slots persist across crashes and know nothing about the state of their consumer(s). They will prevent removal of required resources even when there is no connection using them. This consumes storage because neither required WAL nor required rows from the system catalogs can be removed by VACUUM as long as they are required by a replication slot. So if a slot is no longer required it should be dropped.

47.2.3. Output Plugins

Output plugins transform the data from the write-ahead log's internal representation into the format the consumer of a replication slot desires.

47.2.4. Exported Snapshots

When a new replication slot is created using the streaming replication interface, a snapshot is exported (see Section 9.26.5), which will show exactly the state of the database after which all changes will be included in the change stream. This can be used to create a new replica by using SET TRANSACTION SNAPSHOT to read the state of the database at the moment the slot was created. This transaction can then be used to dump the database's state at that point in time, which afterwards can be updated using the slot's contents without losing any changes.

47.3. Streaming Replication Protocol Interface

The commands

- `CREATE_REPLICATION_SLOT` *slot_name* `LOGICAL` *output_plugin*

- `DROP_REPLICATION_SLOT` *slot_name*

- `START_REPLICATION SLOT` *slot_name* `LOGICAL ...`

are used to create, drop, and stream changes from a replication slot, respectively. These commands are only available over a replication connection; they cannot be used via SQL. See Section 51.3 for details on these commands.

The command pg_recvlogical can be used to control logical decoding over a streaming replication connection. (It uses these commands internally.)

47.4. Logical Decoding SQL Interface

See Section 9.26.6 for detailed documentation on the SQL-level API for interacting with logical decoding.

Synchronous replication (see Section 26.2.8) is only supported on replication slots used over the streaming replication interface. The function interface and additional, non-core interfaces do not support synchronous replication.

47.5. System Catalogs Related to Logical Decoding

The `pg_replication_slots` view and the `pg_stat_replication` view provide information about the current state of replication slots and streaming replication connections respectively. These views apply to both physical and logical replication.

47.6. Logical Decoding Output Plugins

An example output plugin can be found in the `contrib/test_decoding` subdirectory of the Post-greSQL source tree.

47.6.1. Initialization Function

An output plugin is loaded by dynamically loading a shared library with the output plugin's name as the library base name. The normal library search path is used to locate the library. To provide the required output plugin callbacks and to indicate that the library is actually an output plugin it needs to provide a function named `_PG_output_plugin_init`. This function is passed a struct that needs to be filled with the callback function pointers for individual actions.

```
typedef struct OutputPluginCallbacks
```

```
{
    LogicalDecodeStartupCB startup_cb;
    LogicalDecodeBeginCB begin_cb;
    LogicalDecodeChangeCB change_cb;
    LogicalDecodeCommitCB commit_cb;
    LogicalDecodeMessageCB message_cb;
    LogicalDecodeFilterByOriginCB filter_by_origin_cb;
    LogicalDecodeShutdownCB shutdown_cb;
} OutputPluginCallbacks;

typedef void (*LogicalOutputPluginInit)(struct OutputPluginCallbacks *cb);
```

The `begin_cb`, `change_cb` and `commit_cb` callbacks are required, while `startup_cb`, `filter_by_origin_cb` and `shutdown_cb` are optional.

47.6.2. Capabilities

To decode, format and output changes, output plugins can use most of the backend's normal infrastructure, including calling output functions. Read only access to relations is permitted as long as only relations are accessed that either have been created by `initdb` in the `pg_catalog` schema, or have been marked as user provided catalog tables using

```
ALTER TABLE user_catalog_table SET (user_catalog_table = true);
CREATE TABLE another_catalog_table(data text) WITH (user_catalog_table = true);
```

Any actions leading to transaction ID assignment are prohibited. That, among others, includes writing to tables, performing DDL changes, and calling `txid_current()`.

47.6.3. Output Modes

Output plugin callbacks can pass data to the consumer in nearly arbitrary formats. For some use cases, like viewing the changes via SQL, returning data in a data type that can contain arbitrary data (e.g., `bytea`) is cumbersome. If the output plugin only outputs textual data in the server's encoding, it can declare that by setting `OutputPluginOptions.output_mode` to `OUTPUT_PLUGIN_TEXTUAL_OUTPUT` instead of `OUTPUT_PLUGIN_BINARY_OUTPUT` in the startup callback. In that case, all the data has to be in the server's encoding so that a `text` datum can contain it. This is checked in assertion-enabled builds.

47.6.4. Output Plugin Callbacks

An output plugin gets notified about changes that are happening via various callbacks it needs to provide.

Concurrent transactions are decoded in commit order, and only changes belonging to a specific transaction are decoded between the `begin` and `commit` callbacks. Transactions that were rolled back explicitly or implicitly never get decoded. Successful savepoints are folded into the transaction containing them in the order they were executed within that transaction.

Note: Only transactions that have already safely been flushed to disk will be decoded. That can lead to a COMMIT not immediately being decoded in a directly following pg_logical_slot_get_changes() when synchronous_commit is set to off.

47.6.4.1. Startup Callback

The optional startup_cb callback is called whenever a replication slot is created or asked to stream changes, independent of the number of changes that are ready to be put out.

```
typedef void (*LogicalDecodeStartupCB) (
    struct LogicalDecodingContext *ctx,
    OutputPluginOptions *options,
    bool is_init
);
```

The is_init parameter will be true when the replication slot is being created and false otherwise. options points to a struct of options that output plugins can set:

```
typedef struct OutputPluginOptions
{
    OutputPluginOutputType output_type;
} OutputPluginOptions;
```

output_type has to either be set to OUTPUT_PLUGIN_TEXTUAL_OUTPUT or OUTPUT_PLUGIN_BINARY_OUTPUT. See also Section 47.6.3.

The startup callback should validate the options present in ctx->output_plugin_options. If the output plugin needs to have a state, it can use ctx->output_plugin_private to store it.

47.6.4.2. Shutdown Callback

The optional shutdown_cb callback is called whenever a formerly active replication slot is not used anymore and can be used to deallocate resources private to the output plugin. The slot isn't necessarily being dropped, streaming is just being stopped.

```
typedef void (*LogicalDecodeShutdownCB) (
    struct LogicalDecodingContext *ctx
);
```

47.6.4.3. Transaction Begin Callback

The required begin_cb callback is called whenever a start of a committed transaction has been decoded. Aborted transactions and their contents never get decoded.

```
typedef void (*LogicalDecodeBeginCB) (
    struct LogicalDecodingContext *,
    ReorderBufferTXN *txn
```

```
);
```

The `txn` parameter contains meta information about the transaction, like the time stamp at which it has been committed and its XID.

47.6.4.4. Transaction End Callback

The required `commit_cb` callback is called whenever a transaction commit has been decoded. The `change_cb` callbacks for all modified rows will have been called before this, if there have been any modified rows.

```
typedef void (*LogicalDecodeCommitCB) (
    struct LogicalDecodingContext *,
    ReorderBufferTXN *txn
);
```

47.6.4.5. Change Callback

The required `change_cb` callback is called for every individual row modification inside a transaction, may it be an INSERT, UPDATE, or DELETE. Even if the original command modified several rows at once the callback will be called individually for each row.

```
typedef void (*LogicalDecodeChangeCB) (
    struct LogicalDecodingContext *ctx,
    ReorderBufferTXN *txn,
    Relation relation,
    ReorderBufferChange *change
);
```

The `ctx` and `txn` parameters have the same contents as for the `begin_cb` and `commit_cb` callbacks, but additionally the relation descriptor `relation` points to the relation the row belongs to and a struct `change` describing the row modification are passed in.

> **Note:** Only changes in user defined tables that are not unlogged (see *UNLOGGED*) and not temporary (see *TEMPORARY or TEMP*) can be extracted using logical decoding.

47.6.4.6. Origin Filter Callback

The optional `filter_by_origin_cb` callback is called to determine whether data that has been replayed from `origin_id` is of interest to the output plugin.

```
typedef bool (*LogicalDecodeFilterByOriginCB) (
    struct LogicalDecodingContext *ctx,
    RepNodeId origin_id
);
```

The `ctx` parameter has the same contents as for the other callbacks. No information but the origin is available. To signal that changes originating on the passed in node are irrelevant, return true, causing them to be filtered away; false otherwise. The other callbacks will not be called for transactions and changes that have been filtered away.

This is useful when implementing cascading or multidirectional replication solutions. Filtering by the origin allows to prevent replicating the same changes back and forth in such setups. While transactions and changes also carry information about the origin, filtering via this callback is noticeably more efficient.

47.6.4.7. Generic Message Callback

The optional `message_cb` callback is called whenever a logical decoding message has been decoded.

```
typedef void (*LogicalDecodeMessageCB) (
    struct LogicalDecodingContext *,
    ReorderBufferTXN *txn,
    XLogRecPtr message_lsn,
    bool transactional,
    const char *prefix,
    Size message_size,
    const char *message
);
```

The `txn` parameter contains meta information about the transaction, like the time stamp at which it has been committed and its XID. Note however that it can be NULL when the message is non-transactional and the XID was not assigned yet in the transaction which logged the message. The `lsn` has WAL position of the message. The `transactional` says if the message was sent as transactional or not. The `prefix` is arbitrary null-terminated prefix which can be used for identifying interesting messages for the current plugin. And finally the `message` parameter holds the actual message of `message_size` size.

Extra care should be taken to ensure that the prefix the output plugin considers interesting is unique. Using name of the extension or the output plugin itself is often a good choice.

47.6.5. Functions for Producing Output

To actually produce output, output plugins can write data to the `StringInfo` output buffer in `ctx->out` when inside the `begin_cb`, `commit_cb`, or `change_cb` callbacks. Before writing to the output buffer, `OutputPluginPrepareWrite(ctx, last_write)` has to be called, and after finishing writing to the buffer, `OutputPluginWrite(ctx, last_write)` has to be called to perform the write. The `last_write` indicates whether a particular write was the callback's last write.

The following example shows how to output data to the consumer of an output plugin:

```
OutputPluginPrepareWrite(ctx, true);
appendStringInfo(ctx->out, "BEGIN %u", txn->xid);
OutputPluginWrite(ctx, true);
```

47.7. Logical Decoding Output Writers

It is possible to add more output methods for logical decoding. For details, see `src/backend/replication/logical/logicalfuncs.c`. Essentially, three functions need to be provided: one to read WAL, one to prepare writing output, and one to write the output (see Section 47.6.5).

47.8. Synchronous Replication Support for Logical Decoding

Logical decoding can be used to build synchronous replication solutions with the same user interface as synchronous replication for streaming replication. To do this, the streaming replication interface (see Section 47.3) must be used to stream out data. Clients have to send `Standby status update (F)` (see Section 51.3) messages, just like streaming replication clients do.

> **Note:** A synchronous replica receiving changes via logical decoding will work in the scope of a single database. Since, in contrast to that, `synchronous_standby_names` currently is server wide, this means this technique will not work properly if more than one database is actively used.

Chapter 48. Replication Progress Tracking

Replication origins are intended to make it easier to implement logical replication solutions on top of logical decoding. They provide a solution to two common problems:

- How to safely keep track of replication progress
- How to change replication behavior based on the origin of a row; for example, to prevent loops in bi-directional replication setups

Replication origins have just two properties, a name and an OID. The name, which is what should be used to refer to the origin across systems, is free-form `text`. It should be used in a way that makes conflicts between replication origins created by different replication solutions unlikely; e.g. by prefixing the replication solution's name to it. The OID is used only to avoid having to store the long version in situations where space efficiency is important. It should never be shared across systems.

Replication origins can be created using the function `pg_replication_origin_create()`; dropped using `pg_replication_origin_drop()`; and seen in the `pg_replication_origin` system catalog.

One nontrivial part of building a replication solution is to keep track of replay progress in a safe manner. When the applying process, or the whole cluster, dies, it needs to be possible to find out up to where data has successfully been replicated. Naive solutions to this, such as updating a row in a table for every replayed transaction, have problems like run-time overhead and database bloat.

Using the replication origin infrastructure a session can be marked as replaying from a remote node (using the `pg_replication_origin_session_setup()` function). Additionally the LSN and commit time stamp of every source transaction can be configured on a per transaction basis using `pg_replication_origin_xact_setup()`. If that's done replication progress will persist in a crash safe manner. Replay progress for all replication origins can be seen in the `pg_replication_origin_status` view. An individual origin's progress, e.g. when resuming replication, can be acquired using `pg_replication_origin_progress()` for any origin or `pg_replication_origin_session_progress()` for the origin configured in the current session.

In replication topologies more complex than replication from exactly one system to one other system, another problem can be that it is hard to avoid replicating replayed rows again. That can lead both to cycles in the replication and inefficiencies. Replication origins provide an optional mechanism to recognize and prevent that. When configured using the functions referenced in the previous paragraph, every change and transaction passed to output plugin callbacks (see Section 47.6) generated by the session is tagged with the replication origin of the generating session. This allows treating them differently in the output plugin, e.g. ignoring all but locally-originating rows. Additionally the `filter_by_origin_cb` callback can be used to filter the logical decoding change stream based on the source. While less flexible, filtering via that callback is considerably more efficient than doing it in the output plugin.

www.ingramcontent.com/pod-product-compliance
Lightning Source LLC
Chambersburg PA
CBHW080147060326
40689CB00018B/3879

9 789888 406715